"Edith Cord's masterfully crafted portrayal of surviving the Nazis through flight and hiding, as well as the rich and fulfilling life she created in the decades after, serves as an extraordinary example of an individual's will to overcome. In a broader sense, *Finding Edith* also depicts the arc of the refugee experience during the Holocaust and presents a case study of the immense difficulties and trials of hiding under such circumstances. Cord's honest rendering shares a deeply human story, illuminating human flaws and human strengths, and sheds light on the particular texture of the female experience."

—Elizabeth Anthony, Historian,
United States Holocaust Memorial Museum

"*Finding Edith* is a painful book to read—and it should be. In great detail and with unequaled precision, Edith Mayer Cord describes her experience hiding in German-occupied and German-Allied so-called Vichy France as a young girl, and her unrelenting efforts to both get an education and avoid capture. One marvels at her discipline and the courage born of necessity. One also is horrified by the many who exploited her dire situation and impressed by the few who came to her aid. She is brutally honest about her relationship with her difficult mother, who was shattered by the loss of her husband and her son, and by her conditions of dire poverty. One cannot fail to be impressed by the journey that Edith traveled to find herself and create a productive life after so much suffering. I know of few books as candid in explaining the price that was paid for survival."

—Michael Berenbaum, Professor of Jewish Studies,
Director of the Sigi Ziering Institute, American Jewish University

"Through the interweaving story—the odyssey—of the author's and her family's personal experiences, readers learn about the events, the ascent of anti-Semitism that culminated in the death camps, the mass killings of what was termed the Final Solution. There is also mention of some little-known historical information, such as that Italian fascists laid claim to what is now Ethiopia; that Hitler admired Genghis Khan; and the events of the Evian Conference and the Wannsee Conference. Readers learn of the resourcefulness of the author's parents in the face of life-threatening situations, as well as the lessons learned through the experiences of a child and young person during the Holocaust. These lessons Edith Cord carried into her remarkable adult life—survival of painful events and personal losses; assimilation is not enough to grant you safety; resourcefulness and adaptability are the most valuable tools; acquire skills to be able to support yourself; be active on behalf of civil rights and democracy. It is indeed an odyssey of personal growth."

—*Stefanie Seltzer, President, World Federation of Jewish Child Survivors of the Holocaust and Descendants*

FINDING
EDITH

FINDING
EDITH

Surviving the Holocaust in Plain Sight

EDITH MAYER CORD

Purdue University Press ❧ West Lafayette, Indiana

Library of Congress Cataloging-in-Publication Data

Names: Cord, Edith Mayer, author.

Title: Finding Edith : surviving the Holocaust in plain sight / Edith Mayer Cord.

Description: West Lafayette, Indiana : Purdue University Press, [2019] | Includes bibliographical references.

Identifiers: LCCN 2019008629| ISBN 9781557538086 (pbk. : alk. paper) | ISBN 9781612495972 (epub) | ISBN 9781612495965 (epdf)

Subjects: LCSH: Cord, Edith Mayer. | Hidden children (Holocaust)— Europe—Biography. | Jewish children in the Holocaust—Biography. | Holocaust, Jewish (1939–1945)—Personal narratives. | Holocaust survivors— United States—Biography.

Classification: LCC D804.196.C67 A3 2019 | DDC 940.53/18092 [B] —dc23 LC record available at https://lccn.loc.gov/2019008629

This book is dedicated to the memory of my beloved father,
S. J. Mayer, deported to Auschwitz on convoy 31 from
Drancy, France, on September 11, 1942, at age 54,
and to the memory of my wonderful brother,
Kurt Mayer, deported to Auschwitz on convoy 26
from Drancy, France, on August 31, 1942, at the age of 19.
May their memory be for a blessing.

Contents

Preface *ix*
Acknowledgments *xi*

Beginnings
1. VIENNA, AUSTRIA: My Childhood and Early Memories *1*
2. GENOA, ITALY: The Happiest Year of My Life *31*
3. NICE, FRANCE: We Are Refugees *42*
4. MONTLAUR, FRANCE: From School to the Vineyards *68*

In Hiding in France
5. CASTELNAUDARY: The Convent School *113*
6. MOISSAC: In the Hospital *118*
7. MENDE: The English Teacher *122*
8. FLORAC: Christmas Vacation *127*
9. PEZENAS: The Outsider *136*
10. CAHORS: Vocational High School and Centre de Jeunes Filles Déficientes *140*
11. FLIGHT TO SWITZERLAND *148*

Switzerland
12. CLAPARÈDE: The Transit Camp *155*
13. GENEVA: Champel, Le Val Fleuri, Le Centre Henri Dunant *164*
14. CHÉSIÈRES-VILLARS: Alpina *171*
15. ULISBACH AND SPEICHER: The Nanny *177*

Introduction to the Postwar Years *187*

Toulouse, France
16. A YEAR OF FLOUNDERING *189*
17. SCHOOL AT LAST *199*
18. THE SECOND BACCALAURÉAT *215*
19. FACULTÉ DE LETTRES *223*

America
   20. AMERICA: The Immigrant *241*
   21. REFLECTIONS *274*

Life is Sacred *280*
Musings on Old Age and Transitions *281*
About the Author *282*

Preface

After twenty-five years I finally worked up the courage to read the last letters from my father and brother written just before their deportation to Auschwitz. While reading them I was reliving their agony, despair, and loneliness as they were about to be mercilessly murdered. And for what? This unspeakable suffering endured by those who were so brutally killed, dying alone far from witnesses, was caused by the blind visceral hatred that is anti-Semitism.

Sometimes I feel as though I have packed several lifetimes into this one. I recall my own hardships, pain, and despair as an adolescent hiding in plain sight to escape persecution and death in Western Europe. This book is about my odyssey, my struggle to rise out of poverty, to get an education, to transcend hatred, and to come to terms with many traumatic experiences. The circumstances of my life in those days were harsh. The prolonged attacks on my sense of self were relentless and came from many sources. The profound loneliness and despair of those years was so painful that I choose to tell my story as succinctly as I possibly can. I share my story with the hope that we will learn from this terrible past, that we will have men and women with the courage to stand up for our freedom, and that we will not allow ourselves to be silenced by political correctness, indiscriminate terror, or cowed into submission by nuclear, chemical, or cyber threats. We must speak up for our freedom by using words that heal, that enhance our best and noblest understanding of life—for everything starts with ideas.

Ideas work their way across centuries: from the Bible's teachings of the Ten Commandments, individual responsibility and redemption, to the concept of democracy in ancient Greece, to the message of Jesus about accountability, love, and forgiveness, to the Enlightenment, with its recognition of man's intrinsic equality before God and the right to worship in freedom. We are the spiritual heirs of previous generations, and these precious ideas and hard-won insights must be passed on to younger generations. Like a thread, both good and bad ideas weave their way into our consciousness. It is up to us to filter them through our moral compass in order to keep the good ones while discarding the bad ones. It is an unending task. Totalitarianism in all its guises, whether it goes by the name of Nazism, Fascism, Communism, or some other fanaticism hiding behind a religious or political ideology, leads to the same results: a ruthless determination to achieve power by all means. We have little or no control over what life dishes out, but we do have control over how we deal with it. I am sharing my story with the hope of inspiring people. They have a choice; they too can work to build a better life for themselves and a better world for all.

Drawing Edith made during an art workshop representing her climb out of darkness and oppression into light. Included in I Remember: Drawings and Stories by Adult Child Survivors of the Holocaust, *by Tamar Hendel, 1991.*

Acknowledgments

This book took shape thanks to the invaluable help of my assistant and friend, Gabrielle DeMers, whose constructive feedback and technical skills helped to make the book what it is. My daughters, Emily and Louise, have always provided support as well as valuable feedback during the writing phase. I also wish to thank my lifelong friend Leon (Wodowski) Vermont (1929–2019) for his constant encouragement to put my thoughts in writing. Finally, I want to express my thanks to the editorial board of Purdue University Press—especially to Katherine Purple—for their suggestions and technical support during the publication phase of my book.

While I wrote every word in this book, putting it all together is the result of a collective effort, and I am deeply grateful to all those who have helped me along the way.

Edith Mayer Cord
Columbia, Maryland
2019

Beginnings

1. VIENNA, AUSTRIA

My Childhood and Early Memories

As a child, I wanted to be like everyone else. As an adolescent, I yearned for schooling. As a young adult, I just wanted to lead a normal life. In old age, I hoped that the terrible lessons of the Holocaust would be learned and that anti-Semitism would be a thing of the past.

I've come a long way since my childhood in Vienna, where I was born. My parents came from the eastern fringe of the great Austro-Hungarian Empire. Until 1914 both of my parents were living with their families in Czernowitz, then part of the Empire, near the Russian border. Czernowitz had been the capital of the Duchy of Bukovina, annexed as a crown land by the Austrian Empire after the upheavals of the 1848 revolutions in Europe. German was the official language, and my parents and their siblings went to German-language schools. My mother told me that the local population spoke Ruthenian. The city was a major transportation hub and a prosperous commercial center. My mother often talked about the lovely river Prut. Newer buildings reflected the Austrian influence of the *Jugendstil* or art nouveau. After World War I, the province of Bukovina with its capital of Czernowitz became part of an independent Romania. The region was annexed by the Soviet Union after World War II. Today, Czernowitz is part of southern Ukraine.

Shortly after World War I broke out, both families fled to Vienna to escape the advancing Russian troops. My mother, born in 1903, was twelve years old. Her three older brothers were drafted and served in the Austrian army as officers. Karl, the youngest, was killed in 1916 in Italy, a loss from which neither my grandmother, Rosa, nor my mother ever recovered.

My maternal grandfather, Josef Buchholz, was a sophisticated and handsome man with dark eyes and a stylish goatee. Though he had his rabbinical ordination, he never used the title of rabbi. He made his living as a wholesale food merchant, trading sardines by the wagonload, grain by the ton, chocolate and other foodstuffs by the box and barrel. Later, I learned that Jews had lived as merchants in Czernowitz for centuries. Before World War I the Jewish population numbered about 30,000 or one-third of the total population in town. It was a prosperous community judging by the imposing Moorish revival synagogue (now destroyed) and by what is now the Palace of Culture, originally built to serve as the Jewish National House. The rest of the population was made up of Germans, Poles, Romanians, Ukrainians, and more, all living together under the rule of the Austro-Hungarian monarchy. After World War II, members of those different ethnic groups were chased out by the Soviets, with Germans sent to Germany, Poles to Poland, and so forth until only Ukrainians remained.

My mother's family had servants and their standard of living was high. German was spoken at home and all the children attended German-language schools and universities. My grandfather was a highly respected member of the community and the family had what is called *yiches*, Yiddish for ancestry, family status, and prestige.

I suspect the standard of living in my father's family was more modest. My father was the oldest of eight. He was born in 1888 in Horodenka, a small town close to Czernowitz, also within the borders of the Austro-Hungarian Empire. My father was named Schmil Juda, but everyone called him Adolf, a popular name at the time. When my father was one year old, his family moved to Lemberg, now Lviv. When my father was twelve years old, his family moved to Czernowitz where my paternal grandfather opened a clothing store that my mother's family patronized.

Papa's father, Josef Mayer, had a limited command of German. When still a boy, he tried to teach himself the alphabet, but he was caught by my great-grandfather who ripped up the book saying, "*Du wirst dech schmatten!*" ("[If you learn German] you will convert!"). But my grandfather was literate in Hebrew and read the Yiddish newspaper while his written German remained weak. He made amends for what his father had done to him by ensuring that Papa received an excellent secular education. In addition to the required eight years of schooling, my father went to a business academy for four years. As a result, Papa had an excellent command of German and a solid general education. At home, the family spoke mostly Yiddish.

Papa was on the short side with a round face, blue-gray eyes with glasses, very white skin, a high forehead, and thinning blond, straight hair. He was clean-shaven, except for a little, stylish, closely trimmed moustache. As the oldest, Papa often commented that he did not want to have so many children for then they raise themselves. He was very close to his father, which led to resentment among the other siblings (something I learned recently from my Uncle Michael's grandson, Ilan).

When the war ended, Mama's situation in Vienna became precarious. Her father decided to go back to Czernowitz, which had become part of Romania, to see whether anything was left of the family estate. He took his middle son Leon with him and in 1920, while there, my grandfather died of a heart attack. Leon chose to stay in Czernowitz and married a woman named Klara. They had three children: Josef, Rosa, and Karl. In 1918, Mama was left in Vienna with her mother and her oldest brother, Rudolf, who was thirteen years her senior and in his early thirties. They were still living in the same apartment they had occupied during the war. It was on the fifth floor of a nice building in the first district—Werdertorgasse number 17—near the corner of Franz Josef Kai and the Danube Canal.

Vienna was the capital of the once sprawling, multilingual Austro-Hungarian Empire, which was reduced to its German-speaking part after the war. This was the result of President Wilson's Principle of Nationalities, according to which each ethnic group was to have an independent country of its own. That resulted in the dismemberment of the old Empire, leaving in its place small, independent political entities that were not economically viable. This void contributed to the economic weakness and eventual collapse of Central Europe, a decline that opened the way for the totalitarian regimes that followed.

After World War I there were approximately 200,000 Jews living in Vienna, about ten percent of the total population. My family lived in the first district in the heart of Vienna, an area dominated by the soaring Stefansdom (St. Stephen Cathedral) and surrounded by the Ringstrasse where once the city's walls had stood. Now the Ringstrasse was dotted with imposing buildings including the Parliament, the university, the Hofburg (royal palace), two famous museums, the graceful opera house, the Rathaus (city hall) with its gothic spires, the Stadtpark (city park) and its romantic monument of Johann Strauss Jr., all reflecting the city's neoclassical architecture with imposing columns and statues on top of public buildings. The Jews living in the first district were more assimilated than those living in the second district, which had been given to Jews by King Leopold and was known as the Leopoldstadt. In the heart of the first district was the

Judenplatz, the center of the old Jewish Ghetto. When I was five years old, Mama told me that was where they burned Jews in the Middle Ages. And so from early on, I was aware that we were a persecuted minority.

While it is true that Jews were discriminated against and persecuted throughout the Middle Ages and later, the actual burning was done in another location. Both in Vienna and throughout Austria, there had been a series of pogroms over the centuries. These persecutions had some economic motivations, but sadly, they were also the result of the Church's teachings. My reaction to Mama's comment? "I'm glad they don't do that anymore." Little could I know what the future would bring.

When her family moved to Vienna, Mama was sent to a *Pensionnat*, a private girls' school, until she was sixteen. In 1919, Grandmother Rosa died of the Spanish flu in the epidemic that

Edith's maternal grandfather, Josef Buchholz. Photo taken in Vienna, ca. 1918.

killed millions, leaving Mama orphaned and destitute. She had a bourgeois education, knew how to play the piano, spoke some French, and could embroider beautifully, but she had neither marketable skills nor money. The expensive life insurance policy my grandfather had bought to protect her was paid, but the money was worthless because of the inflation raging in Austria. From my mother's sad experience, I learned the importance of acquiring skills to support myself.

Mama's brother Rudolf, together with her legal guardian whose name I never learned, focused on finding Mama a husband. The story she told me was that a *Shiddech* (match) was arranged with an older man who had money. They got engaged, but the engagement was broken by the groom. To compensate my mother, he gave her a substantial sum of money as a quit claim. As a result, Mama boasted that she was a rich girl.

My parents met in Vienna after the war at a party given in honor of one of Papa's sisters on the eve of her wedding. Mama was just seventeen years old. Papa was thirty-two and was being pressured by his family to

*Edith's paternal grandfather, Josef Mayer, and grandmother,
Rifka Rachel Mayer, née Halpern, Vienna, 1920s.*

take a wife. I don't think there was great passion on either side. Mama said only that she liked him, which was very different from the teenage crush she had on a distant cousin, according to the stories she told me.

*Edith's father and his brother, Michael,
Vienna, ca. 1918.*

My father was obviously ready to marry and would often joke that he had searched for her with great care. My mother came from a good family, and that must have settled the match.

After Grandmother Rosa died, Mama continued to live in the apartment with Rudolf, but when he got engaged, he wanted the apartment to himself. Right after my parents' engagement, Rudolf locked Mama out of the apartment. The story I got from my mother was that she was forced to spend the night sitting with Papa on a park bench. Papa took Rudolf to court, which did not improve family relations, and in the end, the two couples were forced to share the apartment. Needless to say, it was not a harmonious relationship.

My parents were married November 6, 1921; Mama was eighteen and Papa was thirty-three. According to Mama, after they were married, Papa visited his parents every night, leaving her alone. She interpreted this as the result of his excessive devotion to his father. Initially I accepted Mama's view of things, but now I wonder if Papa was happy with his young wife. He was fifteen years her senior, a sophisticated and elegant dandy. Mama was an inexperienced young girl with a limited education and a sheltered upbringing. I also suspect that, at least initially, my parents may have quarreled because, again according to Mama, Papa said, "Do you want to quarrel like your parents did?" By the time I was old enough to understand, I never heard my parents quarrel or even raise their voices to each other. When once asked about my parents in school, I remember saying that they got along like two turtle doves. On March 10, 1923, a year and a half after their marriage, my brother Kurt (Mordechai) was born. I came along in 1928, on June 15, and yes, we all still lived in that same place.

Edith's parents' wedding picture, November 1921, Vienna.

Kurt, 3, Vienna, 1926.

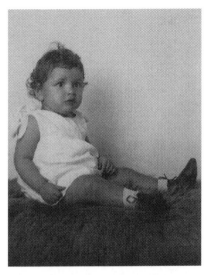

Edith, 1, Vienna, 1929.

Papa, Kurt, and Edith. The caption reads, "Papa and our dear little children," Vienna, 1929.

Our apartment was in a very nice building in the newer section of the first district. By modern standards, the apartment had its limitations. There was a cold water faucet on the landing that served all the apartments on the floor. Inside there was a long hallway. To the left was a toilet used by both families. On the right was a door that led to two rooms occupied by Uncle Rudolf and his wife, later joined by their daughter Alice, nicknamed Lizzy. Mama liked Lizzy, she said, because Lizzy looked like her. Straight down the hall was another door leading to two more rooms occupied by my parents and eventually Kurt and me. Our windows opened onto an inner courtyard, kitty-corner to my uncle's windows, so the families could hear everything going on in the other's living quarters. The families never spoke to each other. As a child, I was well aware of the animosity between the families since their mutual dislike and contempt permeated the atmosphere.

When Mama got engaged to Papa, she'd given him her dowry and, according to her, he'd spent it all setting up his father in business. She resented that. In addition, Mama's relationship with Papa's family was a disaster. She despised all of them and had nothing good to say about any of them, with the exception of my father's sister Anna who died in childbirth soon after my parents' wedding. As for the rest of the family, almost all were very well-off while my family was not. The fact remains that we never socialized with my paternal aunts, uncles, or cousins or got invited to birthday parties, bar mitzvahs, and other life events. Our only contact was through my grandparents or when Mama needed something. Once when we visited an uncle's store, one of my aunts greeted us with, "What brings you here?" Mama took offense and never let it go. So when Mama kept telling me that I looked like Papa's sisters, it was not meant as a compliment and I knew it.

Several years after I was born, Papa took his seventy-year-old parents to city hall to marry them under Austrian law. They had been married according to Jewish law but never got a license because under Austrian law, Jews were required to obtain expensive marriage licenses as the government wanted to keep the size of its Jewish population down. Therefore in the eyes of Austria, all their children were illegitimate and had their mother's name. After the civil ceremony, my father changed our name from Halpern to Mayer. Papa's youngest brother, Oskar, also changed his name to Mayer, but Michael remained a Halpern as did his children.

Papa's concern was always to do things by the book and to adhere to the rule of law. As a former resident of the lost eastern provinces of the Empire, he could choose between Austria and Romania. He proudly chose

Edith's paternal grandparents (front row, center) in Karlsbad, 1925, holding their little cups of mineral water. The photo was sent by her grandfather to her parents in Vienna on a postcard written in German. It is how Edith knew he could write German.

to acquire Austrian citizenship. This was despite the fact that, for reasons only the Austrians in their infinite wisdom could fathom, Papa spent the war years in an Austrian detention camp as an enemy alien. Why Mama's brothers served in the Austrian army and Papa did not remains a mystery.

Edith's Austrian citizenship certificate dated August 9, 1934. It pictured the Rathaus. It was issued after Papa's parents married under Austrian law and reflects the name change from Halpern to Mayer. Edith was six years old and it bears her signature.

Aside from their poverty, my parents had a solid marriage. Papa always treated Mama with respect, lifting his hat whenever he saw her coming down the street. In their marital relations, they observed Jewish law, which meant the monthly trip to the *mikvah* (ritual bath). I had no idea what that meant, and even when I was old enough to learn about it, Mama never taught me a thing and kept me ignorant. I never saw my parents argue. They talked a lot. Papa always filled her in on his business dealings. Mama would sit and listen attentively, usually with some sewing or knitting in her hands. Their conversations dealt with the political situation in Austria and Germany. Financial problems were a frequent topic, and Mama always pushed some idea or other for making money. When my parents did not want us to understand, they switched to Yiddish.

For Mama's birthdays, Papa often bought her a book, which he would read aloud to her while she did her handiwork. Occasionally, for a special treat, they took us to the Yiddish theatre. I was as young as five or six and would usually fall asleep during the first act. When I could stay awake for the second act, I felt proud of myself. I still remember Molly Picon in *Yidl mit dem Fiedl* (The Little Jew with his Fiddle). Papa did not like to go to the movies, so Mama went without him, dragging me along, or she went alone on Sundays while Papa spent the day with my brother and me.

When I was little, Papa still owned a clothing store for men and boys on the Kaiserstrasse, a busy commercial street leading to a suburban railroad station. I remember going there as a little girl. Papa would give me a new *Janker*, one of those grey Tyrolean jackets with green lapels, whenever I outgrew the old one. I also remember getting a trench coat that was too big for me, but I grew into it. After the war, that railroad station was not used as much and eventually it was shut down. This meant less pedestrian traffic and less business for all the merchants. The Depression did not help either. Papa was forced to close his store, but refused to declare bankruptcy and insisted on paying off all his debts. My parents had a small metal lockbox where they kept their cash, and every so often Mama took out some money to buy food until it was all gone. I wore hand-me-downs from my cousins, and I remember standing on a chair crying when I was two or three because my mother had me try on scratchy woolen sweaters from my cousins.

On Saturday afternoons, we often visited my paternal grandparents. They would put peanuts on the large dining room table for us to munch and served us tea with lemon and sugar in glasses set in silver holders. The children sat around the table while the grownups talked in another room. I often played a board game with my cousin Erich Katz, who was my age.

Mama's friends were Finny Seider, younger sister of our next-door neighbor Frau Genia, and Dora Klapholz. As young girls they had been inseparable and were called *Das Drei Mäderlhaus* after a Viennese operetta about three girlfriends. When I was little, she had two other girlfriends whom she visited often. One was Frau Krochmal, whose daughter was one year older than I. We were playmates until she became sick with what may have been cystic fibrosis and died. And so I lost my only playmate. Mama's other friend was a married woman with older children. She lived with her brother, a furrier, in the Leopoldstadt.

Mama loved to talk and when she ran into her friends on the street, I would stand next to her, bored, anxious to leave, often tugging at her coat. I dreaded meeting Frau Dreif, one acquaintance who would pinch me hard on the cheek. She probably thought she was being cute or nice, but she hurt me, and I often wondered why Mama did not protect me from those pinches after I complained about them. One day Frau Dreif was heading in our direction, so I asked Mama to tell her not to pinch me. Mama did, but not without apologizing profusely.

When I was about three, Mama had surgery for an ectopic pregnancy, and I was sent to my paternal grandparents for six weeks. My grandfather was blinded as a result of a streetcar accident just before I was born, and while I stayed with them, I would sit on a low stool next to him and act as his eyes. I would take him by the hand, lead him wherever he wanted to go, and open doors for him, or I would bring him a blanket to put on his knees to chase away the chills. Although I was very little, his blindness made a big impression on me and I tried to help.

My grandmother told my parents that I was no trouble, except that I was a very slow eater. Since chubby babies were considered healthy in those days, they stuffed me with lots of hot cereal. My only defense was to eat very slowly. They treated me well and gave me a doll, but there were no children for me to play with, and I don't recall going out.

Before I was old enough to go to school, Mama would take me shopping to the Karmelitermarkt in the second district. When it snowed, Mama took the sled and pulled me along, storing the groceries between my legs on the way home. In the fall we would walk through the Kaipark, the park along the Danube Canal. I was allowed to gather horse chestnuts to take home. I made holes in them to string them up and make a chain.

Occasionally when the weather was nice on a Saturday afternoon, Mama would take me to the park as a special treat. In the center of the park there was a circle of gravel and grass, called a *Rondo*, with benches all around. There was no playground equipment for children. I could jump rope or play with my *diabolo*—an hourglass-shaped rubber spool that spun on a string connected to two sticks. When it gathered speed, I would toss it in the air and catch it on the string like Chinese jugglers do. It took some practice and I became very good at it.

There were always children in the park, but I did not know them because I went there so rarely. I was too shy to speak to them or join in their play, so I mostly remained an outsider and watched. One incident stands out in my mind. I must have been four and was at the park with Mama on one of our rare outings. The other children were playing a game, something like musical chairs but using trees. They sang a silly nursery rhyme "*Vater, Vater, Leih mir d'Scher, wo ist leer?*" ("Father, father, lend me your scissors, where is it empty?"). You had to leave your tree and get to another one before you were tagged. I was so happy to be included in the game that, when nature called, I refused to leave for fear of losing my place. I ended up wetting my pants, a most embarrassing situation.

Papa was the bright spot in my life. He was charming—playful, funny, and outgoing. He was a master storyteller and I often told him that he was in the wrong profession: he should have been a poet instead of a businessman. Little did I realize that poets too have a tough time making a living. He played the violin by ear and when he came back from his business trips to Italy, he would play Italian songs for us. He also loved to play cards, and he taught us many games including blackjack.

Papa had a tuning fork that he would strike against a hard object, then put to my ear so that I could listen to it hum. Music was an important part of his life and he passed that love on to me. We had a radio that played Viennese waltzes, arias from operettas, Hungarian music, pieces by Brahms and Liszt, and other popular classical music. When Papa came home at the end of the day and the radio was not on, he would exclaim, "How can you live without music?" and turn on the radio. When Papa's taxes were unpaid, the tax collector would come to the apartment to collect the only thing left of value—the radio. Our other valuables, like the silver candlesticks, were already in the pawn shop. Whenever some money came in, Papa would run to retrieve the radio.

I loved to sing and loved music as much as Papa did, but there was no money for music lessons. I knew my cousins were taking dance lessons because they showed us photographs of themselves in ballerina dresses. I wanted to be a ballerina and dance, too. I also pined for a scooter, but it remained an unfulfilled wish like so many others. In wintertime, I remember standing at the fence enclosing the ice skating rink with my face pressed against the cold metal, watching longingly as skaters twirled to the tune of the "Skaters' Waltz."

Mostly I dreamed of owning my very own teddy bear. Whenever we went to visit Frau Genia next door, I was allowed to play with their brown teddy bear and was sad when I had to go home and leave it behind because I secretly hoped she would let me keep it. When I was seven years old, I got sick with a sore throat and high fever. Mama could not take me out and she did not like to leave me alone, so she asked me to stay in bed while she went shopping. When she came back, she gave me a big box. My eyes popped wide open when I found a teddy bear with golden yellow hair, stuffed with straw. It had a black nose and glass eyes. I kept that teddy bear throughout my years on the run.

Papa in Vienna, 1930s.

Papa was a heavy smoker and had three nicotine poisoning attacks. We knew smoking was bad for him, so after the first attack, Kurt and I would encourage him to throw away his half-smoked cigarettes. After cutting down initially, he resumed his habit and had another bout of nicotine poisoning. Kurt and I badgered him not to smoke, but to no avail until the third episode when he became very ill. I vividly recall the scene. We were all standing around his bed with the doctor who pleaded with him to stop smoking, "Mr. Mayer, you have a wife and young children . . ." After that episode, Papa quit cold turkey. Kurt and I never smoked because we witnessed our father's struggle with nicotine addiction.

We vied for Papa's attention and he would often play with each one of us in turn. During the first six years of my life, I spent a lot of time with him. He taught me games—cards, checkers, and chess. He told me stories: I had a choice between grandfather stories, Sherlock Holmes stories—he was a Sherlock Holmes fan—and Bible stories. Much of my knowledge of the Bible came from his bedtime stories.

Judaism was an important part of our lives. Papa was very observant, putting on *tallis* and *t'fillin* (prayer shawl and phylacteries) every morning. My parents kept a kosher home and observed Shabbat and holidays. Every Friday night, the table was set with a white tablecloth and candles, even when the fare was meager. Mama usually managed to buy a carp for Shabbat. We would go down to the Danube Canal and pick out a fish from the holding tank. The fishwife would kill it with a blow to the head, then remove the scales and clean out the insides, and Mama would cook it. Chicken was a rare treat reserved for holidays.

In spite of the importance my parents attached to religion, my religious education was mediocre, in sharp contrast to my brother who started learning Hebrew at the age of four. My parents hired a tutor for me, Mr. Ringel, who was even poorer than we were and who taught me the Hebrew alphabet. The Bible story that he delighted in telling me over and over was the story of Adam and Eve, and how Eve was the one who had tempted Adam to disobey God. Needless to say, I did not learn much, nor did the story he chose paint women in a favorable light.

Kurt and I attended the Seitenstettentempel, the main synagogue on the Seitenstettengasse, where there was a one-hour youth service on Saturday afternoons. (The temple, now called the Stadttempel, was the only one out of the more than eighty temples and synagogues in Vienna that survived the Nazi onslaught.) Papa went to a little shul in the Judengasse where he would spend Friday nights,

Kurt, 10, and Edith, 5, Vienna, 1933.

Saturday mornings, and often Saturday afternoons until Shabbat was over with the *havdalah* ceremony. Many times I would meet him there in the afternoon and stay with him until *havdalah*. The men would fuss over me and my big eyes.

On Sundays Papa usually took us to the museums of art or natural history. Sometimes we went to the park around the castle of Schönbrunn and the Gloriette. I guess Mama never went along because it was her day off and she loved going to the movies. I think that for her, the movies were an escape. When she could spare a schilling she would take me with her. I saw some of Rudolf Valentino's silent films and *Ben Hur*. She told me I should know the classics. I also saw new films, but I confess the kissing scenes bored me no end. As a special treat on birthdays, Papa would take us to the Prater, the big Viennese amusement park, though we couldn't afford the rides. I have a picture of him with me sitting on a *papier-mâché* horse, taken by a photographer. The photo is inscribed by my father to his little daughter on her sixth birthday, and I look happy.

The caption, "As a souvenir of our outing to the Prater on June 17, 1934. Papa and his little daughter Edith Halpern on her sixth birthday June 15, 1934."

In wintertime, cold was a constant companion. Viennese winters were harsh, with lots of snow crackling under foot as the sidewalks were never cleared but only sprinkled with ashes. The apartment, too, was always cold. We had a floor-to-ceiling green tile oven in the wall between the two rooms and Mama had to build a fire every morning. During the night, the fire would die out and by morning, the apartment was freezing until Mama built a fresh fire. I would sit on my little stool freezing, with my hands in my pockets and shoulders hunched, waiting for the apartment to warm up. There were no snowsuits for children back then and we could not afford leggings, so I wore thin cotton stockings and hand-me-down shoes with holes in the bottom. Since we did not have enough money to re-sole the shoes, Mama would stuff newspaper into the shoes every morning, but it would get wet in rainy and snowy weather, so I often sat in school with cold, wet feet.

When I was four years old, Mama sent me to a Montessori kindergarten. I caught everybody's germs and my colds were severe. My mother always treated them with warm milk, butter, and honey—a concoction I hated—and gave me inhalations that I also hated. In preschool I was painfully shy because I was unused to being with other children and I could not stand up for myself. Because of that, coupled with my frequent absences, Mama took me out of school.

The following year she signed me up again. I was five years old, but still had trouble standing up for myself, so they placed me with the four-year-olds. I remember the school very well. It was a stimulating environment where I was allowed to do things that were forbidden at home, like using scissors. I learned to tie the laces of the ankle boots my mother insisted I wear to "strengthen my ankles," or so she said. Of course, the opposite was true and as I grew older, I often twisted my ankles. School was a world apart. I loved the small furniture, custom fit for me. I got along well with the children and related well to the teachers. I frequently volunteered to help serve lunch. The volunteers had to eat first and finish their spinach, so I ate my spinach. Then I was allowed to push the serving cart while a teacher ladled out the soup and served the food. My report card said that I was very sensitive.

For first grade, I went to the public school in the Börsegasse, which was not far from where we lived. Mama always walked me to school and picked me up because she was afraid gypsies might snatch me. While Austria had many gypsies who were known to steal money or small items, my mother's fears were groundless because they did not steal children. By the time I was in third grade, most children went to school by themselves, but Mama insisted on being my chaperone. By then I was chafing at the bit and wanted to be like the other children—independent enough to walk to school on my own.

There were about thirty girls in my classroom. The children came from all social classes and there were a few Jewish girls from wealthy families, but I did not socialize with them. I was keenly aware that they were always well-dressed and hung out with each other. Two children shared a desk, which was fixed to the floor. When we weren't writing, we had to sit up straight with our arms crossed or with our hands folded on top of the desk.

Despite my social isolation, I did very well. The grading system went by numbers: four was the lowest grade equivalent to an F, and one was the

Edith's first grade classroom. Edith is in the second row on the right. Vienna, 1934.

equivalent of an A. I rated an occasional two in gym, sewing, or drawing, and earned ones in all my academic subjects. *"Lauter Einser wie die Soldaten"* ("All ones lined up like soldiers") my grandmother commented when she saw my report card. My parents never praised me for my academic accomplishments. Perhaps they took them for granted or maybe they thought I would get a swelled head. One teacher wrote that I had "quicksilver in my backside," because I had trouble sitting still in class. Even so, I always had a one in conduct.

The students were divided into three sections: A, B, and C. Section A was for the best students and C for the weakest. Classes went from 9 a.m. to noon Monday through Saturday, and we were given an hour of homework daily. Because of our family's religious observance, the compromise approved by the school was that I would go to class on Saturdays, but would not write.

My teachers were older women and they ran a no-nonsense classroom. We learned a lot. With only three years in elementary school under my belt, I was able to read and write German fluently and without mistakes. I practiced my penmanship and covered pages with each letter of the alphabet, learning print as well as Latin script. We also studied *Fraktur* or Gothic script that was heavily used at the time. I had memorized the multiplication table and mastered long divisions. (To this day, I count in German.) The only time Papa helped me with homework was when I had to memorize the alphabet in first grade and later the multiplication table. Otherwise, I was on my own.

Schulnachricht

für _Mayer Edith_

geboren am 15. 6. 1928 zu Wien in Österr. katholisch, evangelisch, A. H. B. mosaisch, konfessionslos;

Schüler/in der 2. Klasse der öffentlichen allgemeinen (vierklassigen) Volksschule für Knaben/Mädchen in Wien, 1. Bezirk, Börse gasse/straße Nr. 5 platz.

Halbjahr	Betragen	Fleiß	Religion	Heimatkunde	Deutsche Sprache	Lesen	Sprechen	Rechnen und Raumlehre	Zeichnen (und Handarbeit)	Singen	Turnen (Körperliche Übungen)	Weibliche Handarbeiten	Äußere Form der Arbeiten	Zahl der versäumten Schultage entschuldigt	Zahl der versäumten Schultage nicht entsch.	Zu spät gekommen	Tag der Ausstellung	Unterschrift der Eltern oder deren Stellvertreter
I.	1	1	1	1	1	1	1	2	1	1	–	–	6	–	–	15. II. 1936	J. Mayer
II.	1	1	1	1	1	1	1	1	1	1	1	–	–	13		4. VII. 1936	

Auf Grund dessen wird diese Schüler/in zum Aufsteigen in die nächsthöhere Klasse für _____ reif erklärt.

_____ Leiter der Schule.

_____ Klassenlehrer/in.

Wurde am _____ 19___ wegen Übersiedlung nach _____ abgemeldet. besucht die Volksschule seit _____ 19___, ist hier eingetreten am _____ 19___ und in _____ heimatberechtigt.

Wien, am _____

_____ Leiter der Schule.

Anmerkung: Die Befreiung vom Besuche eines oder mehrerer Unterrichtsgegenstände wird durch ein in die betreffende Spalte einzuschreibendes „b" (befreit) ersichtlich gemacht.

Notenstufen.

a) Betragen:
1 = sehr gut
2 = gut
3 = entsprechend
4 = nicht entsprechend.

b) Fleiß, Fortgang und äußere Form der Arbeiten:
1 = sehr gut
2 = gut
3 = genügend
4 = nicht genügend.

Städt. Schuldruckforte. Form. III/1. • C. K. • 36. 1. • 54.

Report card for second grade. The report card indicates not only grades, but also religion—Jewish (mosaisch)—and six absences from class. Vienna, 1936.

We learned about Austrian history and the Great War. While in Vienna, I read *The Prince and the Pauper* by Mark Twain in German translation. The story fascinated me, but I skipped over the lengthy and boring descriptions of pageantry, and didn't understand his biting social commentary until much later. I read *Altneuland* (Old New Land) by Theodore Herzl about his dream of a Jewish state. I skipped over the theoretical passages where he described his vision of a Jewish state; I was more interested in the romantic and human part of the story. One of his ideas that stayed with me was that women were working outside of the home. I also read *Das Volk des Ghetto* (The People of the Ghetto), a compilation of stories with mystical overtones. I read *Little Lord Fauntleroy* and tried *Uncle Tom's Cabin*, but could not finish it because it was so sad and made me cry. Of course I read most of Grimm's fairy tales where the good are always rewarded and the bad punished. Early on I learned to admire Schiller and, of course, Goethe. Two poems by Schiller stood out. One, celebrating the virtue of work, was about the forging of a bell called "*Die Glocke*." The other was "*Die Bürgschaft*," a powerful poem about friendship and loyalty. Another book I found enchanting and exotic was *A Thousand and One Nights*. I had few books, so I read my favorites as many as eight times.

When I was four, Papa's father died and Papa decided to try a wholesale business after he closed the store on the Kaiserstrasse. A year later, we moved to an apartment that became available in my grandmother's building on Seitenstettengasse number 5. It was a large railroad apartment, with three rooms and a kitchen, which had running water but no heat. There was a toilet in the apartment, but without heat, going to the bathroom in the winter was a painful experience. I always dreaded it and would put it off as long as I could. There was no hallway either. On the day of the move, Kurt and I ran around the apartment in circles, pushing my doll carriage. I was five years old, Kurt was ten. The apartment had lots of potential. I remember one weekend when Mama, still in her nightgown, walked around and discussed with Papa various plans to improve the apartment. As I watched them, I vividly recall thinking that these were pipe dreams that would never come true, because I was well aware that we did not have the money to make such improvements.

Papa installed shelves and a phone in the largest room and bought dry goods to sell, but somehow the business did not take off. My Uncle Michael had a successful clothing store; so did the two Katz brothers who had married Papa's sisters, Bertha and Dora. Their stores were on one of the major shopping streets, the Mariahilferstrasse. His youngest brother, Oskar, also had a successful store, but no one in the family did business with Papa. It must have been humiliating for him, and I heard Papa complain about it to Mama.

The fact remains that, although Papa could not make a living in Vienna, he didn't leave the city as long as his parents were alive. When our financial situation deteriorated, the wealthier siblings paid for our groceries, perhaps because their mother ordered them to do so. Whatever their motivation, they supported us or we would have starved. They never gave us money, but Mama charged food in a dairy store and they paid for it. While I did not go to bed hungry, my diet was lopsided—it lacked meat, fruits, and vegetables, and consisted mostly of hot cereal, bread, butter, milk, and eggs. I developed eczema on the back of my knees, which was diagnosed as a vitamin deficiency. After that, Mama always made an effort to feed me the proverbial apple a day.

Mama, 34, Vienna, 1937.

There were few family outings. During the summer months we rarely visited the Stadion, a large park with swimming pools, even though summers in Vienna could be oppressively hot. I vaguely remember a couple of excursions to the Kahlenberg just outside of Vienna and to Schönbrunn and the Belvedere, but those trips may have been taken with Papa, not as a family.

We went on vacation twice during the nine years I spent in Vienna. The first time was after Kurt's appendectomy, when he was ten and I was five. He needed fresh air to help him recover during a protracted convalescence. We rented a room at a working farm and Kurt had a wonderful time. The farmer let him climb on the horse-drawn cart and hold the reins. There were farm animals and constant activity. I saw a chicken being killed when the farmer twisted its neck and then, to my amazement, I saw the chicken run around with his head dangling. The image stayed with me and convinced me that killing an animal according to Jewish law was more merciful. Kurt fell in love with the place, and later while we were in hiding, he said he would go to Canada when the war was over and become a farmer. He said farmers never go hungry.

Our second vacation was a year later. I had been diagnosed with tuberculosis, and my parents were advised to take me out of the city to heal in the fresh air. We went to the Burgenland, a rural area not far from Vienna, where my parents rented a cottage near a stream. For many years, I would draw pictures of that little house. Though there was not much to do in that place, it was a welcome change from oppressively hot and dusty Vienna. We often hiked up a steep path lined with blackberry bushes to the nearby village. Kurt would gather berries and once, while leaning too far to get to the riper berries, he fell into the bushes, was scratched by the thorns, and got up covered with blood. Once in the village, Mama ordered a glass of Schnapps—to the innkeeper's surprise—which she used to disinfect my brother's wounds. Later the innkeeper came over to tell us he didn't think Mama was going to drink it.

Anna Buchholz (Mama), 17, and Anna Berler (Tante Anna) with her future husband, Adolf (Alfred) Freudenheim, Vienna, 1920.

These two vacations were paid for by relatives. When Kurt had to recuperate, Mama went to her wealthy cousin, Anna Freudenheim, our Tante Anna, to ask her for the money. I don't know who paid for the second vacation. Tante Anna was my mother's first cousin on her mother's side. She was married to Adolf (who later changed his name to Alfred) Freudenheim. He was an executive, possibly even the CEO of the Montanunion, the Austrian affiliate of Standard Oil. They had no children. He had a sister, Klara

Wachstein, who was divorced. Klara had lost her older child, a boy, to meningitis. She had a daughter, Paula. Klara and Paula lived with the Freudenheims, who treated the little girl as if she were their own. Paula married an engineer from Warsaw and they moved to Poland. Both were killed in the Holocaust.

I loved visiting Tante Anna. She lived on the Schwarzenbergplatz in a spacious apartment with nine or ten rooms. There was a *Herrenzimmer*, a library with dark paneling, to which the men could withdraw to smoke their cigars, drink brandy, and discuss business and politics. There was also a formal drawing room or salon, and a sitting room where we stayed whenever we visited. The place was comfortable and cozy, and especially nice and warm in winter. Kurt and I were always served a tasty snack and then we played with Paula while the grown-ups talked. I thought Paula had such interesting games at her house, especially compared to our home where we only had chess, checkers, and cards. Paula was older than I, and I admired her tremendously. She seemed to have everything I could only dream of: a comfortable home, nice clothes, good food, dance lessons, horseback riding lessons, and vacations. I thought she was very pretty with her dark eyes, black wavy hair, sensitive features, and tall, slender figure. She was always nice to us.

The only bad thing about these visits was in the wintertime when we had to take the long, freezing walk home through the Stadtpark, past the Johann Strauss Jr. monument. Streetcars were just too expensive for us. How I remember those walks! When I was little, Papa carried me. After the age of four, he said that I was too heavy and I had to walk. On rare occasions when Tante Anna visited us in the Werdertorgasse, she would always bring me a bar of chocolate. She was a tall, stately woman, always dressed in good taste, with rounded, attractive features. As a kid, I was struck by her long legs covered with silk stockings.

Tanta Anna in Vienna, 1930s.

In Vienna, housework for Mama was a full-time job. We had no maid and Mama had to do all the laundry by hand. She also had to shop for food daily because there was no place to keep it fresh—we had no refrigeration. On top of that, water had to be carried into the apartment from the landing. Caring for a family of four was hard work.

My parents were strict disciplinarians and demanded respect from Kurt and me. We were required to address them in the third person, as if they were royalty. We also used *"Küss die Hand"* (kiss the hand) as our greeting to them, and I had to curtsy to my grandmother. My parents wanted us to believe that they knew everything and that they were perfect. I recall how shocked I was when I later realized how far from perfect they were. Their attitude toward child-rearing prevented Kurt and me from developing our own judgment and street smarts. Mama's idea of discipline was harsh corporal punishment. She would pull down my panties and spank my bare bottom. Since that hurt her hand, she began hitting me with a wicker rug beater. When I got older, she would slap me across the face. I hated that and recall clearly that I could not wait to grow up so that she could not beat me up anymore.

Mama, 34, and Edith, 9, Vienna 1937.

Kurt and I often squabbled when I was little, but when he became a teenager, we had less interaction. He had a life of his own and I spent all my free time with Mama. Looking back, I would say that Mama did not encourage much interaction between us. It seemed as though everything had to go through her, as if she were the center and we were the spokes of a wheel. Perhaps it was her way of retaining control over both of us. In fact, I would say that my parents wanted to retain control over us, no matter how old we were.

Kurt, the bar mitzvah boy, Vienna, 1936. He received a Kodak camera for his bar mitzvah and after that, the family always had pictures.

Edith, 8, standing by the Danube Canal wearing her first modern shoes and an oversized coat, Vienna, 1936.

Kurt was generally as obedient as I was, but sometime around his bar mitzvah there was trouble. After four years of elementary school, Kurt was enrolled in the Realgymnasium, an academically oriented middle school. He took Latin and needed a tutor who maintained that Kurt was capable of doing the work on his own, but someone needed to stay with him while he was doing it. But something was awry. I was vaguely aware that my parents sought professional help. The counselor recommended that Kurt spend time with people his own age. With our parents' approval, he joined the Betar, a Zionist youth organization founded by Vladimir Jabotinsky. He went to meetings, made lots of friends, and in the summer, he went to a camp in the Salzkammergut on the Wolfgangsee. He came back bubbly, happy, full of stories, and singing the camp's songs. It was one of the happiest experiences of his life.

To make that vacation possible, Mama went to Tante Anna and begged for money. Fritzi, Frau Genia's daughter who was a year older than Kurt, was allowed to join him in the summer camp. While there, Kurt fell in love with an athletic-looking young girl in pigtails. After the summer, he kept in touch with the friends he had made in the camp.

Kurt's Betar summer camp. He is standing, second from the left. Fritzi is next to him, third from the left, 1937.

Though Papa often threatened to spank my brother—he never touched me—I only remember one episode in Italy where he gave Kurt a beating; it may have been because Kurt did not want to go to services on Saturday morning. I was not in the room, but I remember being very uncomfortable. As for Mama, she always yelled at Kurt and me and frequently used sarcasm. She blamed me for everything. One Mother's Day, when I was seven years old, I promised myself to do everything I could to please her, but by 10 a.m. she was already yelling at me.

She knew she had a problem, but instead of doing something about it, she'd say, "I'm nervous. That's how I am." She didn't consider her lack of self-control to be a shortcoming and never tried self-improvement. But she never yelled at Papa, and she was on her best behavior when he was around. Only Kurt and I were her victims. Once Kurt was big enough and strong enough to stop her when she started hitting, he grabbed her arms near the wrist and held them away from his body. Of course that made her even angrier.

As a result of this, plus the Germanic emphasis on obedience and our strict religious upbringing, I was cowed into submission and very shy. When Papa was away, every letter he sent ordered me to obey Mama. Things didn't get better as I got older, which made it hard for me to become a whole person with a modicum of self-confidence. I know my mother used to brag about me behind my back, but to me she was always critical and our relationship remained painful.

Mama also told me I was an accident. That did not bother me because I think I was a wanted accident. That may sound like an oxymoron, but although my parents did not feel they could afford another child, they were emotionally ready to have one. Anyway, there I was and Papa seemed very happy to have a little girl. He was a loving and entertaining companion, and I have warm memories of my early childhood with him.

Mama took care of us, but she never played with us. When my father was away I would ask her to tell me a story. Her answer was always, "I don't know any stories." She tried to treat Kurt and me equally. If she bought me something nice to eat, *einen Leckerbissen*, she would bring Kurt something too. One thing I disliked intensely, though, was getting Kurt's used school supplies. I never had the pleasure of experiencing the feel of a brand new eraser or of a new pencil. I often dreamt that I had a new eraser, so once I decided that I would keep my fist closed in the hopes of finding that new eraser in my hand. Of course when I woke up I found an empty palm.

Despite her conscious attempts at equal treatment, it was clear to me that she favored my brother. He was her firstborn, a boy, and, most important, she said he looked like her side of the family. The truth was that I did not look like her. I looked more like my father, but this was something she could not bring herself to say. She praised Kurt for being a good eater, and denigrated me for eating little.

Perhaps her behavior was the result of her own childhood traumas. When my grandmother was pregnant with Mama, she was very unhappy about it. My grandmother already had three sons and she did not want another child. She even told Mama she tried to cause a miscarriage by hitting herself in the abdomen, but it didn't work. Since Mama was a girl, my grandfather was very pleased and my grandmother reconciled herself. The only picture I have of Mama as a child was taken when she was six years old, soon after recovering from typhoid fever. She looks scrawny and pale as she stands next to her mother, a tall, overweight, elegantly dressed matron. Mama's large brown eyes look straight at the camera and she is not smiling.

Mama said that her brothers abused her and called her *das Traskobjekt* or punching bag. As a result, she never allowed Kurt to hit me, though she more than made up for that herself. Her brother Karl was the only

Grandmother Rosa Buchholz, née Berler, with Mama, 6. Mama was recovering from typhoid fever, 1909.

one who paid attention to her. He helped her with schoolwork, and often made her copy entire pages out of books. As she got older, she would describe her family with visiting relatives gathered around a generously laden dining room table. She would always end her stories with *"Es war schön"* (it was beautiful). While her father was probably nice to her, I have the feeling he was distant. The only one she would talk about was Karl, the youngest of the three brothers, whose photographs and student mementos she kept and treasured until the end of her life. When he was killed in Italy in 1916 during World War I, she lost the one person who had taken an interest in her.

* * *

I was six years old when Papa's mother died. Papa decided to leave Vienna to seek his fortune. Mr. Hirschkrohn manufactured leather jackets and raincoats in Vienna and agreed to fund Papa's expenses as his representative in Italy. And so Papa left for Italy, even though he couldn't speak Italian. He was gone for weeks and months at a time. When traveling in Italy, he continued to eat kosher food by sticking to dairy restaurants called *latterias* and he always carried his *tallis* and *t'fillin* with him in his briefcase.

When he came back to Vienna, he spent more time with his supplier than he did with us. The family saw very little of him during those years, and we still had little money. To make ends meet, Mama rented out two of our three rooms. Two ladies inhabited the large room in the front and an ultra-Orthodox young couple lived in the back room off the kitchen. We kept the middle room for ourselves, which meant we had to walk through the room rented to the two women in order to get to ours. To avoid disturbing them, we stayed in our room as much as possible, and in the evenings we felt like prisoners in our own home. Mama used the rent money to buy produce and occasionally hamburger meat, chicken, or carp.

By 1936, Papa was becoming successful, and we were all unhappy about the long separations. My parents decided to move to Genoa the following year. They decided to wait for Kurt to finish his fourth and final year at the Realgymnasium. That year would also give my mother time to close out the apartment. Mama had time to sell off the furniture, store some things with friends, and get the family ready for the big move.

The other major motivation for leaving Vienna came from politics. My parents had been watching the rise of Nazism in Germany and in Austria with much anxiety. They were well aware of the vicious anti-Semitism of the two Nazi newspapers, *Der Völkischer Beobachter* (The People's Observer) and *Der Stürmer* (The Storm Trooper). They were aware of the concentration camps and of the 1935 Nuremberg laws depriving Germany's Jewish citizens of their basic rights. They expressed dismay when Cardinal Pacelli, who later became Pope Pius XII, signed the Concordat in 1933 with Hitler. This made the Vatican the first state to recognize Hitler and gave him legitimacy and prestige. There was much Nazi agitation in Austria as well. I remember the assassination of Chancellor Dollfuss in 1934, and how shocked I was that he was forced to bleed to death because the four Nazi guards posted at his bedside would not let a doctor near him to provide life-saving care.

Looking back, I don't know why we didn't leave Austria sooner. Perhaps my father would not leave while his parents were alive. To this day I cannot understand the contrast between my parents' political sophistication and their naïveté.

Fritzi (left) and Frau Genia (right) in the Kaipark near the Danube Canal, Vienna, 1937.

They were well-informed. In addition to reading Austrian newspapers, they read Swiss papers—*Die Basler Nachrichten, Die Neue Zürcher Zeitung*, and, more regularly, *Die Weltwoche*. But what did Papa focus on? His Austrian citizenship! And I remember how happy he was when we finally got those papers.

I don't recall saying goodbye to family or friends except for Frau Genia, her daughter, Fritzi, and her old father, Mr. Seider. Papa came to Vienna to pick us up. Most of our stuff was shipped ahead, and we carried just a few suitcases to the station. This was my first major travel adventure, and I still remember the train ride across the Brenner Pass. I was singing a song I had learned in school:

Nun ade, du mein lieb' Heimatland,
Lieb' Heimatland, ade.
Es geht nun fort zum fremden Strand,
Lieb' Heimatland, ade [. . .]
Vom moos'gen Stein [und grünem Gras,]
Da grüß' ich dich zum letzten Mal
Lieb' Heimatland, ade.

Goodbye my sweet homeland,
Sweet homeland, goodbye.
Now it's off to a foreign land,
Sweet homeland, goodbye . . .
From moss-covered stone and green grass
I greet you for the last time
Dear homeland, goodbye.

I was not sad. Papa was with us and I felt we were going forward to a better life. Little did I know that this saved my life. Six months later, Hitler marched into Vienna.

I was nine years old.

What did I retain from these early years in Vienna? Our poverty was a constant source of deprivation, misery, and humiliation. During my adolescence, after many years of abject poverty, always depending on charity, it occurred to me one day that I didn't have to be poor. I could get a job. That was like a revelation. I hated to depend on others. There is a Yiddish expression that says "a poor man is like a dead man, whichever way you put him, that's how he has to stay." So that was poverty. It did not allow for any choices.

From my early childhood, I retained an emotional affinity for traditional Judaism. My parents did not care for the medieval dress of the Hasidim with their beards and long sideburns, but they were not comfortable with Reform Judaism either with its organ music and other features that imitated Protestant services. They wanted to be modern while preserving their traditions. Thanks to my exposure to Yiddish theater, my father's Bible stories, my own reading, and the warmth of our Friday nights and of our seders, I developed emotional ties to Judaism and Jewish culture. At the same time, I was aware that my parents lived mostly in the company of other Jews. Although we lived in a Catholic country, our social contacts with non-Jews, while pleasant, remained limited and superficial. I was also raised with the idea that Judaism was superior to Christianity, because Christian myths and practices were so contrary to common sense. The behavior of Christians with their ceaseless persecution of Jews throughout the centuries only seemed to confirm my parents' opinion.

What else has remained from those years? From my father, I learned to have absolute integrity in business dealings, to immediately pay earned wages to a worker, to show modesty in behavior and dress, to avoid vulgarities in speech, and to only have suitable dinner conversations. I also learned to admire the arts and artists, scientists and writers, to emulate people of achievement, and to respect my elders. Above all, I learned to love books and learning.

2. GENOA, ITALY

The Happiest Year of My Life

It must have been early September 1937 when we left Vienna for Italy. Leaving the familiar for the unknown, I had mixed feelings. But when we went through the Brenner Pass, where the train was stopped for at least two hours to have papers and luggage checked by customs officers, our mood was upbeat. My father was with us and we were looking forward to a better life.

On the way to Genoa, we stopped in Venice. I was excited to be in the city built on water. Kurt and I wanted to go for a ride in a gondola, but Mama was afraid of the water and thought the gondola was unstable, so we contented ourselves with the *vaporetti*, little steam-powered ferries that shuttle passengers along the canals. We were in Venice for only two days, but it was long enough for me to fall in love with the city.

Then it was off to Genoa. Papa had rented a furnished apartment and I had my own bedroom, a luxury I had never known. In Vienna, my mother used to put two chairs by the side of my bed so I would not fall out. But I was nine years old now and I didn't think I needed that, even though my bed was high. Well, on the first night, I fell out of bed, hitting the handle of the night table, which left a square-shaped scrape on my forehead. My parents didn't let me go back to sleep. At the time I did not understand why, but they were obviously afraid I had a concussion. The scar was visible for a long time and my parents always comforted me by saying, "By the time you get married, it will all be gone."

We lived in that apartment for about six weeks until my parents bought a co-op on the Via Zara, a nice street with lovely villas and a few four-story apartment buildings in a residential neighborhood not far from the new sports stadium. My parents bought furniture and Mama happily stayed home. She finally had enough money to indulge her passion for cooking and baking. I can still see her in the kitchen, her lower arms bare, sprinkling flour on a white tablecloth. To make apple strudel, she stretched the dough over the tablecloth until it was paper thin and yet never broke. She spread the dough with apples, raisins, cinnamon, and sugar, then grabbed one end of the tablecloth and rolled the filled dough on itself until she had a long strudel; she shaped it into a horseshoe and carefully placed it in a baking pan. I was allowed to watch but not touch, or even help. She did not even let me spread sugar or cinnamon on the dough, because in her mind, I was a very young, incompetent child.

At fourteen, Kurt wasn't interested in more schooling so Papa, through his business contacts, found him a job at Produzione Industria Tesseli, an elegant clothing store for men in the Galleria Mazzini. The store was run by an Italian family—a father and his three handsome sons, who still lived with their parents. All three were single and all three had mistresses. Of course this immorality greatly displeased my mother. She was afraid that the brothers would exert a bad influence on Kurt, but Kurt was earning good pocket money and he was happy. The brothers took him under their wings—especially Mario—and sometimes invited him to their parents' house. He liked going there and always commented on the lavish three-egg omelets they served, because at home we were used to more frugal fare. As a fast-growing teenager, Kurt was always hungry and often bought sandwiches at the automat between meals. Kurt kept in touch with his friends from Vienna by mail, but Mama always opened and read his letters before giving them to him. To protect his privacy, he had his friends write to him at the post office, care of general delivery.

Kurt's employers: the father and three sons. Mario is in the front, on the right. Genoa, 1938.

As for me, it was back to school. Papa signed me up at the small Jewish day school. Genoa's Sephardic community was old and well-established. Classes were held on the top floor of the new triple-domed Sephardic temple. The sanctuary was beautiful and the school was very modern. Our individual desks and chairs could be moved around and, at first, it struck me as chaotic, especially compared to our fixed desks in Vienna, but it didn't take long before I appreciated the new freedom of movement.

The beautiful Sephardic synagogue in Genoa. The Jewish day school was on the top floor. This photo was taken by Kurt, 1938.

Since I didn't speak Italian, they had me repeat third grade. The teacher was young, quite a contrast to my elderly Viennese teachers. She was lively, pleasant, and tried her best to help me learn the language. I caught on quickly and by the end of the year, I was fluent in Italian. We continued to speak German at home. Mama had brought along my brother's *Gymnasium* literature and history textbooks for me. Before I could read *Pinocchio* in Italian, I read the *Nibelungenlied*, the medieval saga that was the basis for Wagner's *Ring Cycle*. These books helped me maintain and even strengthen my knowledge of German.

My history lessons were very interesting. In Vienna when we studied World War I, we learned that the Austrians and Germans were in the right, the French and British were the bad guys, and the Italians were not much better. In Italian history class, the Italians were the good guys, the French and the English were okay, and the Germans and the Austrians were the villains. Consequently, by the time I was nine, I learned not to trust the printed word. Later, when studying in France, I got the French version of events, which only confirmed my skepticism.

The day school was quite a distance from home, so I was picked up by a limousine that had been converted into a school bus. I thought being chauffeured to and from school was the height of luxury and I was in seventh heaven. I also made lots of friends and was invited to birthday parties and other outings, which was a new experience for me. This was in sharp contrast to my lonely childhood in Vienna where I wasn't even invited to major family events for my many cousins. I was at ease in this Jewish school. In Vienna during the Christmas season, we sang Christmas carols in school, I was absent on Jewish holidays, and I had to go to school on Shabbat. This set me apart from the other children. In Genoa, I learned Hebrew songs, there were no classes on Shabbat or Jewish holidays, and there was no dissonance between home and school.

Best of all, Genoa was sunny and warm with bright blue skies. Gone were the harsh Viennese winters. I loved the way the city looked, too. With a narrow level coastline at the foot of the Alps, most of Genoa was built on the foothills that drop into the Tyrrhenian Sea. The houses on the hilly part of the city looked like children's blocks thrown helter-skelter against the hillside. There were gleaming villas with pastel-colored stucco exteriors looking down on us. At sunset, the hills took on a golden glow. It looked magical. My time in Genoa was the happiest period of my childhood.

Papa was around most of the time. While he did not spend as much time with me as he had in Vienna, I was too busy to miss him because of school, the challenge of learning Italian, and my budding social life. Mama did not do as well. Although Papa was there and she had money, she missed her friends from Vienna. In the spring she had a gallbladder attack and was quite ill. With small changes to her diet she recovered well, though she still complained.

In our building, the flat rooftop had space allocated to each apartment. Each section was the size of a large room and we used our terrace to hang our laundry out to dry. Most of our neighbors did the same thing. A few people turned their space into a little garden or cozy patio. It was all very pleasant and felt safe. In the evening, you could go up there and enjoy the cool breeze from the sea and admire the twinkling lights of the city. One night, Mussolini came to the nearby stadium to deliver a speech. We all went up to the roof and I saw him from a distance. Loudspeakers were blaring so that you could hear him as well as the crowd's chant of *"Viva il Duce, Viva il Duce . . ."*

In March 1938, after the Anschluss (the annexation of Austria by Germany), refugees started pouring into Genoa, mostly from Austria. While in Genoa, we had kept in touch with family and friends in Vienna. Through the temple and the smaller Ashkenazi community that served Jews from Northern and Eastern Europe, my father had lots of contacts with the new refugees from Austria. From these sources, we learned of the petty humiliations inflicted upon the Jewish community, such as cutting off the beards of elderly men, and having middle-aged matrons and old people scrub the sidewalks with toothbrushes. We learned that my uncle Josef Katz, as a prominent and prosperous businessman, had been one of the first to be arrested and sent to Dachau. We also learned of daring escapes over the Alps, and we congratulated ourselves thinking we had left in time. Alas, our sense of security was short-lived. In July 1938, after many meetings, Hitler and Mussolini formed the alliance that became known as the Axis, which was later joined by Japan. For us, this signaled the beginning of the end.

Italy passed racial laws similar to the 1935 Nuremberg Laws and published anti-Semitic propaganda. I can still see the magazine cover of *La Difesa della Razza* (The Defense of the Race, referring to the Aryan race). An article inside compared us to the Hottentots—whoever they were—and showed that we were different in utero. Although only ten years old, I understood that this was pseudoscience. One cover portrayed a Roman face, then a sword, then a caricature of a Jew, then an African. The propaganda was relentless: on posters, in newspapers, at the cinema, on the radio, and, of course, in political speeches.

The irony was that the Italians didn't really know many Jews as there were very few in Italy, and they couldn't tell the difference between a Jew and a non-Jew. Papa, who had blond hair, blue-grey eyes, and very white skin, had an encounter with an Italian lady on a train. She was deep in discussion with two fellow travelers and pointed to Papa as the perfect example of a typical Aryan. To avoid embarrassing her, my father waited for the other two passengers to get off before correcting her. When she still did not believe him, he pulled out his ever-present *tallis* and *t'fillin* to prove it.

After July 1938, Jews were no longer allowed to work in Italy, so Papa and Kurt lost their jobs. My parents canceled their orders for furniture and returned what they could. We gave up the co-op and moved into a single room on the Via Palestro number 15, next door to the French consulate.

We had become refugees.

⚜

The temple and day school were closed. Jewish children were forbidden to go to public school with their Italian counterparts, so we went to a public school in the afternoon while Italian children went to school in the morning. When I was out in the afternoon with my school bag, it felt like everyone could tell I was Jewish. School was a waste of time because they didn't teach us very much and there was no homework. One thing I learned early on, long before George Orwell wrote *1984*, was that when you want to keep people down, you keep them ignorant. In school, we were taught about the *fascio*—a bundle of wheat tied together that was the symbol of the Camicie Nere—the black-shirted Fascists. It symbolized strength through unity because while a single stalk of wheat was weak, a sheath of wheat was strong. It fascinated me to see how totalitarian regimes packaged their ideas for children to make them seem good for society. We were also taught Fascist songs like "*Giovenezza*," but were not taught math, grammar, or any other academic subjects.

Living next door to the French consulate, we witnessed almost daily demonstrations against France by Italian students, mostly teenagers. They usually came after school or on weekends, shouting, "*Voliamo Nizza, Savoia, Djibouti.*" They were calling for the return of the Duchy of Savoy, which had been ceded to France under Napoleon III by the Treaty of Turin in March 1860 at the time of the Risorgimento and the Italian unification movement. Italy was unified in 1861 under King Victor Emmanuel II. The young Fascists also laid claim to a colonial empire in Abyssinia, now Ethiopia. These demonstrations were broken up by hose-wielding firemen who sprayed the demonstrators with strong jets of water. On Saturday afternoons, schoolboys as young as six, led by the Camicie Nere, would parade through town carrying toy guns. It made my parents sad.

Isolated as I was and separated from my friends because the day school was closed, I was very lonely again. Our room overlooked a beautiful garden between our house and the consulate. From my window I could see children playing with their friends and their dogs. I wanted so much to be with them. Instead, I could only watch, trapped inside that room, looking out.

There was a lovely park on a steep hillside at the end of the Via Palestro. In the summer of my tenth birthday, I was finally granted the freedom to go out by myself, a freedom I treasured. Since Kurt had received a camera for his bar mitzvah, photography intrigued me. There was a children's photographer in the park who was always there with his camera ready to photograph parents and children. I often went there to watch what he was doing. Once he had me sit on his lap, but when I felt his hands moving up my thighs I knew something was not right. I climbed off immediately

Via Palestro. The French Consulate is the building on the right. No. 15 is the building next to it with the room where they lived on the second floor. The steps leading to the park are in the background. Photo taken by Kurt, 1938.

and never went back. Another time, a middle-aged man started following me. I was fleet of foot so I ran, dodged, and lost him. After that I became more careful, but I did not tell Mama about these incidents because I feared that she would not let me go out alone again.

In October 1938, the infamous Munich Agreement was signed between France and England on one side, and Germany and Italy on the other, recognizing Germany's control of Austria, ceding the Sudetenland to Germany and breaking up the rest of Czechoslovakia into two rump states: the Czech part under direct German military control and a Fascist, pro-Nazi Slovak state. Despite British Prime Minister Chamberlain's assurances that this treaty guaranteed "peace in our time" for Europe, the talk in my house was that war was inevitable. We had felt for a long time that Hitler would not stop. As young as I was, I understood that and, like the rest of my family, I expected war. It was only a matter of time.

⚜

In the months following the Axis agreement, the Italians kept calling my parents to the *Questura*, sort of a combination police station and city hall. At first it was to provide us with identity papers showing that we were Jews. Later, it was to deny us a residence permit. The officials made it clear they wanted us to leave Italy. My father applied for a visa at the American consulate, but the United States would not have us: first you had to have a sponsor who would provide you with an affidavit of support, and then you had to wait your turn under the quota system based on your country of origin. With the large number of people—Jews and non-Jews alike—seeking to escape the Nazis, the quotas were filled and one had to wait many years for one's turn.

Official document issued to Anna Buchholz on February 2, 1939, stamped with "belongs to the Hebrew race."

This document listing the whole family was issued because of the decree of November 17, 1938, ordering the mandatory census of all Jews in Italy.

In July 1938 President Roosevelt convened a conference in Évian to address the plight of the Jews. As envoy he sent a personal friend rather than a government official, reflecting the low importance he gave to the project. Hitler's initial intent was to get rid of all the Jews in German-controlled lands. He even helped them emigrate, allowing Jews to take along all their furnishings and household goods, provided these were shipped on German lines. They had to leave all their assets to the German government and were only allowed ten deutsche mark per person in currency. Only a few Jews were in a position to take advantage of this opportunity.

Of the thirty-two countries in attendance at the conference, only the Dominican Republic offered to take in 100,000 Jews, provided they would work the land in an undeveloped corner of the island. Initially, only fifty Jews were able to make their way to the Dominican Republic and the Jewish population peaked at about five hundred families, clearly a drop in the bucket given the number of those seeking safety. As the persecution of Jews intensified, an effort was made to save the children through a program that came to be known as the *Kindertransport*. Unaccompanied Jewish children from Germany, Austria, and Czechoslovakia were sent to various countries in Western Europe, including France, Holland, England, and Sweden. Since England took in the vast majority of these children (over 10,000), the *Kindertransport* has become identified with the English rescue operation; however, I personally know children who were sent to France from Germany and to Scotland from Austria. Jewish children from Czechoslovakia were rescued thanks to the efforts of an English businessman by the name of Nicholas Winton. England also accepted Jewish women provided they worked as domestics. These escape routes were closed as soon as war broke out.

As for the Évian Conference, it disbanded with every other country closing its doors, including the United States. Since no one wanted us, it signaled to Hitler that he could do with us as he pleased. In a speech made to his generals in August 1939 prior to the invasion of Poland—as reported by journalist Louis P. Lochner in *What About Germany?* (New York: Dodd, Mead & Co., 1943)—Hitler referred to the forgotten Armenian genocide of 1916 at the hands of the Ottoman Turks. No doubt he expected that the mass murder of Europe's Jews would be equally forgotten. At the infamous Wannsee Conference in January 1942, Hitler's henchmen met to plan the implementation of the so-called Final Solution, and so we died by the millions.

I cannot help but ask myself: did anti-Semitism run so deep? Was it so profound, including in the United States, as to condemn an entire people to the murderous machinations of a dictator? Of course, no one could imagine that Germany would sink so low. But by the time of the Évian Conference in 1938, the humiliating Nuremberg Laws, the seizure of Jewish property, and the concentration camps were already known. Initially, Hitler did not intend to kill us; he just wanted to get rid of the Jewish population in the name of his notion of racial purity. By refusing to accept us and by continuing to treat Hitler as a trustworthy and honorable negotiating partner, the world shares the responsibility for the mass murder of the Jewish people and for the terrible war that followed.

☙

Back in Genoa, my parents were trying to find a hospitable country. I remember poring over maps with my family, looking up every little country in Central and South America and elsewhere. That was one way to learn geography. Papa ran from one consulate to another. We were trapped. Nobody wanted us except for the Dominican Republic and Shanghai. Many times I went down to the harbor to see refugees from Vienna off. Since Genoa was a major port, there were always ships sailing for different parts of the world. The lucky ones got to leave for the United States, Canada, Argentina, Australia, South Africa, or even Lisbon. My family did not have the means to sail to Shanghai, and there was no outside help to get us out.

My parents were probably aware of the Évian Conference, though I do not recall any discussion on the subject, possibly because it did not present a solution to our plight. My father was fifty years old, my brother barely fifteen. No one was in a physical condition to clear the jungle in the heat of a Central American island. We knew about Shanghai, but there again we did not have the means to pay for the three-week ocean voyage for a family of four. And then what? We had no money, no contacts, and no help of any kind.

In desperation, and after months of fruitless attempts to find a safe haven, my parents decided to try to enter France illegally, that is, without visas. Sometime in February 1939, we packed what few belongings we still had and left for Ventimiglia, the Italian border town, to wait for an opportunity to cross into France.

3. NICE, FRANCE

We Are Refugees

We stayed in a *pensione* in Ventimiglia for about two months, and I ate lots of risotto—the cheapest and most filling item on the restaurant menu. Finally on a Saturday morning, the Italian station master, who had previously been contacted by my father, told us that the next day there would be no passport control at the French border because his counterpart had Sunday off. My parents immediately shipped our meager belongings to Nice and prepared us for the crossing. Mama made me put on a little apron over my summer dress. She was thinking of a *dirndl*, the traditional outfit popular in Austria. She thought that would make our family look more casual, when in fact it identified us as foreigners. In her ignorance, she did not know that in a Mediterranean country, only cooks and housewives wore aprons.

On April 23, 1939, the four of us walked to the railroad station to catch the train to Menton, the closest French border town. It was a beautiful Sunday morning. We had no luggage—Papa had his briefcase and Mama took a large purse. That was all. The ride took about thirty minutes and, as promised, no one checked our papers.

In Menton, we took the bus to Nice, the largest and closest city in the area. I will always remember that trip. Papa, Mama, Kurt, and I sat in the back of an empty bus. Papa asked the conductor for four tickets to Nice in his broken French. The conductor hesitated and looked us over, one at a time. I was scared, for even I could tell that he knew we were illegals. Our lives were in his hands. Would he hand us over to the police, or would he let us in? After what seemed like a long time, he handed us the tickets without saying a word and left abruptly. I heaved a sigh of relief. For the moment, we were safe.

Once in Nice, our first stop was the Comité d'Assistance aux Réfugiés (CAR), subsidized by funds from a Jewish charitable organization, the American Joint Distribution Committee (or JDC—usually called the

Joint). It was at 2 Boulevard Victor Hugo, a good walk from the bus station. When we got there, the office was closed because it was Sunday.

By then, it was time for lunch. Mama had brought oranges, which we ate in the office building while sitting on the steps in the stairwell. We didn't want people to notice a family of four eating "on the lam," disposing of the skins in public trash bins, so we left the skins on a radiator in the office building. When we were done, we walked across town to the second address we had been given: the subsidized restaurant for refugees. That too was closed on Sunday evenings. Now we stood in the middle of the street, absolutely clueless, wondering what to do next.

We could not go to a regular hotel because under French law, the management would have to ask for our papers and inform the police of our arrival. As luck would have it, someone spotted us and, in Yiddish, asked whether we needed a place to stay. He took us to a hotel that charged extra for not informing the police. The next day we went back to the office of the CAR. Since the Anschluss, we were officially considered German citizens, because Austria had ceased to exist as an independent country and was now a part of Germany. Since we did not want that, we chose to be ex-Austrians instead, although we had German passports. Once we filled out all the required forms, the CAR assigned someone to accompany us to the police station to legalize our status. With the help of the CAR, my father wrote a supplicant letter to the French authorities:

Nice, April 24, 1939

M. Prefect of the Maritime Alps,

We the undersigned, Schmil, Israel, Juda MAYER born on August 2, 1988 in Horodenka, nationality ex-Austrian, son of Josef Mayer and of Rifka Halpern; and wife Anna Sara MAYER born March 24, 1903 in Czernowitz, citizenship ex-Austrian, daughter of Rosa Berler and of Josef Buchholz, and son Kurt Israel MAYER, born March 10, 1923 in Vienna (ex-Austrian); we have the honor of soliciting from your kindness a residence permit for six months in France to allow us to complete the necessary formalities for our emigration to North America.

We entered France with German passports no. 59/39, 60/39 and 61/39 delivered by the General Consul of Genoa on January 13, 1939.

Of the Israelite religion and as political refugees, we are soliciting from your great kindness the favor of applying the generously
tolerant special laws concerning ex-Austrians so that our status
may be in order with the French authorities.

With our thanks for a hopefully positive response, we ask you
to accept, M. Prefect, the expression of our very distinguished
sentiments.

Family Schmil MAYER
Hôtel du Chateau
3, rue Antoine Gauthier, NICE

The first order of the day was to find affordable housing, for our limited
resources were rapidly running out. My parents found a furnished room
in the old section of town, near the harbor, five minutes walking distance
from the Mediterranean. The room was in an apartment shared by three
or four families, all of whom could use the kitchen.

What I remember most about that place were the cockroaches. They
were big and black, and when you walked around at night, both inside and
outside the house, you could hear them crunch underfoot. When you went
into the kitchen at night and turned on the light, the floor was black and
completely covered with them. So when we had to go into the kitchen,
we would go in, turn on the light, and wait fifteen minutes. By that time,
the roaches had crawled back into their hiding places and the coast was
clear. Since Mama had a profound revulsion to vermin, as did the rest of
us, she did her very best to keep our room free of them. She scrubbed and
cleaned everything and then put a rag soaked in naphthalene or some other
chemical under the door. Whenever we closed the door, we had to push
the rag against the crack at the bottom so the critters would not come in.

Mama would go into a tizzy whenever she saw Kurt talk to one of the
tenants, a young woman who made her living as a prostitute. Although
this woman did not bring her customers to the apartment, Mama did not
like him to talk to her. He had just turned sixteen and Mama had long
conversations with him in code language so that I, at the ripe old age of
ten, would not understand what they were talking about. I eventually
figured out what was going on, but frankly, I had little interest in the
subject. Mama talked about a "7-3-7," her arbitrary code for a prostitute;
I don't remember Papa ever discussing these issues with Kurt. My parents were tough on Kurt who had a strict curfew of 10 p.m. Once, when

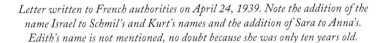

Nice, le 24avril 1939

Monsieur le Préfet des
Alpes-Maritimes
N I C E

Monsieur le Préfet,

Nous soussignés, Schmil, Israel, Juda MAYER
né le 2/5/1895 à Horodenka, de nationalité ex-autri-
chien, fils de Josef Mayer et de Rifka Halpern; et
femme Anna Sara MAYER née le 24/5/1903 à Czernowitz
de nationalité ex-autrichienne, fille de Rosa
Berler et de Josef Buchholz, et fils Kurt Israel
MAYER né le 10/5/1923 à Vienne (ex-autriche); avons
l'honneur de solliciter de votre bienveillance une
autorisation de séjour de six mois en France pour
nous permettre d'accomplir les formalités nécessaires
à notre émigration pour l'Amérique du Nord.

Nous sommes entrés en France munis des passe-
ports allemands n° 59/59, 60/59 et 61/59, délivrés
par le Consul Général à Gênes le 13 janvier 1939.

De confession Israelite et réfugiés politiques,
nous venons solliciter de votre haute bienveillance
la faveur de nous faire appliquer les mesures spé-
ciales généreusement tolérantes concernant les
ex-autrichiens, de façon à être en règle avec la
police française.

Avec tous nos remerciement anticipés, nous
vous prions d'agréer, Monsieur le Préfet, l'éxpres-
sion de nos sentiments très distingués.

Famille Schmil MAYER
Hôtel du Chateau
3, rue Antoine Gauthier
NICE.

Letter written to French authorities on April 24, 1939. Note the addition of the name Israel to Schmil's and Kurt's names and the addition of Sara to Anna's. Edith's name is not mentioned, no doubt because she was only ten years old.

he came home at 11 p.m., my parents locked him out. He stood outside the building talking to my parents through the window. They let him in eventually, but not before giving him a hard time. Such scenes were always very uncomfortable for me.

In the spring and summer of 1939, Nice was filled with refugees of all stripes: Jews and anti-Nazi non-Jews, some wealthy, some not. One of them was an Austrian aristocrat, Count Starhemberg, who frequently associated with Austrian Jews. There was also a group of former secondary school professors from Germany, all Jewish, who let it be known through the CAR that they were willing to give free lessons in French and English. Since some of the refugees were preparing to immigrate to English-speaking countries, it made sense. I jumped at the opportunity to learn French. Both Kurt and I signed up.

Classes were offered three mornings a week. We would take the long walk to the teachers' hotel across town in the newer section of the city. Initially classes were full, but gradually people dropped out until Kurt and I were the only ones left. French grammar did not faze me, as I had already mastered Italian grammar. I was very motivated. I did not want to be placed into a lower grade again because I didn't know French, so I studied my grammar, did my homework, and attended classes faithfully. At bedtime I practiced by telling myself stories in French, though my vocabulary was limited. To complement my grammar classes, Papa enrolled me in the local elementary school. He went to the principal, told her that I did not know a word of French and that I was taking private lessons. He asked if I could attend school in the afternoons in order to be exposed to French, with the proviso that I not be responsible for homework. The principal agreed. In school, I listened attentively to what was being said. One classmate was bilingual because she had Italian grandparents, and she became my interpreter. Within two months, I was able to follow what was going on. The first poem I was able to understand was *"Les Pauvres Gens"* by Victor Hugo. When I told my interpreter the gist of the poem, she enthusiastically raised her hand and the whole class triumphed with me. After that, things got easier. The girls in my class were very nice. One came up to me, pointed to me, and said *"toi"* (you), and then pointed to herself and said *"moi"* (me), and then linked her hands together as she said *"amis"* (friends). My classmates called me *l'Autrichienne* (the Austrian girl).

When school officially began in the fall, I was able to get into a regular French class for my age and keep up with the other students, in contrast to other refugee children who were placed in lower grades because they had not worked on their French in the summer. During all that time, we continued to speak German at home. (I often think this method is a good model for teaching English to immigrant children in America: total immersion plus separate tutoring in grammar for six months or so, regardless of the language spoken at home.) The only casualty was my Italian; with no practice, I lost most of it.

Once school was out after July 14, I went to the beach every afternoon for three glorious months. I was now eleven and Mama let me go out by myself. The beach in Nice was rocky, not sandy, and full of big stones. The rocks were hard to walk on and painful, too, because they were very hot. I learned to keep the old sneakers I had outgrown, cut open the toes, and use them to walk to the water so as not to burn the soles of my feet. Finding a bathing suit for me was a problem because we could not afford to buy one. During that first summer, while I was still flat-chested, I could get away with swimming in my panties. The following year, Mama draped a scarf over my chest like a halter top.

The Promenade des Anglais, in the newer part of town, was an elegant avenue lined with hotels and palm trees that ran along the shore, almost to the harbor. Along its route were privately run beaches that had jute-covered wooden boardwalks leading down to the water. These paid beaches were dotted with beach chairs, restaurants, and cafés, and were completely beyond our means. I swam on the other side of the harbor near the *vieille ville*, the old part of town. There the beach was free, if less glamorous.

Since I did not like to roast in the hot Mediterranean sun, I spent all my time in the water. Although Mama had given me swimming lessons in Vienna, I did not have the confidence to actually swim, so I practiced all the right movements for the breaststroke while holding on to a pole in the

Taken from the park overlooking the Nice harbor with the Promenade des Anglais on the left and the Monument aux Morts carved in the mountainside of the château behind the jetty. Photo taken in 1951 by Edith.

The Casino on the Promenade des Anglais on the Bay of Angels. The casino was destroyed after the fall of France because the Germans needed the steel for weapons. Photo taken by Kurt, 1939.

water. One day, an elderly gentleman who was watching me told me that I clearly knew how to swim. To prove it to me, he waded over and held up my chin while I swam. He was right. I could swim, and after that, I would swim parallel to the shore since I was alone and there were no lifeguards. I loved to float on my back, rocked by the gentle waves of the sea while looking up at the sky. There was nothing in the world but the sea, the blue sky, and me. It was a wonderful feeling of peace and beauty.

As people fled Germany, Austria, and Italy, stories of daring escapes over the mountains or around the shores of the Italian and French Rivieras began to circulate. I imagined that if I had to escape by sea I would have to swim under water, so I trained myself to hold my breath as long as possible. I also trained myself to swim for endurance rather than speed.

⚜

We soon moved away from the harbor area to get away from the roaches and the prostitute. We rented a room on the rue Cassini near the Place Garibaldi, still in the older part of town. That apartment was also filled with refugee families—one per room—with shared kitchen privileges, but I don't remember eating any cooked meals there. Except for a light breakfast, we mostly ate at the subsidized restaurant.

Place Garibaldi in Nice. The Mayer family lived in a room
nearby on the rue Cassini. Photo taken by Kurt, 1939.

During *la Fête de Mai*, the month–long celebration of spring in May, every square in Nice was decorated with colorful lanterns. The cafés put their tables out on the sidewalks and public squares as music blared from loudspeakers. "España," a composition by Emmanuel Chabrier, and "The Carnival of Venice," arranged by Jean Baptiste Arban, were frequently broadcast across the Place Garibaldi. This music remains associated in my mind with the Place Garibaldi and with a time when our family was still together. Sometimes people would dance to the music. For the price of a lemonade, you could sit at a table for hours absorbing the fragrance of spring and savoring the soft night air. So this was *la douce France* that my father always talked about. The spring and summer of 1939 were the last seasons of peace before all hell broke loose.

Unfortunately, my parents ventured out in the evening only on rare occasions. They never took walks along the Promenade des Anglais where everyone would congregate in the evening to stroll, chat with friends, or just sit and listen to the waves. For some reason, my parents felt that we all had to be in after dark—even in those cramped quarters—though fresh air, music, and companionship were simple, free pleasures. One of the benefits of socializing with the other refugees would have been access to valuable information. What my parents didn't realize was that anything they could find out, including rumors, could be useful for our survival.

That summer, Kurt was hired by the CAR as doorman and errand boy, so he had to drop out of the French class and I remained the only student until school started. His job came with an old bicycle, and boy did he love it! He would whistle the tune of *Shalom Aleichem* to get Mama's attention—we now lived on the second floor—because he wanted her to look out the window to watch him riding his bike, hands free. Kurt was a pleasant and conscientious employee, well-liked by everyone. He would occasionally go to the beach on the Promenade des Anglais and hang out with young people his age. One girl in the group, Edith Steinmetz, whose nickname was Putzi, was always surrounded by boys. She was eighteen, wore lipstick, and her body glimmered with suntan oil. She had a nice tan and never went into the water. She just sat on the beach and flirted with all the boys. As a flat-chested kid with pigtails, I stayed away and went swimming by myself.

There were lots of children in Nice. The CAR wanted to do something nice for us so they treated us to a screening of *Snow White*, the popular Disney film. It had come out while we were still in Italy, but at the time we had no money for movies, so I was very happy to see it at last. Outside of this, I do not recall spending any of my time with other refugee children.

Poverty was our constant companion. I often asked Papa for an ice cream cone during those hot summer days. It cost ten centimes. Papa

Refugee children in front of the subsidized restaurant.
Edith is in the front on the right, 1939.

would say that he would have to buy one for each of us, which came to forty centimes, and we could not afford that. As a result, ice cream remained a special treat. Other than the items in my wardrobe that Mama knitted for me, I wore hand-me-downs from charitable organizations, including shoes that gave me blisters. On the rare occasions when I found something nice to wear, Kurt took pictures of me in my new outfits, and I still have those photos.

Papa in Nice, Place Garibaldi, spring 1939. Photo taken by Kurt.

Kurt, 16, Place Garibaldi, spring 1939. Photo taken by Edith.

Edith, 11, Place Garibaldi, Nice, summer 1939. Photo taken by Kurt.

The CAR gave a modest cash subsidy of fifty French francs per month to each refugee family. We would joke that it was too much to die on, but not enough to live on. Even with the subsidized restaurant and Kurt's modest job, life was difficult because we were not allowed to work. Mining and agriculture were the only two industries open to foreigners. Since Mama could sew and Papa knew some tailoring, my parents took in mending, and they also altered clothing for the wealthier refugees. They turned cuffs, sewed on buttons, and resized garments.

Eventually my parents found an apartment in a suburban area, half an hour walking distance from the last streetcar stop on the Boulevard de l'Observatoire. Aside from the healthier air and greater privacy, my parents had been anxious to get out of the shared apartment because they did not like the company Kurt was keeping. They felt that one young man in particular was a bad influence on him. At least, that's what they said.

The new apartment, at number 63 Boulevard de l'Observatoire, had two rooms, a kitchen and a toilet. It also had a large terrace with a view of the Saint Roch neighborhood down below. The building was built into the mountainside and had two floors above street level and two floors below. We had the second floor below street level. Our second bedroom had mildew and was uninhabitable, so all four of us slept in the larger room. We had one box spring shared by Mama and me, with my head at her feet when we slept. Papa and Kurt slept on the stone floor on featherbeds we had brought along from Vienna. The kitchen also served as the living room, dining room, laundry room, and homework room.

The worst thing about that apartment was that you had to walk up a very steep hill to get home. On hot summer days, the hike was murder. In the summer of 1940, when I went down to the sea for my daily swim, the one-hour walk home from the beach negated the refreshing experience, so I gave up swimming because it was not worth it to make the trip back up the mountain.

In addition to doing alterations, my parents began taking in laundry. They picked up the dirty laundry at the hotels, carried it home, washed it, and dried it on our nice terrace. Mama did the ironing and mending, and my parents then carried the clean laundry back to the hotels. To hide their economic activity, Mama covered the laundry with fresh vegetables. Papa helped with tailoring, pick-up, and delivery, and I always helped carry the bundles to and from the hotels when I was not in school.

Edith, 12, with her mother on the terrace. Photo taken by Kurt, 1940.

While we still lived near the Place Garibaldi, my parents signed me up at the École Papon, *Cours Moyen Première Année*—essentially the fourth grade. My teacher was Mme Provençal, a fiercely patriotic woman who taught us songs from the French Revolution and the Napoleonic era. She constantly ranted how the French had been making butter while the Germans were building guns.

Academically I held my own. I was proud to be placed with children my age. We were given monthly tests in every subject. Scores were added up and students were ranked on the basis of their total score. The one with the highest score was first, the next one second, and so forth. Seating in class was based on this ranking so that the good students sat in front and the weak ones sat in the back. During the first grading period, I was ranked nineteenth out of a class of about forty students. The following month I moved up to sixteenth, then twelfth, then seventh, seventh again, then fifth. Every month I would receive praise and an *image*, a little picture habitually given as a reward to children who did well.

During the last month of school I ranked first, which did not please Mme Provençal. Instead of the usual words of encouragement, she told me that the only reason I was first was that the student who normally achieved that rank, Simone Bertolo, was gone. It was unkind and it hurt. What was more significant was that Mme Provençal did not tell me that I should take the entrance exam to the *lycée*. At the time, twelve was the cutoff age for taking the exam and I would turn twelve at the end of that academic year. I had mastered French and arithmetic, and I was ready for the more rigorous curriculum of the French secondary track. Instead, I would end up wasting a precious school year. It was evident Mme Provençal did not have my best interest at heart.

Cours Moyen Première Année. Edith is fifth from the right, back row. Simone Bertolo is third from right, front, 1940.

The girl who usually placed first happened to be my best friend. Simone was blond and petite, with small features and always neatly dressed. I sometimes visited her on the rue de la République where she lived with her parents. I don't know whether her place deserved the designation of "apartment." They had two immaculate but tiny rooms, and Simone slept across the hall in a space not much bigger than a closet. She was an only child and her parents told me that they were atheists. While they called me *la petite juive*, the little Jewish girl, I never felt any negative connotation, especially since they were always very nice to me. In June 1940, the Bertolos fled Nice, fearing the German invasion during

Simone Bertolo, 1940.

the collapse of France. That's why she was not in school at the end of the school year.

I kept in touch with Simone over the years. In 1970–1971, my family lived in Nice for a year and she invited us all to dinner in her new apartment near the École Bischoffsheim. We were very happy to see each other again. She never earned her *Baccalauréat*, married a truck driver, had one son, and did the bookkeeping for her husband. She was as sweet as ever and seemed very happy. Her mother, now widowed, had returned to her Catholic faith. She still lived in the hovel on the rue de la République.

✿

As we expected, Germany did not honor the 1938 Munich Agreement. After staging an incident in Danzig (today's Gdańsk), Hitler accused Poland of starting a war. As planned, German tanks entered Poland on September 1. France and England, who were treaty-bound to defend Poland in the event of an attack, declared war on Germany on September 3, 1939.

What followed was the winter of the *drôle de guerre*, or phony war—also called the *Sitzkrieg* or sitting war—with occasional skirmishes along the Maginot Line where France's stationery guns were facing Germany. But there was not much action until the spring offensive in May 1940, when the Germans attacked France with what came to be called the *Blitzkrieg*, or lightning war. They swept through the low-lying areas of Holland and Belgium to Paris, bypassing the fortified Maginot Line in five short weeks. In school, we were taught to put on gas masks because the Germans had used mustard gas in *La Grande Guerre*, or the Great War. Of course no one expected a second world war to follow so soon on the heels of the first.

Soon after the French declared war on Germany, Papa was arrested as an enemy alien. He was sent to Les Milles, a camp near Marseille. Ironically, he was interned with Nazis because the French made no distinction between those fleeing Nazism and those who might have been a real threat to the country. All were foreigners, all were thrown in together. In fact, the prisoners were mostly Jewish refugees who had fled the Nazis.

Papa was arrested a couple of months after my eleventh birthday. After that I had almost no contact with him. Mama did all the letter writing, and while Papa's letters sent me kisses along with injunctions to listen to Mama and be good, the letters were addressed solely to Mama and she never shared them with me.

Camp des Milles: one of the brick ovens where people were forced to sleep. Used with permission from the Coll. Fondation du Camp des Milles. Mémoire et Education.

I visited Les Milles in the summer of 2013. Except for Drancy, it is the only camp that has a building; the others, consisting of wooden barracks, fell apart so that only memorial plaques are left to mark the spot. Les Milles had been a brick factory. The prisoners slept on the concrete floor in the brick oven or on a metal grid on the second floor. Both floors were covered with straw. Both were infested with fleas, lice, and other vermin. There was dust everywhere from the bricks. The little graffiti that survived on the walls and the few drawings made by inmates gave a picture of what it was like. The prisoners referred to the place as the vermin capital of the world. There were only three toilet facilities and three showers for 500 camp inmates. It is clear that sanitation and cleanliness were of no concern to the French authorities. After the war, Les Milles reverted back to brick making, but in 2012, it was converted into a memorial museum.

France collapsed faster than anyone expected. The British Expeditionary Force, cut off by the advancing German tanks, was trapped near Dunkirk. This episode led to the famous Miracle of Dunkirk when flotillas from England brought the majority of their troops home, along with a few lucky French soldiers. Soon after that, in June 1940, when France fell in what the French call *La Débâcle*, everything turned to chaos. Throughout that winter there had been a mandatory blackout issued for the entire city of Nice out of fear of bombardments. Blue light bulbs were required, and all windows were covered with blue opaque paper. When France collapsed, Mama and I were issued an authorization by the military commander General Lemoine, dated June 12, 1940, a time when France was already overrun by German tanks heading for Paris, giving us permission to re-

This is the official authorization issued by the French Army that
allowed Edith and her mother to remain at their residence until
a decision was taken to send them back. June 12, 1940. Original
at the United States Holocaust Memorial Museum.

main at our address and await the decision to send us back essentially
to where we came from—*"refoulement des ressortissants de la Puissance UN*
necessiteux," whatever that meant.

Rumors were rife. Somewhere Mama picked up information that Jews
were to be taken into protective custody by the French and that we were
supposed to show up at police headquarters. At the time, the government
of the Third Republic had fled Paris for Bordeaux and the French could not
even protect their own. A flood of refugees streamed down from Alsace-
Lorraine and other combat zones in the north.

What did Mama do? She went to downtown Nice, accompanied by
our fifteen-year-old neighbor Rosette, to find out where we were supposed
to go. She packed our bags and we were ready to go wherever they sent us.
Mama left with Rosette around 2 p.m. At dinnertime, Rosette returned
alone and told me they were unsuccessful in their attempt to get help
from the authorities. She described how, by late afternoon, Mama stood
in the middle of the road in front of a truck waving her arms trying to
stop the driver and hitch a ride. The story did not make any sense, nor did
Rosette. In the end, Rosette decided to leave Mama and go home. She had
no idea where Mama had gone.

I waited with our packed suitcases in our empty apartment where there was nothing to eat. At 10 p.m., when Mama was still not home, I decided to go look for her. I started down the Boulevard de l'Observatoire, but it was pitch black and I could not see a thing. Until that night, I had always been afraid of the dark. Groping my way down the boulevard with real things to worry about, my fear left me. After walking a short distance, I realized that I could not accomplish anything, so I returned to the apartment. An hour later Mama was still not home, so I decided to go to the nearby house of another Jewish refugee family. They were very gracious, gave me some food, and invited me to spend the night.

By midnight, just as I was about to settle down to sleep, Mama arrived. Instead of recognizing that I had acted sensibly, Mama was furious with me, and bawled me out for going to the neighbors, eating dinner, and going to bed. How dare I do such things when she was out there wandering in the streets? I quickly dressed and left with her. I have no idea where Kurt was that night, but he must have been safe because Mama did not express any concern about him.

It was a good thing the protective custody Mama sought did not materialize, or I would not be here. As soon as the armistice was signed, the victors did not waste any time. The puppet regime of Vichy was established in the south of France, referred to as Free France, while the northern half of France and the entire Atlantic coastline were under direct German military command. The Vichy government was headed by the eighty-four-year-old Maréchal Pétain, the savior of France at the battle of Verdun during World War I who still enjoyed a great deal of prestige among the French and who was acceptable to the Germans because of his authoritarian political views. The Third Republic and its constitution were replaced by the French State; the motto of "*Liberté, Egalité, Fraternité*" was changed to "*Travail, Famille, Patrie*" (Work, Family, Fatherland). Pétain appointed Laval as his prime minister and, because Laval's extreme right wing views were in line with Germany's, he reinforced France's collaboration in every way, including the persecution of Jews.

Although barely twelve years old, I remember my dread at the uncertain future we were now facing. While mass murder was yet to come, we knew about concentration camps and the treatment of Jews in Germany and in Austria. Besides De Gaulle's speech to the French on June 18, what I remember most was Churchill's famous speech when England stood alone after the fall of France. His determination to continue the fight against Germany gave me hope, and his words "we will never surrender" still ring in my ears. Churchill remains high in my pantheon of heroes as the man who saved Europe and civilization during its darkest hour.

Soon after the fall of France, Papa was released along with all the other prisoners. We were overjoyed to see him, but he had some kind of infection on his belly and had to be hospitalized. The hospital, which was quite a distance from where we lived, kept the wound open with a shunt in order to drain the infection. He was there for a couple of weeks and we went to visit him almost daily until he was released.

It was July 1940 and Papa had been home from the hospital for only a few days when we were awakened at dawn by a knock on the door. Two French policemen came to arrest Papa and Kurt. The order from Vichy was to arrest all Jewish men above the age of seventeen, and Kurt had just turned seventeen. The police gave them thirty minutes to get dressed, pack their bags, and say goodbye to Mama and me.

That was the last time I saw my father.

When Papa was arrested, he took along the precious silver pocket watch that so enchanted me as a child. At my request, Papa would push the knob, and the watch would play a lovely chime. It was attached to a gold chain that he left behind. I know now that when people arrived in Auschwitz, Jews were asked to give any valuables to the guards for "safekeeping." I cannot help but wonder whether some old German, playing the chime for his grandchild, boasts about how it came into his possession. Does he boast "This one, sonny, I took from an old Jew just before I shoved him into the gas chamber"? Or does the new owner ever feel remorse or shame? Whenever I pass in front of a fine jewelry store, I still look for that watch.

Kurt and Papa were sent to Gurs, a concentration camp built in a swamp near Pau in the Pyrénées. It was originally built to house refugees from the Spanish Civil War. There, in order to earn some cash, they did laundry for those camp inmates who had a bit of money. Washing clothes in that setting must have been hard work, especially during the winter months. In Mama's papers, I came across a postcard sent from Gurs by my Uncle Rudolf (the same uncle who threw her out when she and Papa were engaged). He wrote that he ran into Kurt in the camp, and described how painfully thin he looked. I still have trouble reading that postcard because my eyes always fill with tears.

Meanwhile the noose tightened around Mama and me. She was frequently called to the *Préfecture* where our residence permit was renewed for increasingly shorter periods of time: every three months became every two weeks. Since Mama did not speak French, I always went with her as the interpreter. These meetings with the French authorities were a farce. Because we were not allowed to work, we had to show that we had enough resources to live on. The standard procedure was to go to the CAR, borrow 5,000 French francs and then show that money to the authorities. The next day you returned the money to the CAR so they could give it to another refugee for the same purpose. It was a Kafkaesque world.

Mama worked hard to keep body and soul together as she continued to take in laundry. That winter, I spent my Christmas vacation ironing shirts for her customers and helping her carry the bundles to and from the hotels. When I went back to school in January, we were assigned a composition about what we did during our vacation. I concocted a story about visiting my grandmother in the countryside so it would read like the compositions the other girls were writing. I was too ashamed to tell the truth, and I could not reveal that Mama was working and breaking French laws forbidding work by foreigners.

Food rationing became more severe after the German Occupation. Our ration cards were stamped with a J for *JUIF* as were the rest of our documents. The names Sara for women and Israel for men were added to our identity papers to better identify Jews. As a teenager, I was entitled to more food than the adults. For instance, I would get one-and-a half pounds of marmalade or jam a month while Mama got half a pound. This added up to a full can of jam that we sent to Papa in camp while we did without. We did the same thing with sardines or tuna and other items that could easily be shipped. Typically the French guards in the camp helped themselves to at least a portion of the package while Papa and Kurt got what was left. To compensate for the lack of food, I had to swallow cod liver oil, which I hated, and also calcium granules.

Between my inadequate diet and because maintaining proper dental hygiene was impossible, I began to lose my teeth. Whenever I had a tooth-ache, my tooth was pulled, without anesthesia, at a public dental clinic. To rinse their mouths, children in the clinic were given unwashed cups used by other children. Each child stood before a sink in a large hall, dripping blood all over the place. It was gross.

In the spring of 1941 after Papa and Kurt had been in Gurs for a year, we received a postcard with the usual news, but at the edge of the card Kurt scribbled, "Mordechai is coming." Mordechai was Kurt's Hebrew name,

Copy of Edith's new birth certificate with the name Sara added as
a middle name as required by the Germans, 1939. The authorities
also ignored her father's name change from Halpern to Mayer.
Original at the United States Holocaust Memorial Museum.

and we wondered what it meant. We did not have to wait long to find out. A couple of weeks later, Kurt showed up at our door.

He had escaped from Gurs by hiding in a garbage truck. He told us Papa would soon follow. At the time I believed that. Now I realize that, without Kurt, there was no chance Papa could escape. He spent a couple of weeks with us. For the first time, I was getting to know my big brother. I had just turned thirteen, and we were beginning to appreciate each other. Kurt had always been protective of his little sister. I once went to town with him. He wore a white shirt and gray slacks, and I wore a white blouse and gray skirt. I thought we looked like brother and sister in our matching outfits. He was six feet tall and, I thought, good-looking.

He told Mama that girls my age are usually not good looking, but thought I looked nice. I was very proud to be seen with him.

After our initial joy at having Kurt back, we realized it was unsafe for him to stay with us because the police would come looking for him, or so we thought. After many inquiries and much searching, we found a farm outside Nice where a number of young Jews were on *Hachshara*, that is, learning to work the land in preparation for a move to Mandate Palestine, the *Yishuv*. Kurt spent about six weeks there and recovered from camp life. A few photos show him in the com-

Kurt, 18, in Nice right after his escape from the camp of Gurs. He was very thin and looks grim, 1941. Photo taken by Edith.

pany of young people, and he looks happy and well-fed, quite a contrast to his haggard look after his escape from Gurs.

Edith, 12, in front of 2, Boulevard Victor Hugo, 1940. Photo taken by Kurt.

Kurt, pictured in the middle of his friends at Hachshara, two months after his escape from Gurs, 1941.

However, all the people at the farm were "legal" and Kurt's status as an escapee jeopardized all the others, so he was asked to leave. Putzi Steinmetz's father was something of a wheeler-dealer and strongly recommended that Kurt join the Prestataires—a French organization for foreigners who volunteered to serve France as noncombatants under French military command. Kurt was issued a uniform, but kept his ID with his real identity. This was the worst advice Steinmetz could have given us. Kurt should have joined the underground, but in 1941 neither the Jewish nor the French resistance were organized. And of course, as usual, we were trying to do things the legal way. Eventually Kurt was sent along with other Jewish men to work in a quarry in the southwestern part of France. We thought this was an improvement over Gurs and Steinmetz assured us that Kurt would be safe there.

※

During the school year of 1939–1940, we moved to the Boulevard de l'Observatoire, but upon request, I was allowed to finish my term at the École Papon, which was about an hour walk from our new apartment. The following year I registered at the École Bischoffsheim, a good thirty-minute walk at the bottom of the hill, near the last streetcar stop. The principal told me to take the *Cours Moyen Deuxième Année*—the next grade level, and warned me that if I couldn't keep up with the others, I would be put back to the *Cours Moyen Première Année*. On the first day of class, the new teacher called out various math problems—additions, subtractions, multiplications, divisions, and fractions. We wrote the answers on little slate boards and held them up for her to see. At the end of the morning session, the teacher called me over and told me that I knew more than the other students in her class and that I should go to the *Cours Supérieur Première Année*—sixth grade. That was the class that prepared students for the *Certificat d'Études*, roughly equivalent to a general high school diploma in America, requiring a good knowledge of French, arithmetic, (mostly French and European) history, geography, and some science. It also prepared students for the entrance exam to the *lycée*. The course was taught by the principal, a petite woman in her late forties or early fifties, who wore her black hair pulled back into a bun.

Academically that year was a complete waste. Once you knew how to count, read, write, and spell, how many times could you learn it again? On

Cours Supérieur Première Année. Edith, 12, is in the front on the right, spring 1941.

top of that, I was frequently absent because of my trips to the *Préfecture* with Mama, so I missed the monthly tests. I always ended up sitting in the rear of the classroom with the weaker students, as *non-classée*, and in the company of girls more interested in boys than in getting an education. The age range in the class went from eleven to fifteen, with the younger students preparing for the entrance exam to the *lycée* and the older ones repeating the class, several times if necessary, until they could pass the tests for the *Certificat d'Études*—the minimum requirement if you ever wanted to get a job. The official school photograph showed the age range. The teacher had her *chou-chous* (favorites) and made no bones about it.

During that year as the Vichy government consolidated its grip on the country, we learned songs to the glory of Maréchal Pétain, "the savior of France," or marching songs that mimicked those fed to German youth by the *Hitler Jugend*. On July 14, we all marched in a parade to the Monument aux Morts near the harbor singing these songs. We did what we were told. We sang "*Maréchal, nous voilà!*" considered to be the national anthem for the new État Français (French State). Through the song, we promised to follow in Pétain's footsteps so that "*La Patrie renaitra*" (the Fatherland would be reborn).

Throughout that school year I was bored in class. There was a library at the rear of the classroom with books by La Comtesse de Ségur and Hector

Malot. The former talked about the lives of aristocrats—where the disaster of the day was a dog dirtying a little girl's new white dress. Our teacher often read to us from the novel *Mon Oncle et Mon Curé* (My Uncle and My Priest). It was the story of a sassy young girl who was caught between her uncle and her priest: the priest wouldn't let her read certain books in her uncle's library. My world was falling apart and I was supposed to be interested in such insipid stuff? The teacher took no interest in me; it was as if I did not exist. I had a few friends in school, but we didn't socialize outside of school. My friends were nice girls and good kids who were not obsessed with boys, but were definitely not *lycée* material. In the end, I passed the *Certificat d'Études* and took an optional swimming test to earn a *Brevet Sportif.* I was happy about it, though I didn't think that doing a few laps in a pool was a big deal.

At one point, I managed to get hold of *Monsoon*, a novel by Louis Bromfield that was later made into a movie called *When the Rains Came*, starring Lana Turner and Richard Burton. The story was set in India under the British and showed the different layers of society under the caste system—from the Brahmins to the Untouchables—under the umbrella of the ruling British colonials. Everyone in the book was very class-conscious and aware of his place in the hierarchy, but when the rains came, the only thing that mattered was courage, ability, and above all, character. Social class meant nothing. When the monsoon hit, the whole elaborate social structure collapsed. The book made me aware of social class, and I asked Mama to which class we belonged. Her response was *"gut bürgerlich,"* or members of the bourgeoisie. Her father had been a highly respected and wealthy businessman before the Great War, and she identified with that.

Edith, 13, with the neighbor's cat, on her terrace. Papa's only comment from the French concentration camp upon receiving the picture: "The dress is too short," 1941.

In October 1941, I was promoted to the *Cours Supérieur Deuxième Année* after passing the

Certificat d'Études. This was still in the primary track. If you missed out on the entrance exam to the *lycée* because you flunked it or because you were older than twelve, you could continue in the primary system for three more years after the *Certificat d'Études*. The curriculum was similar to that of the *lycée*, but took longer and was watered down. Except for our English course, we had the same teacher for all our subjects while the *lycée* had different professors for each subject. Even so, at last there was more academic substance and I was learning new stuff.

Mme Brun, teacher for the Cours Supérieur Deuxième Année.

My teacher was Mme Brun, all dressed in black because of the loss of her only child who had died of meningitis. She was quite a contrast to the indifferent *directrice* of the previous year. She was an exceptional woman who was kind and took a personal interest in me and my situation. I continued to miss a lot of school because of frequent trips to the *Préfecture* with Mama, and Mme Brun was very understanding. I even asked my brother to come to school to meet her. He was wearing his French uniform and she spoke to him with kindness. Mme Brun started us on English and I imitated her pronunciation until a real English teacher was hired. The new teacher's accent was quite different and I realized that Mme Brun had incorrect pronunciation, so I quickly changed mine. Aside from English, I enjoyed my time with Mme Brun because of her kindness and compassion. She gave me her address and we promised to write after I left Nice.

⚜

America entered the war on December 8, 1941, the day after the attack on Pearl Harbor. Soon after, I recall hearing President Roosevelt declare that in a couple years, America would have so many ships, tanks, and bombers. I remember my reaction to that speech: I didn't think we would last that long. Unfortunately, I was right. The mass murder had already been decreed.

The struggle for survival, for food, for money, the worry about Papa and Kurt, the depressing letters from camp, the drudgery of hauling other people's laundry up and down the hill, being hounded by the authorities—all this did not add up to a normal, carefree childhood. One day on my way home from school, I was walking up the hill and ran into one of my neighbors. She was an attractive young girl, about eighteen, having an animated conversation with her boyfriend. As I passed her, I said hello and, to my surprise, she responded with, "You're so lucky you have nothing to worry about." What could I say? Although still young, I was keenly aware of our precarious situation, but I could not tell her. It was obvious that she had no clue about the dangers we were facing.

Eventually, the Department of the Maritime Alps, which included Nice, was closed to Jews and we were told to leave.

4. MONTLAUR, FRANCE

From School to the Vineyards

Starting in the fall of 1941 through the spring of 1942, Kurt was assigned to work in a quarry with other Prestataires. The French referred to them as *travailleurs étrangers*, or foreign workers. Each Prestataire was issued a military uniform and a military ID but no weapons, and the units were under the command of the French Army. All the men working in the quarry were Jewish refugees who had sought asylum in France.

The quarry was located in a semi-arid region of southwestern France about twelve miles from Carcassonne, a town known for its well-preserved fortified medieval *cité*. Kurt knew from our letters that we needed to get out of Nice, so he contacted the mayor of the nearby village of Montlaur. The mayor, a well-respected landowner, was willing to give us a residence permit, which enabled us to finally leave Nice. By this action, my brother saved our lives. Soon after we left Nice, the Italian occupation troops went back to Italy; the area was occupied by Germans and all the Jewish refugees were rounded up and sent to death camps.

To travel to Montlaur, we took the train from Nice to Carcassonne and a bus from there to Montlaur. The daily arrival of the bus in the village was always an event. When we arrived, there were at least two dozen children swarming around the bus together with villagers who came to pick up packages or meet relatives. Kurt came to greet us. Montlaur was a village of approximately nine hundred people where everyone knew everyone else and their business. Needless to say, as strangers we attracted attention. Nothing was hidden and nothing could be hidden. Soon everyone knew who we were.

The village was off a cul-de-sac on the road connecting Carcassonne to Lagrasse. Grapes for ordinary table wine were the only cash crop. There were a few choice vineyards in the region where sweet grapes were grown to make muscatel wine, and they received more attention and care.

The Prestataire group. Kurt is in the back, sixth from the right, 1941.

During the war, an effort was made to grow wheat and corn in distant fields normally left fallow for lack of water. They were located about an hour's journey by oxcart.

As you drove into the village from Carcassonne, you came upon the main square. To the right was a high concrete wall embedded with broken glass that bordered the vineyard and park of the Château. This is how the villagers referred to the large manor house owned by the Niermans fam-

Kurt in the quarry, 1941.

ily. Rumor had it that M. Niermans won the estate at a gambling table, but no one knew for sure. To the left was a large, classically designed building with the city hall in the middle, the boys' eight-year elementary school on the left, and the girls' school on the right. Several streets led away from the square.

The village had two cafés: *le grand café* and *le petit café*. The smaller one attracted older men playing *la belote*, a card game I never learned. The larger café had a dance hall that was open on Saturday nights. When I first came to the village, I went with other village girls and learned the dance steps by watching people on the dance floor. As the war progressed, the locals decided dancing was inappropriate. This meant that there was no place left for young people to gather on Saturday nights. We ended up getting together on the road leading to Carcassonne.

Kurt was able to rent an old stone house from a couple of well-to-do peasants, the Martinoles. It was on the Grand'rue, an unpaved street that turned to mud when it rained. The house had no running water, no toilet or outhouse, no gas, and no stove. There was a large room at ground level that had a worn tile floor and a large open hearth where I cooked our meals. Mama and I shared the single room upstairs while the loft was later used by Kurt. We used bags of jute filled with straw called *paillasses* as our mattresses on frames with wooden slats. The straw was supposed to be replaced about once a year when the old stuffing turned to dust.

Cooking was an adventure. I would put a pot on a tripod placed over burning wood. This was complicated because I did not know how to build a fire and because the wood at my disposal was green, not dry, and it took me hours to get the fire going. Every fire I built filled the kitchen with smoke. I blamed myself for my failures until much later when I realized that I lacked the basic tools to make a fire: paper, dry grasses, dry twigs or other kindling, and, of course, dry wood.

Next to the large room that served as a kitchen, dining, and living space, there was a *remise*. It was a large space with a dirt floor and was uninhabitable. The villagers used theirs as stables or for storage. We used ours to store the fresh green wood we bought for cooking, and for our human waste bucket. As in all French villages, the houses were attached and there was no backyard, so there was no other way of relieving oneself when not in the fields. In fact, getting rid of human waste was a problem for everyone in the village. Because of the lack of sewers or even septic tanks, the local creek was used as a sewer. You could buy special buckets with rims and lids that served as toilets, but we couldn't afford one and used an old pail instead. Every morning, the village housewives carried their buckets down to the creek. I was too embarrassed to carry our open bucket, so I would put off the task until the pail was full and quite heavy before going down at night to avoid being seen. In the summer, the flow of water was reduced to a trickle, so that everyone's waste ended up on the banks and sat there until the rains came in the fall and washed it away.

View of Montlaur from the hill behind the village. Photo taken in 1956.

The street where Edith lived. Photo taken in 1956.

The worst things about our house were the mice and rats. Every night they came out and nibbled at our bread, leaving their droppings nearby. We had so little food that I simply cut off the part they had touched before eating the rest. In fact, rats were a problem throughout the village. People would put out rat traps. I once saw one filled with five or six rats. The villagers poured gasoline on the rats and set them on fire. There must have been more humane ways to get rid of rodents, but the villagers did what they could.

Water was scarce, especially during the summer. Water for washing, cooking, and drinking came from the fountain in the square half a block from our house. In the summer during the dry season, the fountain was open for only two hours at a time in the morning, at noon, and in the evening. For pure spring water, we walked for ten or fifteen minutes to a pipe fed by a spring. The water came out of the pipe in a thin stream. Before mealtimes, there was always a line of villagers with their carafes.

Our local news was provided by the town crier. He was a handsome young man, about thirty years old, with only one arm. He was employed in the mayor's office. He usually made his rounds at mealtime when everyone was home from the fields. He would stop in the squares near the water fountain, bang on his drum to get our attention, and then shout his announcements, such as, "There will be no water from 2 p.m. to 6 p.m."

Soon after we arrived, Kurt applied for work at the Château. The Niermans family was the largest employer in the village. There was a shortage of manpower because many Frenchmen were prisoners of war in Germany. In addition to that, every eighteen-year-old male had to go to work in Germany for two years in what was called the *Service du Travail Obligatoire* or STO. Not every Frenchman was willing to go, but to escape that obligation he had to go underground, escape into hiding, or join the Maquis—the French clandestine resistance movement. However, in Montlaur everyone went willingly. Unfortunately, there was no Maquis in the area. Had there been one, my brother could have joined. This STO requirement extended to all the countries occupied by Germany, such as Holland and Belgium. In addition to the lack of manpower, gasoline was rationed, so farm machinery remained idle. Kurt got a job as a farmhand at the Château and received permission from his commanding officer to live with us.

I was thirteen years old when I got to Montlaur. At first, I explored the outlying fields and discovered wild fig trees growing in the vineyards. Dressed in shorts, I would climb the trees and eat figs while gathering some to bring home; I had to stop, however, because the manager of the Château complained to my mother that I was distracting his farm workers. I was very frustrated because I could no longer pick free fruit to bring home for my brother and mother. Once in a while, I picked wild blackberries growing along the paths between the vineyards, but I didn't have a basket to carry them in, so I was only able to take what I could hold in my scarf or apron.

As soon as we arrived in Montlaur, Mama got a job at the Château and I followed suit. Work was done by hand as it had been in the Middle Ages. We used cutters, scythes, sickles, hoes, and horse-drawn plows—a man with a horse could hire himself out and earn a good day's wages plowing fields. Once we began working, part of our pay came in the form of one liter of wine a day per person. We didn't drink much, so most of it turned

Edith, 13, in Montlaur shortly after her arrival as a schoolgirl. Photo taken by Kurt, spring 1942.

Edith, 14, as a peasant girl in summer 1942.

to vinegar, and after we had enough vinegar to feed the multitudes, the wine went to waste.

I still remember my first day at work. Mama and I were each given seed-filled bags to tie around our waists. We were also each given a one-foot-long stick and a soup spoon. For the next eight hours we planted beets, working on previously tilled soil. We dug little holes with our spoons and dropped three seeds into each one, covering each hole with dirt. We used the stick to measure the distance to the next spot where we dug the next hole, and so on. We remained bent over as we moved from one hole to the next. We had little time to stand up to stretch and straighten our backs. By the end of that day, neither Mama nor I could stand up straight. We managed to get to a low wall on a bridge and sat down.

Luckily for us, a farmhand working for the Château came by on a horse-drawn cart and offered us a ride back to the village, which was a good distance from the fields. His name was Angel Rosetti. He seemed nice enough. At twenty-one, he was the youngest son of an Italian immigrant family employed by the Château. Their quarters were near the barns. The father and the middle son, Marius, who was single, had salaried year-round jobs. The mother milked the cow and tended to the chickens. In exchange she got milk and eggs. The oldest son was divorced. Angel was a day laborer, *un journalier* like me, and he was single.

A few weeks after we were hired, the manager asked Mama if she wanted to work as a cook for the Niermans instead of in the vineyards. The family had a chambermaid, a young village woman named Georgette, so Mama wouldn't have to clean, and she happily accepted. Working indoors at a job she was familiar with was much easier than working in the vineyards, exposed to the elements.

Mme Niermans, a haughty elderly widow, lived with her handicapped middle-aged daughter. The younger Mlle Niermans walked with great difficulty, perhaps as a result of polio. She walked with a cane, shifting from one leg to the other, with her entire upper body swaying like a pendulum. Both normally lived in Paris, vacationing in Montlaur only during

Anna Mayer's work contract as a farmhand at a salary of FF *18 per day and 1 liter of wine. This was to be added to her application for an ID card as a foreign worker. The contract was for three months.*

the summer, but because of the German occupation and food shortages in the city, she and her daughter decided to sit out the war in the village. Occasionally her son and his family came to visit.

As the cook, Mama got the family leftovers for her meals. If there were no leftovers, Mme Niermans would give her an egg. Mama often brought that egg home for us. Mme Niermans would rummage in the garbage can looking for the egg shells and when she didn't find them, she would yell at Mama for not eating the egg. "The egg was for you, not for your daughter." When there were leftovers, she stored them in a screened

DÉPARTEMENT
DE L'AUDE

ARRONDISSEMENT
DE CARCASSONNE

MAIRIE
DE
MONTLAUR

N°_____

OBJET

ÉTAT FRANÇAIS

Le   19

Certificat

Le Maire de Montlaur soussigné certifie que la nommée Mayer née Bucholtz Anna née le 24 Mars 1903 à Czernovitz Roumanie, de nationalité ex. autrichienne domiciliée à Montlaur — a ses pièces d'identité actuellement déposées à la Préfecture de l'Aude et un dossier de demande de renouvellement en cours déposé à l'Office Départemental du Travail à Carcassonne.

En foi de quoi nous lui délivrons le présent pour lui servir de pièce d'identité,

à Montlaur le 4 juillet 1942.

Le Maire :

Letter in which the mayor attests that Anna Mayer's ID papers had been sent to the Préfecture *of the department of Aude along with her request to renew her work permit. Dated July 4, 1942.*

cube, and since there was no refrigeration, the food would be thrown out within two days. Not once did Madame offer us any food for our family. But every Sunday the Niermans went to church, always sitting in the front pews.

During the last days of the month when our allotted rations were used up, my breakfast sometimes consisted of half a glass of wine and a lump of sugar. Looking back I don't know how I managed because the work was very demanding physically. At lunchtime on my way back from the fields, I would stop at the baker's shop and ask her to sell me a pound of bread without rationing coupons. She never gave me a full pound, but she always sold me something.

Getting enough to eat was a major challenge because our monthly food rations usually sufficed for just twenty days. In the summer and fall, we supplemented our rations with locally grown produce that I bought from the beautifully tended vegetable garden owned by the Noyes family. But during the winter, produce wasn't available. Most villagers had a vegetable garden or a patch of land where they could grow their own produce. The Niermans gave us a little plot of land outside the village so we could grow our own food. Kurt and I worked at it, but by August, the water in the nearby stream dried up and I had neither water nor manure, so nothing grew. Besides not knowing what I was doing, I did not feel safe when I had to go out to the fields alone in the evening because Angel waited for me upon my return.

For the other villagers, the food shortage was not as severe because they were able to supplement their rations with the food they grew and by hunting jackrabbits or trapping them illegally when the hunting season was over. Many raised chickens, the wealthier peasants had a cow, and everyone owned a pig. The pigs were slaughtered in November before Christmas and provided ham and sausage for the rest of the year. After it rained, the villagers also gathered snails to cook escargots.

Every day, I walked to the stable at the Château to meet up with the other farmhands and with the *régisseur*, or manager. He handed out our work assignments and typically, I would be sent out with a group of women led by *la mousseigne* who only spoke the local dialect, not French. She was illiterate and I did not understand her patois. She seemed old to me at the time, but she could not have been much older than forty—though she was wrinkled and usually dressed in black. She was the team leader, like a foreman, and she set the work pace.

I went through the whole cycle of tending vineyards. I hoed in the spring to remove weeds, attached branches to wires to support the future grapes, pruned branches and removed extra foliage to allow the sun to ripen the grapes in May or June, then harvested the grapes in the fall. The harvest was called *les vendanges* and the once-a-year cash crop was eagerly awaited by the landowners. Everyone pitched in including children as young as twelve, who worked with the women's team, because time was of the essence since the grapes had to be picked at their peak.

⚜

After the initial joy of our family reunion in Montlaur, Mama resumed her periodic outbursts. She never needed much to get angry and it was often over trivial things. Kurt was a good kid; he didn't smoke, drink, or run around with girls, and he worked hard for us, giving all his earnings to Mama. I don't remember him ever going out to the local cafés like the other men in the village. Yet Mama constantly found fault. She couldn't beat him up anymore because he was bigger than she was, but, oh, did she scream! And she had a mean tongue. She could carry on for hours, yelling and harping away. After one nasty episode, she brought nineteen-year-old Kurt to tears. He finally yelled back at her, "When I am dead you will cry, but now you are giving me a hard time."

It was August and the grapes were still sour when Kurt was told by his commanding officer that he had to rejoin his outfit within 48 hours. For about three months, he had been detached from his unit. We went to see the *régisseur* and asked him to intervene on Kurt's behalf. At our request, the manager of the Niermans' estate called Kurt's commanding officer and pleaded with him, "He is a good worker, I need him."

"If he does not show up, we will come and get you," was the reply. After that threat to him, the manager made sure that Kurt got to Lagrasse.

Kurt packed his few belongings into his new *musette*, a small canvas bag with a shoulder strap. "You'll escape," Mama said. "Yes," he answered. Looking back, I believe Mama's frequent outbursts may have drained him of his energy and his fighting spirit. I would come to know from my own experience later on how important it was to keep up your fighting spirit—for once you give up, you are done for.

Early the next morning, Kurt left. He had been looking forward to the harvest to fill up on grapes since he was always hungry—but that was not to be. Under the guise of helping my brother, the manager sent Angel to escort him to make sure that my brother got to his unit. The two of them biked to Lagrasse and Angel brought back Kurt's bike. Later that morning, Mama took the bus to Lagrasse with me in tow. When we got to the military headquarters, many Jews were milling around an open courtyard while a few French soldiers stood watch armed with guns. The Prestataires had uniforms, but no guns. All the men from the quarry, some of whom we had come to know, were there as well.

That afternoon, Kurt's unit was sent to Bram. Due to the shortage of gasoline, the group of more than a dozen men was sent out in a flat, open cart pulled by two oxen. The road they took passed within two kilometers of Montlaur, so Mama asked for permission for us to ride along, and it was granted. The men were guarded by two Spaniards, each equipped with a rifle. The two drivers were sitting on a bench with their backs to us and their guns lying on the bench at their side, while the rest of us sat on the flatbed with our legs dangling over the edge.

The whole trip must have taken about two hours. Mama clung to Kurt and urged him to escape; he assured her that he would. Sitting on that cart, I listened to the conversations of the men, most of whom were middle-aged or older. I remember one of the men in my brother's group because he sometimes came to visit us in Montlaur. He was fortyish, an intellectual, soft-spoken, and kind. The treasure he took along with him was a valuable stamp collection that reflected the patient accumulation of a lifetime. It reminded me of Papa and his precious pocket watch. I also overheard a lot of talk about escaping. Sadly, though, it was all negative. Two of the men had escaped once only to be caught later; they complained about the cold, about getting sick, about how hard it was to survive always running, hiding, and searching for food. This put a damper on everyone's thoughts of escape, and so no one tried. When we reached the fork in the road, Mama and I got off and kissed Kurt goodbye. We walked back to the village while Kurt and his unit continued on their fateful journey.

That was the last time I saw my brother.

In my mind's eye, I have replayed that trip on the cart hundreds of times. For a long time, I accepted the sequence of events because I believed we were powerless. As I got older, I asked myself why I didn't say something encouraging to Kurt. At that time, I was utterly dependent on and dominated by my mother who always treated me like an ignorant child. So I sat there, silent, listening to all their defeatist talk. Yet that day was the best day for escaping. The cart was driven by two Spanish civilians, both refugees from Franco's Spain, who were doing it to earn a few francs. They had their backs turned to us and the oxen moved at a snail's pace. It would have been so easy to seize those guns and send the Spaniards on their way with their oxen, or to slip away quietly and hide in the vineyards. I would have gladly brought food and other necessities to my brother. Why didn't

Kurt with Vietnamese workers in Agde. Kurt is in the back row, middle. Kurt sent this photo in August 1942.

I see that the moment to run was at hand? Why didn't I speak up? These thoughts continue to haunt me.

Later we received several postcards from Kurt describing how he had to surrender his uniform, how he went from Bram to Agde and, finally, the last postcard written in a moving train sent before crossing the demarcation line into German-occupied northern France for an "unknown destination."

[Date unknown] 1942
In transit

Dear Mama,

Today, we are going to Bram where we are going to a triage commission within a week. People who are Viennese, Germans, Czechs and Poles are supposed to go as pioneers of the Tri-color Legion. We are supposed to go to Galicia under this Tricolor Legion supposedly under French military command. As far as mail is concerned, we can't get any more. I embrace you mama one more time and hope that we will see each other again.

Kisses for you and dear Papa,

Kurt

23 August 1942
Bram

Dear Mama,

I don't know whether this card will still reach you in Montlaur, I hope, however, that you will be notified in time. All of our military gear, including our blankets, had to be returned. Tomorrow morning we are leaving for an area occupied by Germany via Rivesaltes. I paid M. H [what I owed him]. Otherwise, I don't have much to say. Be well and hopefully we will see each other again in peace. Loving greetings and kisses from your Kurt.

Kurt's last picture before he was deported. He was 19 years old. August 1942.

Dear Edith,

I want to kiss you too one more time.

Your brother,

Kurt

24 August 1942
On the train between Montpellier and Nimes

[This postcard was sent to my father at the Montlaur address. Kurt thought my father had been liberated from Rivesaltes as expected and was already with us in the village.]

Dear Papa,

Don't be too frightened when you find out that I too had to go. I am courageous if I know that you are brave too. Hopefully everything will end well. In the meantime, we are in transit. I don't

*Postcard from Kurt, dated August 23, 1942. The original
is at the United States Holocaust Memorial Museum.*

know where I will soon have the opportunity to write. That's why I
want to say goodbye here. I wish you all the best and I hope to see
you, Mama, and Edith again. With the most heartfelt greetings,

Your son,

Kurti

24 August 1942
On the train between Montpellier and Nimes

[Written in French, all the other letters and postcards were written in German. This last postcard was written on part of an old
envelope, without an address. Kurt must have given it to someone
to mail to us.]

Dear Mama,

Against all suppositions, we went neither to Rivesaltes nor to
Agde. It seems as though we are going there directly . . . If we stop
somewhere, I will write again. If not, don't expect other news. I
don't lose my courage. I hope that everything will end well. I saw
Erika in Bram before leaving.

Your Kurt. I am kissing you again.

All postcards translated by the author from German and French.

As I found out much later, my brother was sent to Drancy, the transit
camp outside of Paris, and from there deported to Auschwitz on August 31,
1942, via convoy number 26.

⚘

While we were in Montlaur, Papa was still held prisoner in the concentration camp of Rivesaltes, near Perpignan. After one year spent in Gurs near
Pau, he was transferred to Rivesaltes. Mama continued her efforts to liberate him, but it was still a Kafkaesque world. We filled out endless forms,
registered our names, and bought special stamps for the official documents
called *papier timbré*. We knew that the order to liberate Papa was in the
office of the French camp commander, and we expected Papa's imminent
release. Recently I found out that, at the behest of Berlin where the mass
murder of Jews had been decreed, Vichy had issued an order not to release
any Jewish prisoners. The Vichy government collaborated fully, as did the
camp commander. My father thought this was a temporary order that
would eventually be lifted.

By the spring and summer of 1942, Papa was spending most of his time
in the camp infirmary. That's how sick he was. Having recently worked up
the courage, I finally read my father's last letters from camp that had been

Map of the Locations of Detention Sites

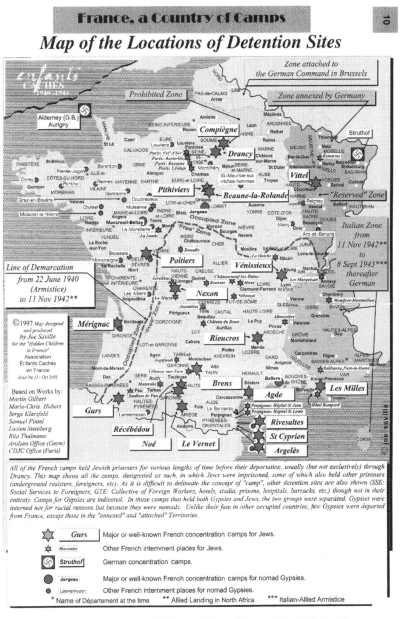

All of the French camps held Jewish prisoners for various lengths of time before their deportation, usually (but not exclusively) through Drancy. This map shows all the camps, designated as such, in which Jews were imprisoned, some of which also held other prisoners (underground resisters, foreigners, etc). As it is difficult to delineate the concept of "camp", other detention sites are also shown (SSE: Social Services to Foreigners, GTE: Collective of Foreign Workers, hotels, stadia, prisons, hospitals, barracks, etc.) though not in their entirety. Camps for Gypsies are indicated. In those camps that held both Gypsies and Jews, the two groups were separated. Gypsies were interned not for racial reasons but because they were nomads. Unlike their fate in other occupied countries, few Gypsies were deported from France, except those in the "annexed" and "attached" Territories.

☆	**Gurs**	Major or well-known French concentration camps for Jews.
☆	Mézières	Other French internment places for Jews.
◎	**Struthof**	German concentration camps.
●	Jargeau	Major or well-known French concentration camps for nomad Gypsies.
●	Lannemezan	Other French internment places for nomad Gypsies.

* Name of Département at the time   ** Allied Landing in North Africa   *** Italian-Allied Armistice

From the booklet "Jewish Children of France During World War II" from a map that was originally issued in French in 2001 by the "Association des Enfants Cachés" (Association of Hidden Children) in France. Produced by Joe Saville, translated by Gerda Bikales in 2003, and distributed by the Friends and Alumni of OSE-USA, Inc. Used with permission from OSE-USA.

Surname	Name	Date	Place	Cit.
LIPSCHITZ	MOISE			
LIVER	ARMAND	4ANS		
LIMERANT	SARAH	28.08.06	VARSOVIE	P
LOEB	JULIUS	13.02.06	WATTERSTADT	A
LOEB	WALTER			
LOEWE	ERICH	17.05.11		A
LOEWENBERG	CHARLES			
LOKIEC	ESTHER	15.11.07	POLOGNE	P
LOKIEC	DAVID	06.04.28	PARIS	F
LOPPER	MAYER	31.12.90		A
LOWY	MICHAEL	19.07.96	BRISBRUG	AUT
LUBETSKI	NATHAN	15.01.32	PARIS	F
LUFT	STANISLAS			AUT
LUKIERMAN	JOEL	03.01.08		APA
MAJER	ACHILLE			
MAJUFES	ROZIA			
MALINIAK	ADOLF	01.02.01	PAWA	P
MANE	EDWIG			
MANE	GUNTHER			
MANE	SALLY			
MANE	WILKI			
MANN	DAVID	05.01	VARSOVIE	P
MANNA	BERNARD	16.04.39	PARIS	F
MANNA	CZARNA	OO	BIALA	P
MANNA	MENSCHEN	03.02.31	VARSOVIE	P
MANNHEIMER	N.BRIKENFLO			
MANNHEIMER	MAX			
MARCUS	JOHN	15.09.83		
MARX	ADOLF	18.11.93	MANNHOIS	A
MARK	OTTO	29.04.04	ALCHEN	A
MARKIEL	SZYGA			
MARKIEM	ANNA			
MARKIEM	HENDEY			
MARKOVICZ	JEANINE	08.05.34	PARIS	F
MARMUREK	CHAVA	09.03.10	LODZ	P
MAROKO	GOLDA			
MARTIN	HANS			
MARWEL	SMUL			
MARWEL	MAURICE			
MARWEL	SURLA	04	LODZ	P
MARX	ERICH	10.04.07	MENNHEIM	A
MASLER	MONIQUE			
MATOUSSOVSKY	CHARLOTTE	13.12.95	KIEW	R
MATZNER	JACOB			
MAUNER	JULIA	01.08.25	VIENNE	AUT
MAUNER	FELICITAS	08.01.24	VIENNE	AUT
MAUNER	LISELOTTE			
MAUNER	ROSA	29.05.99	CZENAUTI	AUT
MAUNNER	MAX			
MAYER	BERTIA	30.04.21	MAHDENDORF	A
MAYER	MARGARET	12.09.23	MAHDENDORF	A
MAYER	BURT	10.03.23		AUT
MEDRYNA	DAVID			
MEDRYNA	JOSEPHINE			
MERENHOLC	PERLA	13.08.31	VARSOVIE	P
MERIN	IGNAZ	14.08.95	BENDZIN	APA
MENKES	HERBERT			
METZGER	RUDOLF	03.10.00		A
MEYER	SIGMUND	29.03.07	BREISER	A
MEYER	JACOB	03.06.85	HANOVRE	A
MICHAELIS	CECILE			
MICHAELIS	WALTER			
MICHEL	JOSEPH	02.04.77	ALTDORF	A
MILER	JANCKEL	21.08.23	BALTI	RO
MICNER	RIVKA	05	VIAGROW	P
MILSTEIN	BASIA			
MILSTEIN	ROJRIEZ	01.04.93	TOMASZOW	P
MINHAUSER	NATHAN	25.05.93	CERNAUTI	AUT
MISLER	EMMANUEL	26.06.09	LENBERG	AUT
MOGER	ESTERA			
MONCZARZ	ADELE	35	PARIS	
MONCZARZ	SUZANNE	17.07.38	PARIS	F
MONCZARZ	SALOMON	06.11.33	PARIS	F
MONCZARZ	RACHEL	16.05.32	PARIS	F
MONCZARZ	DWOPA	20.01.08	PARCZEW	P
MORGENSTERN	SARAH	10.11.90	BREST LITOWSK	P
MORSEL	SAM	03.02.11	WLAMAR	P
MOSES	SAMUEL	25.06.88	KIRSHEN	A
MOSKONIC	CHWANA	26.06.11	RADOM	R
MOSTZKOWICZ	JACQUELINE	04.06.38	PARIS	F
MUHLRAD	ABRAHAM	21.06.06	LANCUT	IL?
MUHLRAD	HIRSCH	22.04.12	LANCUT	LU
MUHLRAD	JAKOB	27.11.08	LANCUT	LU?
MULLER	GUILLAUME	14.09.94	BILSTOCK	A
MULLER	KURST			
MUNZER	DONAT	20.10.82	LEOPOLD	P
NACKMANN	STEICK	23.03.88	VARSOVIE	P.
NADEL	CYPRA	29.09.39		
NAJER	KATARZYNA	14.08.06	SZERESZ	P
NASSELSKY	REBECCA	17.02.18	PARIS	F
NEUMANN	ISAAC	07.11.12	CZIESZANOV	AL?
NIKBAN	ERNESTINE			
NUDELMAN	HENRI	12.04.31	PARIS	?
NUDELMAN	LAJA	01	SZYDLOWICE	P
NUDELMAN	RACHEL	28.02.40	PARIS	F
NUDELMAN	SARAH	20.09.34	PARIS	F
OBSTRAUM	SARA	30.05.12	VARSOVIE	P
OLCZAK	LEIBA	94	ZARRAYNIMIN	P
OLCZAK	SUZANNE	09.04.34	PARIS	F
OLSZAK	MOERSCH	13.03.94	VARSOVIE	P
OPALEK	MALCA	05	POLOGNE	P
OPALEK	NINA	37	PARIS	F
OPALEK	BENJAMIN	28.05.34	PARIS	F
OPALEK	JOSEPH	28	PARIS	F
OPALEK	HENRI	27	PARIS	F
ORMANN	ARTHUR			
ORONSKI	DESSA			
OSTROWSKI	PENKUS	01.02.00	SULMIAZYN	P
OULITZKY	LEON	31.12.94	KICIO	P
PANTIEL	JACOB	19.11.01	JUWITZ	A
PARAWAN	BELA	12.07.23	VARSOVIE	P
PECKEL	KURT			
PECKEL	ADOLPHE			
PECKEL	FRANIA			
PERLMOUTER	LAJA			
PERLMOUTER	PEISAKH			
PERELMUTER	ZACHWELTA	08	OPATON	?
PERELMUTER	RYWKA	26.11.06	VARSOVIE	?
PERELMUTER	GISELE	09.10.39		?
PERELMUTER	CHANA	02.02.27	MELITOPOL	?
PHILIP	RICHARD	03.04.25	EFFENBECK	?
PIENKNA	GURA	23.09.07	LUKEW	?
PIENKNA	SUZANNE	13.12.39	CAEN	P
PIORKOWSKI	HANS	08.06.88	BERLIN	A?
PLESNER	ESTERA	10.11.14	BESSIER	?
PLEVINSKI	HENRI	08.07.33	NANCY	?
PLEWINSKI	JEANINE	13.08.38	NANCY	?
POLICNER	ETLA	13.01.06	VARSOVIE	?
POLLAK	FRITZ	21.10.95	BUDITS	A?
POMMER	SARAH	01.01.00	BERLIN	A?
POMMER	SIEGMUND			
POSENER	MANFRED	01.06.24	BREME	A
POSNER	MANFRED	15.04.16	CHEMNITS	A
PREJZEROWICZ	GITLA	02.08.05	TSCHENTOCHAU	?
PRZEDNOWEK	MALKA			
PREZEROWICZ	JAKOB		03	TCHETOCHOWA	?
PRISAND	WOLF	14.05.84		A?
PRISAND	JACOB	02.09.88	PRZMYSLANY	A?
PROTH	NORBERT			
PRYNC	DANIEL	05.12.25	WIELM	?
PRZYTYKOWICZ	JEANNE	21.11.39	PARIS	?
PRZYTYKOWICZ	RYFKA	03	KUKOW	?
PSZNICA	RAJLA	02	TARNOWICE	?
PUZAJOSER	MARJAM	10.06.12	VARSOVIE	?
RAAB	LADISLAS	06.05.01	BUDAPEST	A?
RAJMAN	ROBERT	6 ANS	PARIS	?
RAPHAEL	ALFREDE			
RAPPAPORT	CHARLOTTE			
RATH	HEIM	08.05.99		A
REICH	BERTHE			
REICH	HENNY			
REICH	PEPE			
REICH	MINDEL			
REICHENFELD	GEORGES			
REICHER	SURA			
REIN	HENRI	25.09.21	TARNOW	?
REIN	JACOB		89 OBERTIN	?
REIN	ROSA	15.02.25	TARNEFF	?
REINMAN	GRETA	16.07.88	MANHEIM	A
REISS	MAURICE			
REMINGER	FRITZ			
ROBISECK	ESTHER			
ROCHOW	LEON	07.11.20	VARSOVIE	?
ROLNIK	LAJA			
ROLSEVNAS	HELENE		05 VARSOVIE	?
ROSEN	JOEL			
ROSEN	MIRLA			
ROSEN	RACHEL			
ROSEN	HELENE			
ROSENBAUM	ARTHUR	18.03.00	GAMAHEIM	A
ROSENBACH	RODOLPHE			
ROSENBERG	FRANCINE	21.06.12	VARSOVIE	?
ROSENBERG	SARA	21.06.01	VARSOVIE	?
ROSENBERG	TOBA	21.03.07	ZELECHOW	?
ROSENBERG	ELISE	29.11.84		A
ROSENBERG	LEON		PITHIVIERS	
ROSENBERG	GEORGES	40		
ROSENBERG	RYWKA	13.03.95	CZORKOW	?
ROSENBERG	JULIUS	11.10.00	BRISACH	A?
ROSENBERGER	JACKY	37	PARIS	?

Excerpt from lists prepared by French and German authorities prior to deportation, showing Kurt's name, typed as EURT MAYER, date of birth, and citizenship (AUT = Autrichien or Austrian). Reproduced in the book Le Memorial de la Deportation des Juifs de France *by Serge Klarsfeld, 1978. Used with permission from Serge Klarsfeld.*

in my possession since my mother's death in 1990. From them, I learned that he was quite ill. I knew that he suffered from dysentery and he had high blood pressure. In a previous letter, Papa told us that he had been seen by two medical commissions who declared him unfit to work, since working was the pretense for sending people to Germany. But the third commission said he was fit. In one letter he writes that the doctor ordered two days of complete bed rest, so I think the camp doctor initially tried to help him. But to no avail. His last letter from the train was written while traveling in the infirmary car, which is an indication of how sick and weak he must have been.

His last letters show his hope, his frame of mind, and the bitter disappointment before his deportation:

12 August 1942
Camp de Rivesaltes

Most beloved Annerl,

I am waiting impatiently for a call so that I can go to you and our children. It can't be much longer because I was liberated by Vichy a month ago. Thank God I feel good and for the moment I am content. In the meantime, you no doubt found out that my case has received a delay. How long it will take before I can see you again, I really don't know. Whether and when I will be able to leave the infirmary, I do not know. In fact, several of my fellow camp inmates have been transferred from here . . . In the infirmary I am able to rest well and not get any infections. I see the doctor every day and he takes care of me . . . How do you feel? How are you all doing? I think that since everything is working, I will be able to talk it over with you in person. This is a great need of my heart after twenty-one-and-a-half months of absence. In the prefecture of Perpignan, it might be easier to find out when I can be liberated. But who can talk to them about it? Or could you or better yet, Kurterl, contact the prefecture in Carcassonne!!! . . .

My dearest Life,

I myself would be happy to be able to tell you that I am on my way to you. If I am lucky and the papers that were approved by

Vichy via Perpignan arrive here, then it is quite possible. I think that again I poured out my heart to you in great detail and you understand me well. I am happy and satisfied, thank God. I am expecting an imminent liberation, God willing, no later than this month. Everything else, you can do as you think best. I am hugging you with deep feeling and with warmest kisses as well as for our dear children.

Your faithful happy Adolf

Also, this time especially for our dear Kurt and also many kisses from Papa to Ditterl. As soon as they stop suspending liberation, then I will be released immediately. But when?

13 August 1942
Camp de Rivesaltes

Beloved Annerl,

Since last night, I know for sure that my liberation papers are here, however, all releases for Jews are now stopped. When this interdiction will be lifted is not known . . . Today I was added to a list where I indicated that my family lives in Montlaur and that our son is working for the French government as a foreign worker; he is detached from his outfit to work in Montlaur. I see this as a favorable sign. But it is possible that Kurterl is added to some sort of list. I don't agree with his trip to the city of his birth. It is better if he remains on his current work assignment. [My father thought that my brother was still with us. Camp prisoners were encouraged to give the address of other family members under the pretext that they will be "together" for this supposed "resettlement," but it was so that they could find us and deport us as well.]

My most beloved life,

I supplicate daily to the Almighty that he may reunite us and that He preserve our health.

Kisses,

Your Adolf

17 August 1942
Camp de Rivesaltes

Here, nothing has changed. I am optimistic that my liberation will soon become a reality. In the meantime, I have to be patient I think up to the end of the month . . . Write to me good things about yourself and the children . . .

Do not worry. Everything will be fine. Courage and faith in God. This waiting time will also pass. Then we will see each other again with the help of God. Courage. So I shouldn't forget, I greet and kiss our dear little daughter Ditterl many times. Papa would like to see his little daughter, see her and admire her and be happy with her. Soon, soon I will be home. I was very happy to read your note and wouldn't my son write something to his Papa? He too is Papa's little son of whom I think lately with gratitude. Greetings for him too.

This month, I am expecting finally a denture and I am happy about it. My mouth is all sore because I no longer have any teeth. I also can't speak very well. Lately, I am calm, even if I don't know the exact date of my liberation yet, but my hope for liberation is great. Only the when is unknown to me. Patience and more patience . . .

Waiting! I am so-so. I am still in the infirmary, but I don't know for how long . . . I myself am hoping that when the suspension of the liberation of Jews is lifted, I will be able to join you soon. Vichy liberated me, and that makes me feel calm . . . The best thing is if I were already out and with you in every respect. I feel with you and know how right you are, just patience. Here I don't have anything to wear anymore. Everything is worn-out rags in need of mending by your hand. Just imagine that. It's easy to understand after 22 months in camp life, I lack a lot and am living with the hope that you will be able to put me together again in physical appearance. I am also troubled by the heat. You know how someone with high blood pressure like me suffers in the heat. Whether I will be home this month is unknown. Maybe. If [I am liberated], I will telegraph you immediately. Otherwise, my beloved, everything orally. If my mail got lost, then just take out one sentence and that is that I am at this time in good spirits, full of hope. For the moment, I am not being transferred. The doctor during his daily visit still has much to say about me. Write your husband soon. I was just ordered at this moment absolute bed rest for two days. I'm happy about that.

Many kisses from your Adolf

25 August 1942
Camp de Rivesaltes

My best wife, my most beautiful life in the world, my dearest Annerl,

I am using this opportunity to give you a sign of life as long as I am here. Whether I will have the chance to write to you is questionable, although I will take advantage of every opportunity to keep you informed about my fate as well as my whereabouts. Today is supposed to be a break, but things can get going by tomorrow. I don't know exactly what will happen because here everything is happening so fast. My letter from yesterday is not exactly cheerful, but we have to bite into the sour apple. Today I can see that I should have requested leave in order to see you. But who could have known that such measures would be taken so suddenly. You can see that the order for my liberation was given by Vichy. Now it's over. I am ready and I am asking you, too, to accept your fate. Of course I would have liked to see you and to speak to you before, but alas. Destiny! So don't do anything foolish and accept. Rather than have you separate from the children, I prefer that you should stay with them. You can comfort each other. Courage is needed in order to get through the crisis. Children up to the age of 17 are spared. Past that age even those children must go to Germany. [My father wrote "children up to the age of 20." The censor corrected that to the age of 17.]

Believe me, Annerl, my heart is full, and not a word is crossing my lips. But my thoughts are in constant turmoil. I am living the novel of my own life. I now really feel my loneliness, and I will continue to feel that way. Up until now I at least was in contact with you and I had the hope of seeing you soon again. And now you are disappearing from my horizon, without the slightest hope of seeing you again. I take refuge with the Almighty in heaven. It is from Him that I await the long hoped for help. I pray constantly. I want to keep my courage in order not to collapse emotionally and physically. And you, my beloved, you are a hero; endure our separation with the same courage. Our Lord is testing us and He alone will give us back our good fortune. Meanwhile my soul is suffering great torment. Everyone understands my sad situation. So close to the goal, the orders for my liberation came in from Vichy, and in the last moment "No liberation for Jews," and, finally, "transport to Germany."

My dearly beloved life! Never—perhaps—to be able to embrace you, not be able to look into your dear, loyal eyes, not to be able to share long talks with you and especially not to be able to lighten your everyday burden, all this causes me much pain. Remember how fast I left you and [now] in what uncertain future our reunion.

I don't want to give advice to the good Lord; it is still possible that things will change for the better even if I, a little man, do not know how. As long as I can keep my eyes open, I want to turn my gaze toward heaven. My bags are packed and I await being shipped to Germany. May God keep me healthy and alive for your sake.

And you, brave and never tiring Annerl, remember your Adolf who always loved you deeply, who still loves you and who will always love you. Like you I am honest and I have provided you throughout my camp stay with detailed and abundant mail. Of course I prefer to give you only the best and most pleasant news. Unfortunately some circumstances are so serious that I am forced to tell you about less pleasant stuff.

Tomorrow I will write to you before we leave and after that I don't know whether it will still be possible. With affectionate kisses.

God willing, as we are about to start the Jewish New Year Rosh Hashanah on September 12 and 13, our situation will change in our favor. To all Jews and to the whole world I wish peace and tranquility, a return to normal economic activity and harmony. Goodbye my good, my beloved, my golden Annerl and don't forget your Adolf. Best wishes for the New Year, hopefully together, Amen.

My dear children Kurti and Edith,

To you too an affectionate goodbye and all the best for the new year. Grow up to become good people in life. May God bless you your whole life! If it is not granted to your Papa to be with you, then a miracle is always possible. Keep hoping with me and the old true good Lord will not abandon you and me. Be obedient and get along well with each other. Give your dear Mama much joy. I embrace you and kiss you,

Your Papa Adolf

Don't cry, but pray to God for your Papa in German hands!!!! Perhaps we shall leave even today!!!! So goodbye my loved ones,

Kisses,

Your Papa Adolf

3 September 1942
Camp de Rivesaltes

My beloved little wife Annerl,

Goodbye! To you and our dear children Kurti and Edith. I have been prepared for the transport. Unfortunately without you, which I regret deeply. Who knows when I will see you again? May the Almighty protect us all and may He bring us together soon in joy and peace. Amen. Remember your Adolf and pray for him. Enjoy life with the dear children. If you could manage to meet with me somewhere, then do it so we can remain together. I embrace you with many kisses.

Your Adolf

3 September 1942
Camp de Rivesaltes [postcard pictured]

Dearest beloved Annerl,

At this moment we are being shipped to Germany and I am send-ing you from here an affectionate GOODBYE. Be well, all my loved ones. May God allow that we will all meet very soon some-where so as to share our destiny together, just as long as we are together. Don't be upset. It is the will of God. Think of me and keep loving me. I kiss you and the dear children,

Your Papa Adolf
Be blessed. Amen.

4 September 1942
In transit

My beloved life,

A heartfelt goodbye and many greetings and kisses from my trip to Germany. Today at 10 a.m. we passed Carcassonne. The station drew a bitter smile. I had imagined my arrival in Carcassonne otherwise. I assume that you will join me and that you will go through the camp of Rivesaltes. The committee from Perpignan gave each one of us 100 francs. You can have fruit in Montlaur so stay even if you're not with me. I am traveling in the infirmary car. Be well and happy and the children. Many kisses.

Your Adolf

All postcards and letters translated by the author from German and French.

On September 11, 1942, via convoy number 31, Papa was deported from Drancy, the same transit camp outside Paris through which my brother and tens of thousands of other Jews passed on their way to their deaths. Like my brother, he was sent to the killing camp of Auschwitz in a sealed cattle car.

A copy of her father's last letter, translated in the text by Edith. The original is at the United States Holocaust Memorial Museum. (Continued next page.)

Meine gutste Frau, mein geliebtes Leben auf der Welt, mein liebstes ...

Ich benütze noch die Gelegenheit, solange ich hier bin, Dir ein ... zeichen von mir zu geben. Ob ich noch Gelegenheit haben werde, ... ist fraglich, obwohl ich jede Gelegenheit wahrnehmen werde Dir über mein ... resp. mein Befinden etwas zu lassen — der heutige Tag ... eine Pause ... kann es schon losgehen. Ganz genau weiß ich noch nicht, denn es kommt ... alles so plötzlich. — Du wirst über mein gestriges Schreiben wenig erbaut sein, doch man muß in den sauren Apfel beißen. — Heute scheint, daß ich Dich ... Urlaube hätte erbeten sollen, um Dich zu sehen, aber wer konnte wissen, daß plötzlich solche Maßnahmen getroffen werden? Du siehst doch, daß ... der Tat meine Liberation in Vichy geben werden. — Nun, vorbei! Ich bin ... gefaßt und bitte auch Dich Dich ... zu finden. — Gewiß hätte ich vorher noch gesehen und gesprochen, aber leider, Bestimmung! Mache ... keine Dummheiten und füge Dich. — Bevor wir von den Kindern ge... werden, ist mir lieber, Du bleibst bei denen und räumt Ihr Euch gegen... zeitig ... — ... ist jetzt nötig nur die Kriegszeiten zu überst... Kinder ... Jahren bleiben derweil verschont über dieses aber hin... müssen doch alle nach Deutschland. — Glaube mir, mein He... ist voll und es kommt kein Wort zu niemand über die Lippen. — Dagegen ... meine Gedanken dauernd in Aufruhr. — Ich erlebe jetzt einen Roman ... meines eigenen Lebens. Jetzt fühle ich erst recht meine Einsamkeit und werde sie auch in der Folge empfinden. Bis jetzt hatte wenigstens Kontakt mit Dir und Hoffnung Dich bald wiederzusehen. — Und jetzt entschw... denn Du meinem Horizont, ohne jede ... Hoffnung Dich zu sehen. — Ich wollte jedoch ... vom Allmächtigen im Himmel und von diesem erwarte ich die langersehnte Hilfe. — Ich bete dauernd. Ich will just meinen ... hochhalten, um nicht seelisch u. physisch einzu... Und Du mein geliebtes bist eine alte Heldin ... unsere Trennung ... heldenhaft. — Unser Herrgott prüft uns und Er allein wird uns ... Glück wiedergeben. Einstweilen leidet meine Seele große Qual... Jedermanns versteht meine betrübliche Lage. So nahe am Ziel nach ... "Liberation aus Vichy" erreicht und im letzten Augenblick "Liberation für Juden gesperrt" und als Letztes: Abtransport nach Deutschl...

Postcard from Edith's father dated September 3, 1942,
translated in the text by Edith. The original is at the
United States Holocaust Memorial Museum.

Surname	Given name	Date	Place	Code
KARNI	GETSEL	23.10.89		R
KARSEBOOM	ANNA	16.11.16		B
KARSEBOOM	CHARLES	08.01.00		B
KASZEWSKI	BLANCHE	13.05.34	REIMS	F
KASZEWSKI	ANNA	.98		P
KASZEWSKI	SZMUL	04.01.86	KALUSZYN	P
KASZEWSKI	TAUBA	08.03.23	VARSOVIE	P
KASZEWSKI	ZICHA	15.04.26	VARSOVIE	P
KATZ	AARON	21.01.07		R
KATZ	JOSEPH	17.06.04		R
KATZ	LEOPOLD	09.06.95		A
KATZ	PAULINE	12.11.05		R
KAUFMANN	ARTHUR	18.08.11		A
KAUFMANN	MAX	22.12.67		P
KAYLER	NICHEM	.92		P
KENIK	ROSA	23.03.03		P
KERBES	TOBIAS	09.02.01		AUT
KERBOTHANE	ISAK	15.02.07		P
KERN	GRETE	02.11.08		A
KERFEN	HANS			
KESSLER	MARGOT	28.09.00		A
KIBEL	BERTHE	17.02.32	LODZ	P
KIBEL	HENRI	01.05.37	PARIS	F
KILSZTOK	PISZEL	28.04.01		P
KILSZTOK	ZALA	26.08.04		P
KIMMER	TONI	03.10.05		P
KLAJES	HERSCH	04.05.88		P
KLEINBERG	AKOS			
KLING	ERNEST	01.05.00		A
KLING	RUTH	10.01.06		A
KLINZELLER	ARNOLD	08.12.85		TC
KLIPPER	KATE	03.05.84		AUT
KNOPF	MAURICE	18.05.15		APA
KOHNIGSHOFER	LEO	13.04.86		A
KOHN	CHAIM	30.01.96		P
KOLATZY	ELKAN	21.03.88		P
KOLLIK	MEYER	01.01.01		R
KOPILEFF	MARTA	25.01.03		R
KOPRAK	SZLAMA	24.03.12		P
KORN	SARAH	02.02.10		P
KORNBERG	ISAAC	25.07.05		P
KORNBLUM	ISAAC	10.09.93		F
KORNBLUT	CHANA	15.06.88		P
KORNBLUT	RACHEL	29.01.29		B
KORNBLUT	SULIM	21.01.96		P
KOSSIAKOF	MARIA	16.07.03		R
KOSUBSKI	ESTHER	21.06.85		P
KOSUBSKI	JANKIEL	03.09.76		P
KOSUBSKI	SYLVAIN	18.08.38		F
KOWARSKI	RIJVA	28.08.98		P
KOWARSKI	SWORJRA	28.11.24		F
KRAMBOLC	CHAIM	19.12.98		F
KRAMBOLC	DAVID	04.94.33		F
KRAMBOLC	RACHEL	.00		P
KRAMBOLC	SARA	26.04.26		P
KRAMBOLT	MOISE	13.11.24		P
KRAUTER	JACOB	31.12.10		H
KRAUZE	FANNY	03.03.05		P
KRESS	SAMUEL	19.06.95		A
KRIESSER	PEPI	05.06.99		P
KROCHMAL	MOISE	02.07.83		P
KROMENBERG	RUTH	12.10.14		A
KROTOSCHIN	EWALD	16.10.99		A
KRUGGEL	TONI	02.06.03		AUT
KUHN	JOHANNA	04.10.87		A
KUEN	WILHELM	22.03.87		A
KUPERMAN	ARON	03.04.01		P
KUPERMANN	FELIX	23.02.15	STRYKOW	P
KURZ	ABRAHAM	09.08.85		P
LACHONTCH	MADELEINE	14.10.18		P
LACHS	MAIER	24.02.97		P
LACHS	PAULA	25.04.08		A
LADENBURGER	PAUL	05.04.04		A
LAMBERT	BERTHA	09.02.00		A
LANCMANN	ANNA	.02	SOSNOWIECZ	P
LANCMANN	ARMAND	27.12.23	MEEZ	F
LANCMANN	JACHETTA	.83	SOSNOWIECZ	P
LANCMANN	LEO	10.05.81	SOSNOWIECZ	P
LANCMANN	SZLAIDA	28.05.97	PILICKA	P
LANCMANN	ZILA	17.11.83	SOSNOWIECZ	P
LANCMANN	SUZANNE	16.06.26	METZ	F
LANCZER	DINA	18.09.06		AFA
LANCZER	JACQUELINE	27.11.34		F
LANDMAN	ISRAEL	04.08.08		P
LANG	DAVID	05.05.03		A
LANG	ADOLF	25.03.02		P
LANG	ILSE	17.08.09		A
LANG	ROSEL	04.09.07		P
LASMANN	LEA	02.08.82		P
LASNIARZ	JOSEPH	13.08.07		P
LAUB	GEORGES	18.04.31		P
LAUB	MARCUS	12.12.93		B

Code	Surname	Given name	Date	Place
R	LEHMANN	JANTA	20.05.05	
B	LEIBOWITZ	MANDEL	08.12.01	
B	LEIBEL	PAUL	12.06.14	
F	LEMBERGER	TONI	02.11.08	
P	LERER	ERNA	18.04.11	
P	LERER	SARAH	24.04.30	
P	LEVIE	ARNOLD	01.06.25	
P	LEVINE	BARNETT	20.03.97	
R	LEVY	ALFRED	07.05.97	
R	LEVY	ALFRED	30.11.92	
A	LEVY	BERNARD	05.02.81	
R	LEVY	BERTA	02.12.95	
A	LEVY	KRUNHILDE	03.05.00	
P	LEVY	BRUNO	27.03.97	
P	LEVY	ELSA	.95	
P	LEVY	EMILIE	26.08.76	LANDAU
AUT	LEVY	MARIANNE	12.11.83	
P	LEVY	MARIE		
A	LEVY	MATHILDE	17.06.85	
	LEVY	META	20.02.96	BRESLAU
A	LEWI	MOSSET	06.12.14	
P	LEWIN	ERICH	11.08.09	
F	LEWY	MAX	13.07.08	
P	LICHTENSTEIN	SIEGFRIED	12.11.93	
P	LIEBER	REGINA	03.06.01	
P	LIEBERMAN	FRIEDA	11.07.06	
P	LIEBERMAN	HIRSCH	15.07.98	
	LILLE	SAMUEL	10.10.94	
A	LIND	STELLA	24.04.13	
A	LION	HERZ	12.11.20	
TC	LIPINSKI	MICHEL	26.02.96	
AUT	LIPSCHITZ	GELA	15.12.21	
APA	LIPSCHUTZ	SAMUEL		
A	LIPSZIG	KOPEL	14.05.06	
P	LIPSZYG	HAIM	13.08.18	
P	LIPSZYG	SALI	02.06.18	
R	LIPSZYG	MOTTEL	17.05.87	
R	LIS	SIMON	02.11.10	
P	LOEWENSTEIN	JULIUS	15.04.98	
P	LORCH	ALFRED	14.08.22	
P	LORCH	FRITZ	14.11.88	
F	LORCH	JENNY	16.03.91	
P	LORLACHER	MARTHA	04.05.97	
B	LOSZYCER	BERNARD	26.02.30	PARIS
P	LOSZYCER	CHAIM	01.08.93	VARSOVIE
R	LOSZYCER	RIFKA	26.03.93	KICHINEFF
P	LOWENSTEIN	ANNA	05.01.96	
P	LOWENSTEIN	EMILIE	29.12.82	
F	LOWENSTEIN	GUNTHER	13.06.24	
P	LUBLINSKI	MAX	01.07.00	
P	LUBLINSKI	PIERRE	05.11.38	
F	LUBLINSKI	ROSIETTE	06.05.10	SLATINA
F	LUX	MYRIAM	21.10.01	
P	MAIER	HERMANN	06.03.85	
P	MAJZNER	ANNA	16.08.26	PARIS
P	MAJZNER	JEANINE	16.02.36	PARIS
H	MAJZNER	JOSEPH	26.04.29	PARIS
P	MAJZNER	MAURICE	26.04.31	PARIS
A	MAJZNER	RENEE	18.03.31	PARIS
P	MANDL	EMMANUEL	30.12.94	
F	MANN	HEINRICH	15.07.06	
A	MARKUS	MAX	05.02.02	
A	MARX	BERTA	07.05.29	
AUT	MARX	HILDA	20.10.87	
A	MARX	OTTO	27.07.88	
A	MASS	REBECCA	04.02.00	
P	MASS	CARMEL	30.11.93	
P	MAUS	ILSA	02.11.33	
P	MAUS	OTHLA	06.10.95	
P	MAUS	RUTH	02.06.25	
P	MAY	MARTHE	10.03.11	
P	MAYER	JULIUS	11.02.03	
A	MAYER	OLGA	01.06.07	
A	MAYER	SHINIL	02.08.88	
P	MEHLER	HERMANN	16.01.11	
F	MENDELSOHN	PAULA		
P	MERZNER	WALTER	07.07.25	
P	METZGER	LUDWIG	15.05.94	
P	MIESSTANTER	ERIKA	30.04.14	
P	MINC	BELLA	17.02.95	
F	MOCH	BERTHOLD	13.09.05	
AFA	MON DOLPHO	GERARD		
F	MONK	HERMANN		
P	MOSES	WALTER	18.05.07	
A	MOSCOWICZ	ABRAM	15.08.06	
P	MOSKOWICZ	MALIE	19.01.07	
A	MOSCOWICZ	MICHEL	31.12.35	
P	MOSKOWICZ	MIRYAM	28.02.38	
P	MUELLER	KURT	01.07.11	
P	MULLER	CHARLOTTE	22.12.36	
P	MULLER	MARIE	18.11.37	
B	MULLER	MICHEL	19.07.12	

Excerpt from lists prepared by French and German authorities prior to deportation from Drancy, showing Schmil's name, typed as SHIMIL MAYER, date of birth, and citizenship (AUT = Autrichien or Austrian). Reproduced in the book Le Memorial de la Deportation des Juifs de France *by Serge Klarsfeld, 1978. Used with permission from Serge Klarsfeld.*

In the camp of Rivesaltes, the authorities had asked the prisoners to give them the names and addresses of other members of their families, so they could be "reunited in the east." Since my father believed the German's diabolical lie about resettlement in the east, he wrote that he hoped we would join him "so we can share our fate." The image of my father's and my brother's suffering is haunting, and I cannot allow myself to dwell on it lest I lose my own composure and strength. At the time, while fearing the worst for their lives, we swallowed the lies and kept up our hope.

While the Jews under Vichy's control were rounded up and deported, my mother and I remained in Montlaur. Isolated as we were in that rural corner of France, we were not even aware of rumors. Of course had we known . . . but who knew? And who could imagine that in the country that gave us Bach, Kant with his moral imperative, Goethe, Schiller, and Beethoven, the Germans at the Wannsee Conference in January 1942 would decide to murder an entire people? And who could have imagined that France, the land of liberty, equality, and fraternity, the birthplace of enlightened rationalism, would agree to hand over the very people who had sought refuge in France to their German victors as part of the armistice agreement (Article 19 of the Armistice, signed June 22, 1940)? And who could have imagined that the civilized Christian world from the Vatican to the United States would stand by without even raising its voice to demand an end to this abomination?

✿

Mama and I still had to survive. For the harvest, the government issued extra rations to the farmhands due to the hard physical labor they had to do. The fact that we were doing hard, physical labor the rest of the year was not taken into consideration. With Papa gone, we no longer sent food packages to him, so we had more food for ourselves. But I was still hungry, so the grape harvest was wonderful because I could eat grapes to my heart's content. I began by eating one grape at a time, but there was no time for that. Eventually, I took whole bites out of bunches of grapes and put the rest into the basket. The grapes were unwashed and had a sulfur residue on them from being sprayed to prevent mildew. The harvest lasted about ten or twelve days and by the end, my mouth was sore from the acid on the grapes' skins. I eventually solved the problem of my burning lips by squeezing the insides of the grapes into my mouth without touching my lips. Needless to say, with this high consumption of grapes, we all had to stop often for what we called sentinels. We used vine leaves to wipe our derrieres.

Each of us was given a basket that we filled with grapes clipped from the vine. When the baskets were full, the men came to pick up the grapes. They had large woven baskets strapped to their backs. They would kneel so we could dump our basket into their containers. Once the containers were full, they would walk back to the end of the row and dump the contents into a waiting cart before returning to collect more grapes from the pickers. Our work had a certain rhythm. The harvested grapes were processed in the local cooperative to produce ordinary red table wine from Languedoc.

After the harvest, the men clipped the vine branches called *sarments* close to the trunk or *souche*. The women gathered the cut branches from the ground, tied them into hand-sized bundles, and then tied eight bundles together to form a fagot. This was used as firewood, since each bundle fit neatly under the tripod in the fireplace hearth. I remember the difficulty of tying these branches and bundles together because we did not have real string. We had to manage with string made from grasses, which was not very strong.

The branch-gathering was done in the fall during the rainy season. It was backbreaking work, and we stood on soggy ground with wet feet, bending over to pick up the branches. Decent shoes were unavailable because of rationing, and I couldn't even afford the wooden shoes the peasants wore. I had no gloves, so my hands were badly scratched. The chilblains—or sores due to the cold weather—and scratches left my fingers swollen and oozing and they did not heal until spring. On rare occasions in November, I was able to work in the barn preparing corn for animal fodder.

One day, the manager sent me out to cut down corn stalks with a team of three men. At the time there was little field work to be had, and perhaps the manager thought he was doing me a favor by giving me work. It was very rare though that a woman was sent out with a men's team. I was sent out alone, far from the village, in the company of three farmhands.

Angel was one of the men on the team. Immediately after Kurt was gone, Angel had become more aggressive. He would put his arm around my shoulders and try to steal kisses. If someone saw us together, he would say: "*piano bassano.*" I didn't understand what he was muttering, but when

I figured it out, I was humiliated because he was telling everyone that he intended to have me. The others on the team that day were Bazaga, a twenty-year-old refugee from Franco's Spain, and a thirty-five-year-old peasant whose wife was in a mental institution.

The work entailed cutting down corn stalks less than ten inches above ground. I had a dull sickle and, as a fourteen-year-old girl, I could not keep up with the men. This meant that when they stood up to stretch their backs, I would continue to work. No one offered to help. Instead they made sexual jokes about me. One of them found an ear of corn and made a vulgar gesture that I did not understand—I was that ignorant. In my naïveté, I thought Angel would protect me. I had read stories from the medieval period like *Ivanhoe*, and I knew the rules of chivalry. But instead of protecting me, he made jokes with the rest of the men. They said that he should go first since everyone in the village knew that he was running after me.

At first I thought they were only joking, but they egged each other on with "*chiche*" (I dare you), and I became frightened. Looking around, I searched for a way out, but there was no escape. They were all bigger and stronger than I, and we were in the middle of nowhere. I was trapped. With no possibility of escape, I became terrified.

That's when I saw the manager approach. Someone must have been looking out for me up there, because the manager never went out into the fields. We were three hours into our four-hour shift and the manager stayed with us until it was time to return to the village for our lunch break. I have no idea why the manager came. Perhaps he had second thoughts about sending a fourteen-year-old girl out with three men. The manager had a daughter, Mathilde, who was about my age. Whatever the reason, he never again put me in a similar situation.

After the episode in the cornfield, I did not even want to talk to Angel, let alone be seen with him. I did not want to have anything to do with him. During a chance encounter in the village, I called him *salaud*. He responded by calling me a dirty Jew, *sale juive*. Needless to say, it hurt. This whole experience bothered me for a long time. When I left the following summer, the gossips in the village assumed it was because I was pregnant, as I found out later. This episode reminded me of the biblical injunction to care for and be kind to the widow and the orphan. With Kurt gone, Mama and I were unprotected and vulnerable.

Since then I have come to better understand the French social structure. The truth was that Angel, too, was an outcast, an outsider low on the social ladder. He was a handsome man, blond, with a little moustache, well-built and strong, but he was a foreigner and he did not own any property. The village girls would not go out with him, so he picked on me. As a foreigner and a hunted Jew, I was even lower on the social ladder than he was.

⚖

In November 1942, the Germans occupied Vichy France—the area south of the demarcation line. No more so-called Free France, although the Vichy government remained in place. We were not aware of this important change because without radio or newspapers, we were completely cut off from the outside world.

In winter, there was no farm work and that reduced our meager income even further. In November, someone from Carcassonne told Mama a maid was needed for a young couple with a new baby. I accepted the job. The couple owned and managed a small hotel in town. I took the bus to Carcassonne, got to the hotel, and found it full of German soldiers. I connected with one of them. He was a sixteen-year-old Hungarian boy who could not wait to fight for the Führer. His older brother was already at the front, and he was chomping at the bit to get there. He didn't even have peach fuzz on his face. Since he was barely two years older than I, I thought we both belonged in school. I felt sorry for him because he was so brainwashed. Of course I could not tell him what I thought. While I did not tell him who I was, I spoke German with him, something I should not have done. Fortunately, nothing happened.

The family I worked for was different from what I was used to. Though there was plenty of water and indoor plumbing, the woman washed her infant's scalp with *eau de cologne* and used soap and water only on the baby's tush. Occasionally after lunch, her husband would grab her breasts in front of other people. It made me uncomfortable as I was not used to that sort of behavior. I helped serve the family meals, did laundry—especially the baby's things—and took the baby out for walks. I liked the walks because I was able to explore the city. The new part of the town was built in the valley at the foot of the medieval fortified city. I learned my way around Carcassonne.

The old walled cité *of Carcassonne. The new part of town was in
the valley outside of the walls. Photo taken by Edith, 1956.*

There were lots of German soldiers stationed all over Carcassonne, not
just in my hotel. To this day I can hear the echo of their goosesteps on the
cobblestones that paved the streets. The marching songs of the German
platoons and the sound of their boots hitting the pavement still resonate
in my ears and send chills up and down my spine.

The best part of my job was that I had enough to eat. For sleeping,
they gave me a bed in a room that doubled as storage space for wine bottles. One night, the owner came in and made a lot of noise while getting
some bottles, which woke me up. Startled, I wondered what was going
on. When I saw the owner, my boss, I grumbled a bit and turned around
to go back to sleep. Perhaps he had other things in mind besides fetching
that bottle of wine.

About four weeks after I started working at the hotel, a sweater went
missing from the laundry line in the attic. I was accused of stealing it and in
spite of my protestations of innocence, I was promptly dismissed. Looking
back, it was probably just as well. The German soldiers were part of the

occupation troops sent to Vichy France, and this was not a safe place for a Jewish girl with all my identity papers showing that I was born in Vienna, not to mention the dumb risk I took in speaking German to a soldier.

Once back in Montlaur, Mama worried about me being idle, so she pleaded with the local seamstress to take me on as an apprentice without pay. The woman reluctantly agreed. I learned nothing, but stitched a lot of hems and sewed on many buttons. I had outgrown my clothes. When my brother left, he took with him his good pants and left behind an old worn-out pair. I took the leg part of the pants and made a simple A-line skirt. I also took a dress I had outgrown and made a blouse. I wore these two garments for the next few years. When spring came, I went back to work in the fields.

At one point, Mama received a summons to appear at the police station of Carcassonne or at the local *gendarmerie* to get her identification papers and her rationing cards stamped with the big J or the word *Juif* in keeping with a law passed on December 11, 1942. According to the summons, she would be held responsible for the actions taken against her by the *Procureur de la République*, subject to penalties according to the law, and also responsible for expenses. If she did not show up in person, a ruling would be made against her, but if she appeared in person, then she would simply pay a fine of about eighty-three French francs, an enormous sum for us, given our meager income.

Since she failed to comply within a month after the proclamation of this law, she was called to appear in criminal court in Carcassonne to be questioned and to defend herself as to why she did not appear before the authorities to have her papers stamped. Going to Carcassonne was not a simple matter. First of all, it cost money to take the bus for the round trip for both of us—money we did not have. It also involved applying for a permit or safe-conduct to travel. I had to go with her to serve as interpreter because her French was not that good. For us, this meant that the noose continued to tighten. By making a census of the Jews and confirming their place of residence, this ordinance would facilitate the arrest and deportation of the remaining Jews.

ASSIGNATION A PRÉVENU

ORIGINAL

L'an mil neuf cent quarante trois

le Deux avril

A la demande de M. le Procureur de la République près le Tribunal de première instance d **CARCASSONNE**

_____ qui élit domicile en son

parquet sis audit lieu.

L'HUISSIER SOUSSIGNÉ AVERTIT PAR LE PRÉSENT ACTE

M BUCHHOLZ Anna f. MAYER 39 ans, s;p. À MONTLAUR

ci-après nommé.

Que M. le Procureur de la République de **CARCASSONNE**

1' assigne à comparaître en personne le Huit avril 1943

_____ mil neuf cent quarante trois

à neuf heures _____ pardevant le Tribunal Correc-

tionnel de **CARCASSONNE** séant

au Palais de Justice de ladite Ville _____ pour :

Etre présent e___ à l'instruction qui s'y fera, être interrogé e___ et se

défendre comme prévenu e d'avoir, à Montlaur, étant de

race juive, omis de se présenter dans le délai d'un

mois à dater de la promulgation de la loi du II

décembre 1942, au commissariat de police ou à la

brigade de gendarmerie de sa résidence pour faire

apposer la mention " Juif" sur la carte d'alimenta-

tion et la carte d'identité.

Fait_ prévu_ par l'a arix loi du II décembre 1942.

Huis. 3, Trib. 456

57H . Allain - Elbeuf C

Visé pour timbre à
et enregistré à
Débet, décimes compris

le

_Convocation letter, dated April 2, 1943, for Anna Mayer to appear on
April 8 at 9 a.m. at the Palace of Justice. (Continued next page.)_

et en outre répondre aux conclusions qui seront prises contre elle
par Monsieur le Procureur de la République d'après l'instruction à l'audience et s'entendre condamner aux peines prévues par la loi et aux frais.

Défaut sera prononcé contre elle s-i elle *ne se présente* pas. *Néanmoins si la présente signification est faite à personne, le prévenu pourra, nonobstant son défaut, être jugé contradictoirement (Art. 149, alinéa 4, et 188 du Code d'Instruction criminelle).*

Copie du présent acte a été remise par

M⁼ Je soussigné, Jean CARBONNEL, Huissier près le Tribunal Civil de Carcassonne, résidant à Lagrasse

à M BUCHHOLZ Anne f. MAYER, étant à son domicile et parlant à sa personne

Coût : Quatre vingt deux francs 40 Cmes.

Employé pour la copie Une feuille de papier du

format du timbre à six francs en debet.

Safe Conduct to Carcassonne, March 5, 1943, to appear before the Palace of Justice. This was requested after the first summons, which is why the date is in March. It specifies why this trip was needed—"convocation for a judgment"—and what means of transportation used—the bus. Original at United States Holocaust Memorial Museum.

COUR D'ASSISES

Carcassonne, le ~~8 AVR 1943~~ 19___

de l'Aude

PARQUET

Le Procureur de la République de Carcassonne invite la

nommée *Buchholz Anna p. Mayer 39 ans*

s.p.

à Montlaur.

poursuivi pour délit de *défaut d'opposition de la mention*
"juif" sur carte d'alimentation et sur carte d'identité.

commis le *courant 1943*

à se présenter volontairement à l'audience correctionnelle de

Carcassonne, le *15 Avril* 19*43*

à neuf heures du matin.

**Faute par lui de comparaître ce jour-là, il sera cité par huissier
et à ses frais pour l'audience suivante.**

Le Procureur de la République.

NOTA. — *Prière de vouloir bien détacher cette feuille et de la faire remettre
immédiatement au Prévenu.*

This letter, dated April 8, 1943, states that Anna Mayer will be cited because she
failed to appear to have her papers stamped with the word Juif. She is to appear in
court voluntarily because she ignored the previous request. If she does not appear,
then she will have a citation and expenses for the following convocation.

༄

My teacher from Nice, Mme Brun, had kept up her correspondence with me and sent me a few French classics for children. It was very kind of her, though I must admit that they really bored me. I could not get excited about the antics of a little goat in one of the stories by Alphonse Daudet. I had previously read books written for adults. For example I recall reading *Gone with the Wind* while still in Nice at age thirteen. There was no library in the village. Without interesting books, I was left to my own devices. I recall writing a play about aristocrats trading places with their servants, a classic plot in many seventeenth- and eighteenth-century plays. Without other outlets, I simply lived like the other village girls. Occasionally there was a film on Saturday night shown in some barn. Once I went on a pilgrimage with other young people from the village. I think we went to Rocamadour. We traveled in the back of an open truck, and I learned a mountain song about the Pyrénées. I remember it as a pleasant outing that broke up the monotony of village life.

After the *grand café* closed its dance hall, all the girls went for walks on the main road that led out from the village. One Saturday evening, I was out with them as usual and was talking to one of the French soldiers stationed nearby. All of a sudden, Mama showed up and whacked me across the face in front of everyone before leaving in a huff. After that, no one dared even to talk to me. That was her idea of protecting my virginity.

During our time in Montlaur, we became friendly with one family, the Duponts, who owned some land and a horse. They had two sons: Jean, who was eighteen, and Paul, nicknamed Popo, who was my age. The family worked for others during the week and tilled their own land in the evenings and on weekends. They had two hunting dogs who received only table scraps, something I noticed when Mama and I were invited to supper with them. The dogs would approach us while we ate and M. Dupont would kick them in the ribs to chase them away, but they always came back. I felt sorry for the poor animals.

Mme Angèle Dupont was a tall woman in her forties with a round face, red cheeks, and a gentle smile. I sometimes played with Popo, who would tease me and call me *unocento* (innocent). I had trouble understanding the local dialect, which was closer to Spanish than to Italian. Jean had willingly gone to Germany for the *Service du Travail Obligatoire*. After two years in Germany, Jean returned and became the manager of the local cooperative.

During the long, cold winter months, Mama and I often went to the Duponts' after dinner. Their fire was fed by the slow-burning trunks of grapevines, and it was warm. We would sit in the dark and talk in the glow from the hearth. Many times we got too close to the fire and our blood vessels would show through the skin of our legs. If you did that too often, your legs would become permanently marbled, as could be seen on many of the village women.

The other family we came to know was the Noyes. They were the second wealthiest landowners in the village, after the Niermans. M. Noyes was an *ingénieur agronome*—he had a university diploma in agricultural engineering and managed his own estate. He had a large garden where he raised fruits and vegetables for sale and I went there to buy produce. They had two sons, Jean, who was bright, and his brother, who was slower, perhaps because of a case of childhood measles. Madame, an attractive, elegant woman, often went to church twice on Sundays—at 7 a.m. and again at 11 a.m. The village gossips said she did it to show off her outfits. The family had a full-time maid, Jeanne, who raised the boys and was very devoted to the family. I once watched her stuff geese, a sight that could cure people from ever eating pâté de foie gras.

In the fall of 1942, after the mass deportations from France began, I was out working in the fields when Mama was contacted by a member of the Sixième, a code name given to the clandestine branch of the Eclaireurs Israélites de France (EIF, the Jewish Scouts of France). They now focused their dwindling resources on the rescue of children. The young man tried to convince Mama to let me go into hiding. Her first reaction was to say no, but he then explained that if I were arrested, I would be sent to a concentration camp and might be sexually abused.

My initial reaction to the idea of leaving my mother to go into hiding was to say no as well, but when I was told what the possible consequences of an arrest would be, I decided to go. Given how I was raised, shaming and sexual abuse would have been a fate worse than death for me. In the end, it was my decision to leave. Perhaps I was afraid of being denounced by Angel after I refused to have sex with him. The fact remains that the possibility of being violated in camp was enough to push me to go.

It took about six months after our initial contact with the Sixième before we were notified that a hiding place had been found for me and that it was time to leave Montlaur. I was told to appear with my belongings at an address in Carcassonne on a certain day. I needed a safe conduct permit to make the trip and my pretext was that I had to see a dentist.

Mama had to raise money for a bus ticket to Carcassonne. We had no money and not much left to sell. When I was little, I remembered seeing Mama work for years on a *petit point* embroidery. I had watched her in Vienna as she recreated a seventeenth-century Gobelin design on canvas. Later, she had the finished embroidery mounted on a frame to create an elegant purse. Now she took that purse to Mme Noyes who bought it for fifty francs, enough to get me to Carcassonne and leave me a little change.

I knew Carcassonne as a result of my stint at the hotel, so finding my contact was no problem. When I got there, my official legal ID papers were taken from me and destroyed. Edith "Sara" Mayer disappeared. I was given a new name, Elise Maillet, with ID papers to match, and was asked to memorize my new story, a fiction I could easily maintain. My story was that my mother lived in Nice, my father was a POW, and I had no siblings. My parents were non-practicing Catholics, not uncommon in France.

I never forgot the day I left Montlaur. It was July 3, 1943, two weeks after my fifteenth birthday. Soon after I got my papers and my story straight, I boarded a train for Castelnaudary accompanied by a member of the Jewish resistance. Castelnaudary was a nearby town of about 3,000 people, where a convent school was located. As we waited in the station, my escort offered to buy me a book and, to his surprise, I chose a biography of Pericles. On the train I took out my new identity card and examined it. That's when I noticed my thumb print was missing. My guide quickly took out his fountain pen to create an inkblot, and I pressed my thumb on the false document. My new identity card was now officially complete.

I was fully aware of the dangers that awaited me. I knew my life was now in my own hands. In French schools there was roll call every morning, and I was afraid that I would not react quickly enough when Elise Maillet was called. To make matters worse, I was anything but self-reliant. I had never been separated from my Mama, not even for a sleepover at a friend's house or a summer camp experience, and I was utterly dependent on her. Now that I was on my own with no one to tell me what to do, I resolved to be very strict with myself. Of course, I hoped to see my parents again and when I did, I would be able to tell them everything so they could be proud of me. I knew absolutely nothing about Catholicism even though I had always lived in Catholic countries. I had only had the most superficial contact with non-Jews and I wondered what they were like. All this inexperience added to my stress.

Ville de MONTMEDY

Département de la Meuse

EXTRAIT des minutes des actes de
NAISSANCES.

Le quinze Avril mil neuf cent vingt-
huit est né à trois heures dix un enfant du
sexe féminin qui a recu le prénom de
 E L I S E
Fille de Charles, Jules MAILLET
Et de Eliane Marie CHAUVIN.

Fait à Montmédy, le seize Avril mil
neuf cent vingt -huit.
 L'Officier d'Etat-Civil.
 Signé: illisible

*Fake birth certificate. Elise Maillet, daughter of Charles Jules Maillet and Elaine
Marie Chauvin, was born in Montmedy on April 15, 1928—the wrong date,
which did not correspond with the fake ID card, a dangerous oversight.*

❧

In the summer of 2014, I visited Neuengamme, a former slave labor camp near Hamburg. Among the many buildings was one named The Hut. I learned that it was used as a brothel. The SS would bring girls and women from the other camps to serve as prostitutes for the inmates. They would use the women to manipulate the prisoners and reward the more cooperative ones with permission to use these women. It became clear to me at last that in 1942, at the age of fourteen, I had made the right decision.

For a long time I wondered how the underground found us. How did they know who we were and where we were? We certainly had not registered with any Jewish organization in Carcassonne or elsewhere. I think I solved the mystery a few years ago. Inmates in French concentration camps were told to give the authorities the names and addresses of family members on the outside so that the Nazis could "reunite families." My father alluded to that in his letters.

There were two social workers in Rivesaltes where Papa was held. The social workers knew about the reunification sham and the concentration camps, and they told the prisoners not to give information about their families to the authorities but to them instead. My father may have given them our names and that is how I was found and saved. Years later I met Simone Weil-Lipman, one of the social workers, who explained the whole story. She was a lovely lady in her eighties and an aunt by marriage of one of my close friends in New York City.

❧

After the war, Mama and I went back to Montlaur several times. We kept in touch with some neighbors, especially with the Martinoles who rented us the house on the Grand'rue, with the Duponts who lived across the street, and also with the Noyes. Since Montlaur was the last address known to Papa and Kurt, Mama made sure that the post office always had our forwarding address in the vain hope that they had survived.

I went back with my husband, Steve, and again with my daughters, Emily and Louise. After the war, Jean Dupont married Mathilde, the daughter of the manager of the Château. Popo was married to the daughter of the village carpenter and was living in her house on the Grand'rue. As for the Noyes, Jean went into electronics and eventually landed a job with

Madame Martinoles and Edith, summer 1956.

From right to left: Edith, Paul (Popo) Dupont,
his wife, and their relatives, 1956.

IBM-France. He married a girl from a well-to-do family from a nearby village. His brother married a local girl who had less education. I also learned that neither Angel nor his brother Marius ever married. After the war, the main streets were paved, water was brought to the village from the Pyrénées, and there was indoor plumbing everywhere. The banks of the stream were covered with cement and a little channel was left in the middle for water during the dry season. The village population had shrunk to 650.

My most recent visit was in the summer of 1999 with my son, Daniel, and his wife, Leigh. The park of the Château now had a swimming pool for the exclusive use of guests of the Château where several rooms on the ground floor had been modernized to serve tourists for what the French call *gite touristique*. Even the Rosetti apartment near the stables had been converted into a *gite*. The population of the village had shrunk even further. Popo had died, but I met Jean. Together we made a tour of the Château. In the kitchen I could still hear the imperious voice of Mme Niermans calling my mother.

On a sadder note, Jean told me that his father had offered to hide my brother in some cave in the area and to bring him food. Kurt refused, he said, because he wanted to be with our father to take care of him. My brother expected that our father was about to be released from Rivesaltes—he even wrote as much in his last postcard to us. If such a conversation ever took place, my brother never shared that information with me. I wonder whether my mother had been informed about it. I certainly never heard it. Then there is the possibility that Jean was not quite telling it the way it was, since everyone wants to look good in hindsight. But then what interest would he have now in making up a story? So many questions shall remain unanswered. This revelation just reopened old wounds.

In Hiding in France

5. CASTELNAUDARY

The Convent School

We arrived in Castelnaudary that same afternoon. It was a very hot summer day, and I remember the long walk as I carried my suitcase up a steep hill from the train station to the convent. My guide left me at the convent door, and I began my new life as just another Catholic high school student. The nuns were running a girls' vocational high school with a commercial curriculum and a home economics track.

The nuns were divided into Mothers and Sisters. Each Mother was from an upper-middle-class family, had a good education, and usually brought a dowry with her to the convent. Mothers served as both teachers and administrators. The Sisters had peasant or blue-collar backgrounds and less education. They did all the hard work and drudgery: laundry, cooking, cleaning, and taking care of the rabbits and the chickens. I stayed at the convent through the summer, and I got to know some of the nuns. Even as a non-Catholic, I had put all people of the cloth on a pedestal. But I discovered that nuns were people just like the rest of us with foibles and egos, tempers, and attitudes. I also remember thinking that the Sisters were often kinder and more compassionate than the Mothers.

I shared a room with four other girls. One of them, Naomi Zoé, was teased a lot because she was awkward and her name sounded funny in French. It wasn't vicious teasing, but it was constant. Normally, I would have said something in her defense, but under the circumstances, I was almost glad of that, as it deflected attention away from me. I was trying hard to blend in and was careful to observe the other girls and imitate whatever they did when they prayed or crossed themselves. We took our meals in the large refectory while one of the nuns read inspirational literature to us.

On my first Sunday at the convent, I noticed that there were fewer girls at breakfast. I assumed they were allowed to sleep in because it was

Sunday. After breakfast, I went to church with all the students. I followed them to the altar and took communion, carefully mimicking their gestures—the folded hands, the downcast and pious look upon returning from communion, the silent prayer while kneeling at my bench. Imagine my surprise when, upon returning from church, I was greeted with dismay. I wondered how I had given myself away after only a few days. Apparently I had committed a mortal sin: I had eaten breakfast before taking communion, and you were not supposed to do that. The reaction of the nuns and of the students surprised me because, in my mind, mortal sins should be reserved for major transgressions, not for eating breakfast before communion—especially given the injustices and horrors we were witnessing all around us.

My action provoked an uproar among both the nuns and the girls. The nuns asked me if I had had my first communion. Of course I had not. Was I baptized? I said I didn't know. So the good nuns took it upon themselves to write to the priest in the village where I was supposedly born. I hoped that the Mother Superior would put a stop to these investigations and interrogations, because I had been told that the Mother Superior knew I was Jewish. Now I wonder if she was really aware of that. In their zeal, perhaps the nuns failed to tell her that they were writing to the village priest, an action that could blow my cover. They may also have been attempting to convert me in order to "save my soul." The reply from the village priest came two weeks later and, of course, there was no record of me. Then the nuns asked me if I would be willing to take catechism. I said yes. I was prepared to do whatever I had to in order to survive. I was scheduled to start catechism in September with the new school year.

For me, survival was a full-time job. I worried about giving myself away by talking in my sleep. I had to be alert at all times, to remember yesterday's lies, and to always be conscious of what I was saying or doing. I complied with the Catholic rituals as best I could in order to save my life. As for the teachings, I did not have the luxury to evaluate what I learned. That had to wait until later, when the war was over and I was free to think.

There was only one month left in the school year when I arrived, and I was put into the home economics curriculum that normally attracted the less able students. We studied a little bit of literature and some arithmetic, easy stuff. I think I read Molière's *Bourgeois Gentilhomme* while there, at least parts of it. But again, school turned into a waste of time.

When summer vacation began, I was asked if I would be willing to stay in the convent and work. Since I had no place to go, I accepted. I shared a room with another girl who volunteered to stay and work, but she went home every weekend. Her name was Catherine. She had an oval face with a pointed chin, long brown hair, and curls above her forehead as was the fashion. Catherine was a gentle soul, but not once during those two months did I confide in her in any way, tell her who I really was, how I felt, or what was on my mind. And she didn't ask any questions.

During the summer, the nuns ran a day camp for preschoolers. The children arrived late in the morning and we fed them lunch. Lunch consisted of a porridge cooked outdoors in two huge cast-iron kettles that I had to clean every morning. It was hard work because the kettles were almost bigger than I was and were very heavy. The worst of it was that the food had worms in it. You learned not to eat the hot cereal by the spoonful but to pick through it. After my initial revulsion, I learned to set the worms aside and eat the rest.

After lunch we took the children for a walk to the grassy banks of the nearby Canal du Midi, where we let them rest for a while before playing with them. Though the weather was very hot, there was no pool or water play of any kind, and there was no playground equipment either. We played games, taught them songs, and, after a few hours, walked them back to the convent where they were picked up and taken home.

I enjoyed working with the children and playing games with them. I was in charge of lining them up in rows before walking to and from the canal. I vividly remember one little girl who always refused to get in line when it was time to go home. She was one of the youngest in the group, not verbal yet, and she would throw temper tantrums every day when it was time to leave. She would throw herself on the ground, kicking and screaming. I would pick her up and usually managed to get her to comply. On one particular day, try as I might, I could not get her to cooperate. In desperation, I spanked her by slapping her on her thigh.

This attracted the attention of Mother Marie-Rose, a tall, bespectacled, slender, and rather young woman with aristocratic airs. She called me aside and gave me such a tongue-lashing that I began to cry. That did not stop her. Instead she added, "It's good that you should cry," and she continued to lay into me. The irony was that neither she nor the other nuns ever helped me with this child. It was always up to me to get this little girl

*The convent school in Castelnaudary. Edith is in the front row, left.
Catherine is in the middle row, fifth from the right. Naomi Zoé
is in the back row, third from the right. July 15, 1943.*

to walk back. Now that I have more experience with children, I realize
that this little girl was a battered child. She was always disheveled and
badly dressed, often dirty, and her head was infested with live lice. Lice
are easy to kill even if eggs, or nits, are not, so although lice in children
were not uncommon, live ones were. I caught lice from her. The question
I ask myself now is why did the nuns not realize what this poor child was
going through? She only threw her tantrums when it was time to go home.

On weekends when Catherine went home, I worked with one of the
Sisters on Saturdays cleaning out the rabbit hutches and cutting branches
from the weeping willows for the rabbits. Though I never confided in
her either, she was more outspoken about the war and gave vent to her
anti-German feelings. As a result of her kindness and honesty, I felt closer
to her than to any of the nuns.

Toward the end of the summer, the nuns allowed me to go out with
some of the other girls. We went down to the canal where there were tippy
little boats called *périssoires* for rent. They were made of wood and were less
stable than canoes. We dared each other to paddle across the canal. Two
of us climbed into one of these boats, and of course, it capsized. Since I
knew how to swim, I swam across the canal fully clothed and had to sneak
back into the convent, dripping wet. It would have been a funny story to

tell, but the canal was polluted and a few weeks later, I suffered the dire consequences.

Soon after that, as school was about to start, I was called to the office of the Mother Superior. Word came to her that I had been "burned." One of the students at the convent had relatives in Montlaur and when she went home for vacation, she showed the class photo to her relatives. The young owner of the *grand café* in Montlaur recognized me and told her my name was Edith Mayer, not Elise Maillet. My cover was blown, and I had to leave the convent in a hurry.

I was gone the very next day.

6. MOISSAC

In the Hospital

In the rush to get me out of Castelnaudary, there was no time to find another hiding place, so I was sent to Moissac, where the home run by the Éclaireurs Israélites de France (EIF, or Jewish Scouts of France) was still functioning. Moissac was one of many *maisons d'enfants* (children's homes) that took in Jewish children whose parents were threatened, deported, or languishing in French concentration camps. Many of the children were foreign born and had come to France on a *Kindertransport*.

All these *maisons d'enfants*, most of which were operated by the Oeuvre de Secours aux Enfants (OSE), were officially recognized and registered, which made it easier for the authorities to find and arrest the children. In the OSE home in Chabannes in the Creuse, ten of the older boys were arrested on August 26, 1942. Five were deported immediately (only two came back), and the remaining five were released thanks to the intervention of M. Chevalier, the French director of the home. In another home in Izieu near Lyon, all the children were arrested by Klaus Barbie, known as the butcher of Lyon, deported to Auschwitz, and gassed immediately. When it became clear that the Germans were out to kill all the Jews and the French authorities were cooperating by arresting children and handing them over to the German authorities for deportation, hiding places had to be found and the homes had to be closed. I was lucky that in Moissac, the headquarters of the EIF, the home was still open.

My stay in Moissac was to be temporary. The plan was to send me to work for two weeks to help with the harvest. That would give the Sixième time to find a hiding place for me and after that, schools would open and I would be placed in one of them. The children's home was still full, though plans were underway to find hiding places for everyone because it was too dangerous to keep so many children together in one place.

It was harder to hide children who did not speak French or those who spoke with a German accent. The counselors told the German and Austrian children to say they were from Alsace-Lorraine, a region in France where German was still spoken. I was fortunate for I spoke French like a native and linguistically, I could pass. I watched the children in Moissac memorize their "stories" as they got ready to leave. The older ones could be placed in schools as borders, like I had been. For the younger children, families had to be found that would take them in. It was an enormous task for the Sixième, for the OSE, and also for the Mouvement de Jeunesse Sioniste (MJS). They were the principal clandestine networks focused on saving the children in Nazi-occupied France, and they worked together and helped each other to get false papers—including rationing coupons—find hiding places, and maintain contact with children in hiding and their families, when possible.

I got to Moissac early on a Friday. That evening one of the counselors, two other girls, and I went to the movies. When we came back, I went to bed feeling sick. I woke up the next day with a very painful sore throat. I could not swallow, was running a high fever, and felt utterly miserable. I was rushed to the hospital where I was diagnosed with diphtheria. The people who ran the home were extremely concerned because the children were about to be sent into hiding and could not afford to get sick. They nicknamed me *la pestiférée*, or the plague-ridden one, and my room was thoroughly fumigated.

At the hospital, I was injected with horse serum, then the standard treatment for diphtheria, which was supposed to provide the antibodies to help my body fight the illness. The serum caused unbearable itching and there was nothing to relieve it. This went on for weeks. I also remember getting the inside of my throat daubed with some kind of blue medication to relieve the pain and reduce the swelling. But swallowing remained painful and the high fever persisted.

The doctor placed me in the hospital pavilion for contagious diseases. A woman in her thirties in the room next door had scarlet fever, and we shared the same nurse who cared for both of us, going from one to the other. After four weeks in the hospital I finally began to feel better when I got sick again, this time with scarlet fever. For me, this was the coup de grâce, the last blow.

There I was in the hospital in Moissac, sick as a dog again, depressed, with all the fight gone out of me. I could not take it anymore and I was ready to give up. I was no longer able to fight for my life. For me, the persecution had been going on for five long years, starting in July 1938 in Italy; it was now October 1943. I felt that sooner or later we would all be killed. There was no point in continuing to try to hang on to life, and I wanted to die with my Mama instead of alone like an abandoned animal. I wanted to go back to Montlaur so we would at least die together.

I wrote all of this in a letter to my mother. Since I had no stationery, I wrote on toilet paper. For mail, the Sixième had worked out a system. With censorship, it was too dangerous to send letters through the post office. To communicate with my mother, I would give my letter to a *resistant* (counselor) who would give it to another, and so on until someone would personally hand her my letter. Her mail to me was handled in the same manner. I handed my toilet paper letter to a *resistant* who visited me at the hospital.

Physically and emotionally at the end of my rope, I was resigned to die. The doctor who examined me said I was run-down and malnourished. With rationing, the hospital food was not very nourishing. I got a lot of cabbage, rutabagas, turnips, onions, celery, and little protein, so the people at the children's home decided to supplement my diet with their own food. Twice a day, they sent two children to the hospital to bring me their food. This allowed me to be a bit more selective. The home sent some much needed food with protein. Because it was harvest time, I also got chestnuts, persimmons, and grapes. I learned to eat larger quantities in order to get more nutrition even though it wasn't good for my waistline. After four more weeks in the hospital, I recovered.

While I was there, the lice in my hair and scalp multiplied and thrived. When I arrived, I was too ashamed to tell the nurse that I had lice. But when I came down with scarlet fever and had at least another four weeks stay in the hospital, I decided to tell the nurse. Lice fell out of my head by the dozen whenever I ran a comb through my hair. I discovered that lice bite your scalp. The nurse applied a medication that killed the live ones, and she did it more than once. I had started out with fashionably long hair in the style of Rita Hayworth, but after I left the hospital I got a very short haircut.

While I was getting better, I was also very bored without books and with nothing to do. The kind nurse brought me materials to make a little tote bag. She dyed some old sheets a bright red and brought me a large piece of cardboard. I cut it up and sewed the red fabric over the cardboard, using the additional fabric for the gussets and the handle. The bag turned out to be very useful as a small piece of hand luggage. I had also brought along my old winter coat that showed signs of wear. While convalescing, I undid all the seams, turned the fabric inside-out, and sewed everything back together by hand.

I finally left the hospital in November. It was cold, and I was shivering. When I got to the home, I found it almost empty as most of the children had been placed. I shared a bedroom with two other girls. Since we did not have enough blankets, we took spare mattresses and put them across our beds in lieu of blankets to keep out the chill. After a few days in the home, I was sent off to my next hiding place, the Collège Moderne de Jeunes Filles in Mende (Lozère) in the Massif Central, approximately two hundred miles northeast of Moissac.

7. MENDE

The English Teacher

It was mid-November and the weather was miserable. I had begun to doubt my own survival and, worse, I was losing the will to fight and to resist. Death was all around us, and it seemed like just a matter of time before I too would get caught in the dragnet and be killed. It was the lowest point of my life.

I traveled to Mende by train with a female *resistant* whose wartime nickname was Belette (weasel). At one point, the door to our compartment opened and two men came in and asked for our papers. As we produced our false identity cards, I was gripped by fear. This was the first time my false papers were put to the test. Would they pass? Did they look authentic? Control in trains was common as there was little chance of escaping from a fast-moving train, and the exit of the compartment was blocked by the two inspectors. One man, who seemed pleasant and polite, handled the procedure. He was tall and wore a gray raincoat. The other one supervised and was the more menacing of the two. He was even taller and wore a dark winter coat. As they inspected our cards, the man in the gray coat noticed that our ID cards were issued by the same town of Orange. The inspector might have suspected something, but he simply asked, "Are you related?" Thinking quickly, Belette replied, "Yes, she is my niece." With that, the cards were politely returned to us and the men left our compartment. I breathed a sigh of relief.

Hiding under a false identity was not a simple matter. I was still not used to being on my own and worse than that was the constant lying. I had to be on my guard at all times. Every word, every gesture had to be controlled and scrutinized to see whether it was safe. This created a constant state of tension that escalated with each passing day. It also created an incredible sense of loneliness since I could not share my thoughts with anyone. I couldn't even keep a journal because if someone found my notes, it would put me and everyone around me at risk.

Leaving Moissac depressed, miserable, scared, and lonely, I arrived at a huge boarding school in Mende. The building was cold and gray and, like all French *lycées*, it was forbidding and prison-like. The school had an iron gate and a fence with wrought iron spikes. As a boarder, I was not allowed to leave the premises except for group outings, like the weekly trip to the public showers and the customary Sunday afternoon walks. Only an authorized person was allowed to sign me out.

Unlike my stay in Castelnaudary, I was not alone in this untenable situation. There were twelve other Jewish girls in this school. They were placed there by the clandestine branch of the OSE and by the Sixième. I recognized one of them from my brief stay in Moissac, and soon I knew all twelve girls. Though we knew it was dangerous to stick together, we still tended to seek each other out. There was some comfort in being able to speak openly, even if we had to use code language like apples for Germans or pears for Poles.

The huge dormitory may have housed as many as forty girls. The beds were lined up in two rows against the walls. They had iron headboards and small night tables, where we put most of our possessions. The room was dimly lit, unheated, and drab—just like the rest of the place—and it was quite uncomfortable.

Classwork was a disaster for me. I arrived at school six weeks into the trimester and had no textbooks. In French secondary schools, students had to purchase textbooks and all school supplies themselves. The Sixième was too busy saving lives to worry about providing their charges with textbooks, so my grades were bad. I began to think of myself as stupid when I saw my math tests come back covered in red ink, and so I convinced myself that I had a mental block for math. Looking at my report card for that school, I noticed that my grades for spelling, reading, and geography were good as were the comments by the professors. No matter. I was fixated on the results of my math tests.

And then the English teacher appeared. At first, she was just one of my many teachers. She was young, dark-haired, tall, slender, and well-groomed. I thought she was pretty. After a few days, she gave me a textbook. Then she helped me with the chapters I had missed and checked my homework. Thanks to her support, I caught up with the rest of the class

ACADÉMIE de MONTPELLIER

Département de la Lozère

Collège Moderne de Jeunes Filles

Année scolaire 1943-1944

BULLETIN de Mademoiselle *Maillet Élise*   Section *1re Moderne*

Notes obtenues pendant le 1er trimestre

MATIÈRES	Moyennes	Compositions	Place	OBSERVATIONS des PROFESSEURS
Morale et Inst. civique				
Composition française	absente			Arrivée en fin d'année
Lecture expliquée	14,5	14,5		A l'air de s'intéresser à son
Orthographe	12	absente		travail S. Traité
Langues … Anglais	absente			
Histoire				Travail satisfaisant
Géographie	11	absente		S. Traité
Mathématiques	absente			
Physique				
Chimie				
Histoire naturelle				
Dessin	absente			
Écriture *Allemand*	16,7	16,75	2e	Bien, beaucoup de facilité
Gymnastique	absente			
Chant	13		6e	
Économie domestique				
Enseignement ménager				
Couture	15		3e	
Conduite	15,9			

Moyenne générale : 13,40   Place non classée   élèves.

Observations : Trop d'absences pour être jugée

Les Parents :   La Directrice :

Report card for first trimester at the Collège Moderne de Jeunes Filles. The comments for subjects are satisfactory. Edith placed second in German, third in sewing, and sixth in singing. The bottom comment is "too many absences to be evaluated" since Edith arrived in the middle of the trimester, which meant that she wasn't ranked. 1943.

rather quickly. I do not remember this young woman's name, but my report card has the initials SL. When I realized that she was taking a special interest in me, I asked the other girls whether it was safe to trust her; they said it was. I never told Mademoiselle L who I was and she never asked me any direct questions, but I am convinced that she somehow figured out which girls were in hiding.

One day she asked me whether I had a winter coat and warm socks. I was flabbergasted. No one had ever asked me anything about my own needs—not even the nuns or the Mother Superior at the convent, who clearly knew who I was. I almost burst into tears when she gave me some yarn and knitting needles so I could knit myself some socks. She also asked me if I would like to become a girl scout. I accepted enthusiastically. I went to meetings that were run by her and held in a remote corner of the *lycée*, studied my scout manual, and prepared for my Promise. I appreciated the break in the drab routine, and I liked the scout values and ideals since they complemented and reinforced my own. I had only spent a month with the troop when, just before Christmas vacation, suspecting that I would not return, Mademoiselle L asked whether I wanted to make my Girl Scout Promise before I left. I accepted joyfully and became an official girl scout in record time.

The high point of my stay in Mende came when Mademoiselle L invited me to her house. Even though it was only for a few hours, it was so nice to be in a home that was comfortable, warm, and had real furniture. It felt wonderful to be away from the institution. But above all, it was such a privilege to be with someone I looked up to and who took an interest in me. Mademoiselle L treated me to a *goûter*, the customary French mid-afternoon snack, and we spoke at length. She asked me whether my mother had explained the facts of life to me. I was fifteen-and-a-half, and I told her I knew something about it. Before I left that afternoon, she wrote in my memory book:

> *Que seulement je fasse de ma vie une flûte simple et droite pareille à un roseau que l'on puisse emplir de musique. —R Tagore*

> May I make of my life a flute, simple and straight like a reed that can be filled with music.

> *A l'éclaireuse que j'estime et regrette, pour qu'elle en fasse le mot d'ordre de sa vie.*

To the girl scout whom I esteem and [whose departure I] regret so that she may make this the motto of her life.

Mademoiselle L's farewell note in Edith's memory book, 1943.

It was a line translated from the Indian poet Rabindranath Tagore. I took it to heart and never forgot it. Soon, Christmas vacation came and it was time for me to leave. I never saw Mademoiselle L again.

8. FLORAC

Christmas Vacation

Dedicated to Peter Feigl to help him remember.

It was December 1943 and time for Christmas vacation. Staying in school was out of the question as all the schools closed for the holidays, but the children in hiding could not go home. So the Sixième organized a scout camp, where we pretended to be Protestant scouts. A counselor took me from Mende to the small town of Florac in the mountains of the Massif Central in France.

I got to Florac on a cold, dark night. The ground was frozen. I was shivering and stood there, alone, wondering whether I would ever be warm again. Gradually other people began to trickle in as I waited in the dark, shoulders hunched, freezing. One of the new arrivals asked me if I knew how to dance the hora, an Israeli folk dance. I said I didn't, so he offered to teach me. Others joined us, we formed a circle, and those who knew the songs sang and danced at the same time. Soon, everyone was dancing and we warmed up quickly. It was a wonderful start to the camp and it lifted my spirits.

Once everyone had arrived, our counselors took us to our quarters. We were housed in wooden military barracks that offered little shelter from the bitter cold. While there was a wood-burning stove in the middle of each barrack, the walls had no insulation. With about twenty to a barrack, we were assigned bunk beds, four to a section, with two bunks on the bottom and two on top. There were mattresses and rather drab, scratchy blankets. At the far end of the camp was a cement building that contained the toilets and showers, so we had to cross the length of the camp to get there. During the day this presented no problem, but at night, if nature called, we would leave the barrack, turn the corner, and relieve ourselves in the open. One of my three bunkmates was a twelve-year-old girl from Germany we shall call Valerie. She was soft spoken, with olive skin, regular features, a gentle smile, shoulder-length black hair, and puppy eyes. That night, Valerie refused to go out in the cold and she wet her bed. After that, we made sure that she slept on the bottom bunk.

The next morning, we were awakened at 7 a.m. by the shrill whistle of the head of the camp, Chef Pierron. I threw on clothing and left the barracks for our early morning calisthenics outside on the frozen ground. After our exercises, we had free time for washing, dressing, and breakfast. At 9 a.m. we had roll call. There were about eighty children in the camp, mostly teenagers, and about twenty scout leaders. I recognized several of the adults because whenever I was transferred from one hiding place to another, someone had to accompany me. Some had also visited me to bring me letters from my mother. We all gathered outside around the flagpole for the raising of the French flag while someone played reveille on a trumpet.

After roll call, our counselors laid out the general guidelines for our camp activities, including chores. We were responsible for keeping the barracks clean, sweeping the floors, and stacking wood for the stoves in the barracks. We would have assignments to clean the toilets, and kitchen duties such as washing dishes, pots, and pans and peeling potatoes. Some of the kids would do so grudgingly, but often one of the camp leaders would peel potatoes with us, so it became a time for stories and for sharing. In general, chores were kept to a minimum as our counselors filled the days with other activities. We were given enough free time to take care of our personal needs such as letter writing and washing our clothes or going to town.

We played a lot of ball games, in particular *ballon prisonnier*, which was similar to dodgeball. The children were divided into two groups. Behind each group, a line was drawn that served as the threshold of the prison. The ball was thrown by one child to hit a child in the other group. If you caught the ball, you could throw it back, trying to hit a child in the opposite camp. But if you were hit, you were made a prisoner and you had to go behind enemy lines. You were basically out of the game until you were rescued by having someone from your team throw the ball to you over the heads of the children in the enemy camp. If you caught it, you were free to return to your team. We all participated, and it was a wonderful activity to warm us up in the cold mountain air.

In the evening, we all sat together around long wooden tables in the barrack that served as a dining room. There was plenty to eat—I have no idea how they managed it. We all had an insatiable desire to talk, to compare experiences, and to share with one another because while we were in hiding, we were forced to keep everything to ourselves. Like everyone else, I wanted to know where people were from, where their parents were, if they had brothers or sisters. I also wanted to know where they were hidden—what town, what kind of school or convent. We talked about academics too. I also wanted to know where my fellow campers wanted to go after the war. No one thought of going back to Germany, Austria, Poland, Hungary, or wherever they were from. Some kids mentioned going to Palestine, which would have been my choice if no one in my family survived.

Many of the campers talked about Le Chambon-sur-Lignon, a farming village tucked at the foot of the Cevennes in the Massif Central with 5,000 inhabitants, about ninety percent Huguenots. Some among us were hidden in Le Chambon including Simon Liverant and Peter Feigl, while others stopped there for shelter on their way to other hiding places. It wasn't until much later that I learned about the heroic efforts of the villagers of Le Chambon. It was their pastor André Trocmé who, at the beginning of the German occupation, inspired his flock to keep on fighting with "the weapons of the spirit." And so Le Chambon became a refuge for as many as 5,000 people—adults and children. Miraculously, the entire village remained unscathed except for the pastor's nephew, Daniel Trocmé, who was arrested and murdered. Many years after the war, Pierre Sauvage, one of the Jewish children who was saved, went back to interview the peasants for his documentary *The Weapons of the Spirit*. The peasants did not see themselves as heroes. They remembered what it was like to be persecuted as Huguenots and so they acted with incredible kindness and compassion in spite of great personal risk.

We were keenly interested in each other's lives. We were very eager to share our experiences and felt free to tell each other our real names until our counselors cautioned us that if we were caught and tortured, we might give each other away. So, we learned to limit ourselves to sharing feelings and thoughts, but we refrained from giving out possibly compromising information.

After dinner, we were told to organize ourselves into troops by age and gender. We had to choose a mascot and a motto and compose a song that had to rhyme. There were about a dozen girls in my group and I remember huddling around the stove in the middle of the barrack while we brainstormed. We chose the *cabri*, the mountain goat, as our mascot and our motto was *Tiens bon!*–stand firm or hang in there, referring to the mountain goat's ability to climb steep rocky mountain terrain without slipping. We chose a familiar scout song to which we made up our own words. To this day, I remember our song's refrain:

> *Sur les monts comme dans la vie,*
> *Disons-nous je suis un cabri*
> *Difficultés nous franchirons,*
> *Grâce à notre devise: Tiens bon!*

> On the mountains, as in life,
> Let us tell ourselves we are mountain goats
> Difficulties we will overcome,
> Thanks to our motto: Tiens Bon!

I also remember the older boys' motto because I liked it. It was "*On les aura!*" (We will get them!) yelled out loud, and the echo's answer in a softer tone was "*On les a eus!*" (We got them!).

Each Friday night, we had an *oneg shabbat* with *kiddush* (blessing over wine and bread), *benshen* (grace after meals), and we sang *zemiroth* (Shabbat hymns) to our hearts' content. We would sing for hours, or so it seemed to me. I learned most of my repertoire of Hebrew songs during camp. We were way out in the boonies, so no one could hear us, but at the time I wondered how safe we really were. Recently I found out that our counselors took turns standing guard around the camp to make sure outsiders did not come in. We got lots of religion through fun and singing and fellowship rather than through dry lectures or sermons. The leaders also gave freely of themselves, sharing stories about dangerous actions and many close calls. They taught us about courage, standing up for truth, honor and life, and fighting for the values they believed in—all by their example.

We called our counselors chieftains and used their scout nicknames. Giraffe (Raymond Winter) was young, tall, and, of course, he had a long neck. Moulin (windmill) was a woman (Franceline Bloch) who had escorted me from one hiding place to another. Chameau (camel) was much older than the others, and later I found out that he was Frederic Shimon Hammel, a founding member of the Sixième. Eventually he went to Israel and wrote a book called *Remember Amalek*. Chef Pierron was young, about twenty-five, handsome, and engaged to be married. I was only too aware of the dangers our counselors were facing in order to protect us and save our lives, and I was full of admiration for all of them.

At the camp, every day was filled with activities. In addition to playing ball games, we went on hikes and outings in the surrounding countryside. For some of us, our clothing and shoes were inadequate for hiking, so we looked a bit bedraggled and didn't hike so well. Once we were tired after a particularly long hike, so we hitchhiked and some of us were picked up by truckers. Those who had money for shopping or the beauty parlor were free to go to town in their spare time. I didn't have any money, so I never went.

I thought that some girls were prettier and more mature than I. A few of the seventeen-year-old girls were attractive and, at fifteen, I felt like a little kid compared to them. Some girls were better dressed. I also knew that I had less schooling than the others since I had left school at thirteen and had never gone to a *lycée*. There was one girl, Henny, whom I remember as being rather condescending and vain, always primping herself and talking down to me. I preferred her younger sister, Ginette, who was in my troop. Both girls came from Germany. I had less interaction with the boys, though we talked a lot, played ball, hiked, and of course peeled potatoes together.

The counselors also tried to be surrogate parents. They prepared a talk for those seventeen and older on "Love and Friendship: Is there such a thing as friendship between a boy and a girl?" No one in my group was included because we were "too young." I felt left out as I too was interested in the subject.

Toward the end of the camp, we decided to prepare a soiree with skits. Each troop had to prepare one or more skits. Henny took charge of ours, which was a little bland. We sang a silly English song called "The Three Little Kittens Who Lost Their Mittens." We borrowed mittens and meowed like cats. Henny played the mother cat and we fell in line. The older boys produced biting satires and political comedies. I liked them, because it was a way of relieving our frustration. Besides ridiculing current political leaders, they acted out satirical skits about tyrants through history, which were wildly successful. One of the skits dealt with Lajos Kossuth who briefly held dictatorial powers in Hungary. Everyone cheered when someone talked back to a tyrant. The skits were staged and the older boys even managed the illusion of costumes and sets. It was a very entertaining and successful evening.

The two weeks flew by fast. At the end of camp, the chieftains wrote a camp song summarizing our adventures, while poking fun at ourselves. This was the refrain:

Nous sommes cent synthétiques
Qui campons tous à Florac
Dans un camp aspécifique,
Bien planqués dans des baraques.

We are one hundred fakes
Camping in Florac
In a non-specific camp,
Well-hidden in barracks.

I remember that, at the time, I did not know the meaning of the words *synthétiques* and *aspécifique*. The verses were:

Le matin la gymnastique
Vient faire notre bonheur
Et nous rassemblons nos cliques
D'un même cri du cœur. (Refrain)

Afin que nul n'en ignore
Marchant dans les rues de Florac
Nous filons comme des pandores
Presque tous d'un même pas. (Refrain)
[. . .]
Parfois nous allons en ballade
Marchant dans la bonne direction
Et nous revenons d'promenade
Montés sur des camions. (Refrain)

Les filles toujours coquettes
Défilent chez le coiffeur
Et reviennent avec des bouclettes
Qui conquièrent tous les cœurs. (Refrain)

Après ces cinq belles strophes
[. . .]
Car il serait peu philosophe
De dépasser la Sixième.

In the morning,
Calisthenics make us happy
And we gather our troops
With the same heartfelt shout. (Refrain)

So as not to be ignored
We march in the streets of Florac
Parading like peacocks
Almost all in step. (Refrain)

[3rd stanza missing]

Sometimes we go on hikes
Walking in the right direction
And we return from our promenade
On top of trucks. (Refrain)

The girls, always vain
Parade to the beauty parlor
And they come back with curls
That conquer every heart. (Refrain)

After these five beautiful stanzas
[missing line]
It would not be very wise
To surpass the Sixième.

The last refrain was changed to:

Nous sommes cent synthétiques
Animés d'un même espoir
Et bientôt dans un monde pacifique
Nous irons faire nos devoirs.

We are one hundred fakes
Filled with the same hope
And soon in a peaceful world
We will go and do our duty.

The chieftains admirably succeeded in what they set out to do. Besides giving us a place to spend our Christmas vacation, they provided us with much needed psychological and physical respite from the difficult and lonely days in hiding. We also had plenty to eat and had a chance to be ourselves and act like normal adolescents. They succeeded in boosting our morale while at the same time giving us a heavy dose of Judaism. They inspired us to keep going while continuing to hope for a better future.

As a result of this experience, I was *gonflée à bloc* (pumped up to the max) and ready to resume the struggle for my survival. Toward the end of the camp, I was called in to see Chef Pierron. Naturally, I wondered what I had done wrong and expected to be bawled out—why else would

The scout camp in Florac. Edith is on the ground in the middle between two boys. Behind her is Chef Pierron (Roger Klimovitsky; wartime name, Climaud), December 1943.

Le Camp de Florac: the boys. Souris (Marcel Gradwohl) is standing on the left; Giraffe (Raymond Winter) is behind him; Jacques Majerholc, standing, fourth from the left; Chef Pierron (Roger Klimovitsky) standing on the right. Peter Feigl is in the middle of the front row, third from the right. Photo given to Edith by the archivist at the Mémorial de la Shoah in Paris, December 1943.

Le Camp de Florac: the girls. Edith is in front, second from the left in her gray Tyrolean Janker with the green lapels and the skirt made from her brother's slacks. Ginette is standing sixth from the right. Photo given to Edith by the archivist at the Mémorial de la Shoah in Paris, December 1943.

he want to see me? Instead, Chef Pierron pulled out the desperate and depressing letter to my mother written on toilet paper, the one from the hospital. Chef Pierron told me he had taken the liberty of reading the letter and never gave it to my mother because he thought it would make her feel bad. Now he asked me if I still wanted him to transmit it to her. By the time he finished talking to me, I was in tears. I tore up the letter and wrote another one.

I searched for Chef Pierron for many years after the war, but I did not learn his real name until I read Frida Wattenberg's book *Organisation juive de combat—France 1940-1945* (first published in 2002) about the Jewish Resistance in France. Frida refers briefly to this Christmas camp, but without mentioning the powerful effect it had on us and how successful it was in lifting our spirits so we could continue the fight. In it, I also found the wartime code names and real names of our chieftains. Chef Pierron's real name was Roger Klimovitsky and Climaud, a diminutive of his last name, was his false name. He was arrested after D-Day, tortured by the infamous Klaus Barbie, and deported to Auschwitz. He came back to Paris physically wounded but emotionally strong. He later married his sweetheart and they had three children. Those of us from the group who lived in and around Paris would visit him and provide support. He died in 2000 before I had the chance to thank him personally. His name is inscribed on the walls of the Mémorial de la Shoah. During a visit to France in October 2004, I paid my respects at his gravesite.

9. PEZENAS

The Outsider

After the camp, the Sixième took me to another boarding school in Pezenas, a town about halfway between Montpellier and Beziers. The school primarily served students from the surrounding rural areas. All the girls boarded during the week and went home every Sunday and often on Thursdays too. (There was no school on Thursdays at that time.) The place was not geared toward someone like me, who depended entirely on the school for basic necessities. There were no showers, no laundry facilities, and there was not much food. The school was a *lycée* that went up to the *troisième* (equivalent to ninth grade in American schools). If the course was completed, students could take the exam for their *Brevet Elémentaire*. If the students wanted to continue for the *Baccalauréat*, which required three more years of schooling, they had to transfer from this school to a regular *lycée*.

In Castelnaudary and Mende, we were taken every week to the public baths for our showers. In Pezenas, the girls went home to bathe while I remained dirty. We were only able to wash our hands and face in cold water, and brush our teeth during scheduled times and under staff supervision. I couldn't wash my hair or my private parts. When I had to present my comb for inspection, I wiped it on the towel. After a while, the edge of my towel was black with dirt but the comb was clean. Students were expected to provide their own sheets, something the Sixième promised to give me but didn't. Initially a student lent me two sheets, but after a week she wanted them back and I ended up sleeping on the mattress covered with a scratchy blanket.

The school required our clothes to be neatly folded on a shelf next to our beds. Initially my clothes were clean, but they were not ironed, so folding them neatly was difficult. Eventually all my clothes were dirty, and so was I. I was not given the opportunity to wash myself or my clothing.

A word here about my clothes—I only had my "pant" skirt, two blouses, a sweater my mother had knitted, a threadbare coat, several panties, two pairs of socks, and two bras. I wore these same clothes every day for a couple of years.

I had gotten my first menstrual period three months after my fourteenth birthday. Fortunately, I only got it twice and then it stopped for a long time, probably because of malnutrition. Under the circumstances, it was a blessing because I could not have kept myself clean.

The worst part about Pezenas was hunger. The other girls would come back every week with baskets stocked with ham, sausage, cheese, bread, and other food. I depended entirely on the food the school served us. We got watery soup, two tablespoons of pasta, and once a week, a quarter of a candy bar—or one-fourth of the government ration. During a school break, I remained in the school while the other students went home. I ate with the kitchen staff and noticed that they ate very well and helped themselves to our rations. Mme l'Econome held the keys to the larder, but I wonder what she did with our food. Years later I ran into her; she gave me such a big hello, but I had trouble believing her sincerity after the way I had literally starved under her care.

In addition to the tiny quantities of food they gave us, the quality was so bad that the other girls turned their noses up at it. Every day, after meals, they would go to their baskets and eat their provisions. No one shared anything with me. One girl, who must have come from a poorer family than the others, would run out of supplies by midweek. The others shared their food with her, but not with me. Eventually my hunger pangs were so bad that the smell of food drove me crazy. I got into the habit of retreating to the toilets while the girls ate their goodies.

Classwork was a disaster again. I had no textbooks. When I asked classmates to lend me one of their books, they told me that they needed them for their own homework. I got terrible grades and was never able to prepare for class. That only reinforced my conviction that I was stupid.

In this school, I clearly stood out because I was different, because I lacked basic supplies, and because I had to stay in on weekends. After a while, the girls began to spy on me. They constantly asked me if my mother had sent me any letters. I usually said yes, and that I had gotten my letters days earlier. But they were watching me because they would retort, "No, you didn't." Mail call was done in front of everyone so that everyone could hear who got letters.

The *directrice* (principal) did not help matters either. She looked like a witch and acted like one. She was a middle-aged woman with wiry graying hair who usually wore a gray coat and walked around with a cane. It was January 1944 and lots of girls came down with colds and coughs. She would walk into the dining hall and demand that we all stop coughing. I remember almost turning blue and red, trying to suppress my cough. Our gym teacher would work us hard, and it was harder on me because I did not have much energy. What did the *directrice* do? She yelled at the gym teacher in front of the students for working us so hard, and then had the nerve to add, "I am feeding them to do mathematics, not gym."

During the early February break, I pleaded for permission to do my laundry. The *directrice* had me put my dirty clothes out on the floor in the presence of other school personnel. When she saw my bra, she picked it up with the tip of her cane and flung it across the room saying, "You don't need that." I felt humiliated. I could not understand her. Didn't she know who I was? I had been led to believe that the heads of the schools where the Sixième placed Jewish children always knew who they were, so the principal's behavior left me puzzled. I never did get to do my laundry in that place. For more than six weeks I went without washing myself. My hair was dirty, my clothes were filthy, and I was hungry, cold, and miserable. Had I not been physically invigorated and emotionally strengthened by the inspiring and morale-boosting experiences of Florac, I wouldn't have made it. Eventually my health began to suffer. I had a pimple on my elbow that developed into a large sore; my cold never went away, I coughed for months, and I developed chilblains, too. Fortunately, sometime in late February a counselor picked me up and I left Pezenas. I must have told her all about the place because they did not send me back.

The counselor took me to a house in a small town or village. We arrived in the evening after dark on a very cold night and the ground was covered with snow. Other girls were there, some of whom I remembered from my two weeks in Florac. On the first night, I was happy to find a clean bed with clean sheets. The house must have served as a home for younger children because the beds were small—too small for us—but no one complained. I spent the entire next day washing myself, my hair, and doing laundry. That evening I was told that I would be leaving early the following morning, so I quickly ran outside to pick up the laundry I had hung up to dry and found it was frozen stiff. I took the laundry off the line and arranged the pieces around the wood stove so it would dry in time for my departure. Some of my things were so close to the stove that they were scorched. That was a small disaster since I couldn't replace anything. That evening, the girls and I talked until late into the night, sharing confidences about our hopes and dreams for the future. It was an intense experience that I will always remember.

I spent only thirty-six hours in that house, and it was the only hiding place whose location remains a mystery to this day.

10. CAHORS

Vocational High School and
Centre de Jeunes Filles Déficientes

The next morning I went to Cahors, a larger town in southwestern France on the Lot River. Cahors was an old town known for its famous fourteenth-century bridge, Le Pont Valentré, with its three distinctive towers. Like the convent in Castelnaudary, the school was a vocational high school for girls with a commercial and a home economics curriculum. It was much nicer than the usual *lycée*. It had a campus with an open feeling; there was a lawn, and once a week we were taken to the public showers.

I could wash my hair and do my laundry. And the staff did not steal our food rations in Cahors like they did in Pezenas. In Cahors there were six of us in hiding. Everyone had been placed there either by the Sixième or by the OSE. With the school's more adequate amenities, it was a livable place.

I was placed in the home economics section. The school gave us fabric to make a blouse in sewing class. Working with a pat-

Le Pont Valentré. Photo taken by Edith, 1950.

tern, I made myself a simple, royal blue blouse that became a much-needed addition to my wardrobe. The school also provided each of us with textbooks. Classwork was easy and it wasn't much of an academic challenge.

Edith, front, bottom right, with fellow students and
a teacher in the Cahors vocational school, 1944.

My fellow students were much nicer than the girls in Pezenas and I became friendly with a few, though I still did not confide in anyone.

The lighter school workload left me time to write a poem for my mother for her upcoming birthday. In addition to sending her birthday wishes, I wanted her to know that she wasn't forgotten and I also wanted to lift her spirits. Mail was still handled the same way, but I wanted to make sure she got my letter in time for her birthday, so I dropped it in a mailbox without putting a return address on the envelope. It would be the only time I broke the rule about writing directly.

A MA CHÈRE MAMAN POUR SON ANNIVERSAIRE

Qu'il est doux de se dire, se dire et se redire
«J'ai une Maman, au loin, qui m'aime.»
Oh Maman, que je t'aime!

J'aime tes pleurs et j'aime ton sourire,
Je te vois toujours, et je t'admire;
Sans cesse tu es présente à ma pensée
Ton image est toujours devant mes yeux

Quoique loin de toi
Je suis toute à toi.

Mon âme, mon cœur, mon amour
T'appartiennent tour à tour.
Tout me semble facile
Tout au long de la journée
Et rien ne m'est pénible
Dans l'épreuve à endurer
Quand, quand . . .
Devant les yeux tu m'apparais.

Je ne vis que pour toi, chère Maman!
Car mon travail, mes espérances, mon avenir,
Tout a pour but de te faire plaisir.
Maman ! Je veux te rendre heureuse
Te faire oublier par mille petits soins
Les malheurs qui tant de fois ont mis sur toi la main.

Ainsi, le jour où nous serons tous réunis,
Quand de nouveau sera créé le sein de notre famille
Dans le souvenir duquel, aujourd'hui
Nous puisons tous un si grand appui,
Tu te souviendras dans la joie
De toutes nos peines
Et tu songeras alors à l'immense foi
Qui fit bouillonner le sang dans nos veines.

C'est grâce à Celui qui réside là-haut
Que nous triompherons de l'oppressant fléau
Ce fléau qui veut nous réduire en poussière
Et qui est causé par cette terrible guerre.
Mais, Maman, par la suite tu verras
Que le succès nous appartiendra.

Maintenant que ton anniversaire arrive
Anniversaires fêtés jadis avec tant d'allégresse
Sois courageuse quoiqu'il arrive
Et sache dominer et vaincre la tristesse.

Songe à notre famille dispersée un peu partout
Qui lutte et luttera avec ténacité jusqu'au bout.

Nous pensons tous à notre Maman chérie
Qu'aucun de nous jamais n'oublie.

Ta petite fille,
Elise (mon nom de guerre)
Cahors (Lot) mars 1944

To my dear Mom for her birthday

How sweet it is to say again and again,
"I have a Mom far away who loves me."
Oh Mom, how much I love you!

I love your tears and I love your smile
I see you always and I admire you.
You are always in my thoughts
Your image is always in front of my eyes
Though far from you
I am all yours.

My soul, my heart, my love
belong to you in turn.
Everything seems easy to me
All day long
And nothing is painful
In the hardship I have to endure
When, when . . .
You appear before my eyes.

I only live for you, dear Mom!
My work, my hopes, my future
Are all meant to give you pleasure.
Mom! I want to make you happy
And make you forget through a thousand little attentions
The misfortune whose heavy hand rested on you so often.

And so, on the day when we will all be together again
When our family will be reunited
In whose memory
We find so much solace today
Then you will remember with great joy
All our suffering

And you will think of the deep faith
That coursed in our veins.

It is thanks to the One up there
That we will triumph over this oppressive plague,
This plague that wants to reduce us to dust
And that is caused by this terrible war.
But Mom, you will see that in the end
Victory will be ours.

Now that your birthday is coming
A birthday celebrated with much joy in the past
Be brave whatever happens
And know how to overcome sadness.

Think of our family dispersed everywhere
That is fighting and will continue to fight with tenacity to the end.
We all think of our dear Mom
That none of us ever forgets.

Your little daughter,
Elise (wartime name)
Cahors (Lot) March 1944.

Translated by the author.

Several weeks into my stay, the idyll was over. One morning at 11 a.m., the principal burst into our classroom and told us that the German Army had requisitioned the school for use as its headquarters. We had to vacate the premises by 5 p.m. that same day. Everyone was sent packing, including the six girls in hiding. What was the principal going to do with us? There was no time to contact the underground, but our resourceful *directrice* found us a great hiding place: the nearby home for mentally deficient girls (Le Centre de Jeunes Filles Déficientes).

Since we were obviously not mentally handicapped, the Centre left us to our own devices. We shared meals and went on outings with the others, but otherwise we were left alone. By then, it was late March and the weather was mild. We could sit outside mending our clothes while one of us read aloud from the classics. One book I remember reading was *Jocelyn* by Lamartine.

To be around mentally disabled girls was a novel experience for me. There were teenage girls who could only read at first or second grade level,

*Six Jewish girls in hiding at the Centre de Jeunes Filles Déficientes
in March 1944. Edith is in front, second from the right.*

or they were learning to scrub floors. But there were also girls who had no
other place to go. I remember one fifteen-year-old, a very nice girl, whose
parents were alcoholics. Social Services put her in this home for her own
protection. The Centre seemed something of a catchall, and it was sad to
see how normal kids were warehoused among the mentally disabled. This
would change in France after the war with more specialized facilities to
meet different needs.

We spent two weeks there until Easter, when our fearless leaders were
able to place us with families in rural areas for Easter vacation. I was told
not to discuss anything with my assigned family. I have no idea what they
knew, but they listened to the BBC in front of me, something that was
forbidden under the Vichy government. At the dinner table, they liked to
tell anti-German jokes and felt free to express their political views. The
best part was that there was plenty to eat, and the food was good. The worst
part was getting to the indoor toilet. I had to walk through the parents'
bedroom to get there, and they always slept late, so I could not "go" before
10 a.m. That was torture!

This couple had a nineteen-year-old daughter who, I was told, was
engaged to be married. She had a friend visiting—a handsome young
man in uniform. After lunch, I would join the daughter and her friend
for a walk. They walked ahead of me and they were always kissing. That
surprised me because I thought that being engaged to someone required

Edith during Easter break, 1944.

fidelity. Someone took a picture of me during Easter week. I was wearing my famous "pants" skirt and the blouse I made from a dress—I don't look skinny and I am smiling.

After Easter vacation I was sent back to the vocational school in Cahors. The Germans decided they didn't want it after all. I stayed there for another month. Then Belette from the Sixième picked me up and brought me to a hotel in Clermont Ferrand, a nearby town. I had learned not to ask questions and I assumed that I was going to another hiding place.

⚜

During my whole year in hiding, I lived like a hunted animal, always on the run. The close calls and constant fear gave the whole year the aspect of a nightmare. One day in May, while still in Cahors, I wrote down some thoughts of a non-compromising nature. It dawned on me that the unassuming English teacher from Mende had something other people did not have. I did not know what it was, but whatever it was, I wanted to have it too. It had to be powerful, for this woman acted like no one else.

She cared, she took risks, and she showed compassion, going beyond the role of teacher. She radiated light amidst all the darkness. Where did she get her courage, her strength, her character? She did it all so simply, with humility, without affectation or grandiose manners.

Although I had known her for only five weeks, she remained an inspiration and a role model for the rest of my life. The only other person in her league was Mme Brun, my teacher from Nice. These women had a special quality of being. They weren't sugarcoated; they had character and caring. I wanted to know what made them that way because I wanted to be like them. They were my heroes, and their moral support and faith in my ability to succeed proved invaluable after the war.

That day also proved to be a turning point. I was waking up to the life of the mind and of the spirit, though I did not realize it at the time. That day, I realized that I had ambition; I wanted to make something of my life. I did not want to stay down in the dumps. I wasn't sure I would do anything great, but I knew I wanted to be somebody. I did not want to remain ignorant and unskilled. I was becoming my own person, separate from my parents, with my own identity and clear goals. I was not quite sixteen and I thought I was waking up late. I believed that those who had the benefit of schooling woke up much earlier. I now know that some people never wake up.

Because I was forced to keep things inside over such a long period of time, I developed an intense inner life and became very introspective. I also learned to control what passed my lips, even in anger. And I turned to the God of my childhood and to the prayers I had been taught to sustain me during those difficult times.

11. FLIGHT TO SWITZERLAND

After two or three days at the hotel in Clermont Ferrand, the counselors assembled about thirty children. I knew some of them from Florac and from other hiding places. But until that evening, the counselors didn't tell us why we were there. I assumed I was just going to another hiding place. Soon, however, we discovered the answer: they told us that they were going to smuggle us over the border into Switzerland.

We were told to take only what we could carry and to wear two layers of clothing, so we would have something to wear once we got to Switzerland. If we had real papers, we were to take them along. I watched one lucky boy who had real papers sew them into the lining of his coat. We were told that, if stopped, we should say that we were going on vacation to a summer camp, though that was an unlikely story since it was May and schools were still in session. Nor did we look like children going to camp, with our wooden-soled shoes, coats, and handheld bags. Nevertheless, that pretext gave us confidence. We were told to leave our other belongings behind—that they would keep them for us.

I recall that, as I packed, I did not necessarily choose the most useful items. I put my only other blouse, one pair of underpants, some socks, a towel, a comb, a handkerchief, my false papers, and a little food from breakfast into the red bag I had made in the hospital. I also packed my memory book—where the English teacher had written her dedication and my other friends had left notes—a fountain pen, and photos of my family. I left behind most of my belongings, including my precious Pericles book. I wore the blouse I had made in Cahors and the coat I had turned inside out in the hospital.

We were told that the Swiss accepted girls and boys up to the age of sixteen. A couple of the boys were seventeen, and they made themselves appear younger by wearing short pants to look more convincing. Since most of us had no documents, the Swiss would be forced to take our word for everything, something they did not like. We were told that we were the second large group of children smuggled into Switzerland by this counselor who worked with the Mouvement de Jeunesse Sioniste (MJS) and the Sixième. The first group of twenty teenagers had made it across successfully just the week before.

That night, there was a little party in my hotel room with several kids from the group. We shared some cookies and I was very pleased with this little get-together, which was in sharp contrast to my lonely days locked away behind bars in some boarding school. After everyone left, I sat down to express my feelings in this poem:

TRISTESSE

Que je me sens drôle ces jours-ci
Il me semble que je ne suis pas moi-même.
Le monde me parait si petit
Et je sens comme c'est doux quand on s'aime.

Oh oui, aimer,
Ne point connaître le vilain côté de ce monde,
Mais c'est trop rêver,
Et il faut songer à l'orage, la-bas, qui gronde,

Il gronde, fort,
Il fait trembler la terre entière
Il ne ménage pas les morts
Et sème partout tellement de misère.

Orage, orage, quand t'arrêteras-tu
Afin que chaque homme sans crainte d'être pendu
Puisse exprimer librement
Jusqu'à ses plus profonds sentiments.

Moi aussi je voudrais pouvoir exprimer
Mes pensées en toute franchise
Mais je me sens comprimée
Comme dans une cage, prise.

C'est alors que ces noires idées tourbillonnent dans ma tête
Et me dépriment pour toute la journée
Je deviens méchante comme une mauvaise bête
Sans vouloir le faire exprès.

Oh papier! Je ne veux rien te cacher . . .
Comme seul confident tu sais si bien soulager.

(Clermont Ferrand, Le 20 mai 1944)

SADNESS

How strange I feel these days,
I don't feel like myself.
The world seems so small
And I feel how sweet it is to love one another.

Oh yes, to love one another
Not to know the ugly side of this world,
But that's too much of a dream,
And we must remember the storm that rages over there.

It rages, loud,
It makes the whole earth tremble
It causes so many deaths
And sows so much misery everywhere.

Storm, storm, when will you stop?
So that each man without fear for his life
Is free to express
His innermost feelings.

I too would like to be able to express
My own thoughts in freedom,
But I feel compressed
As though trapped in a cage.

That's when those black thoughts swirl in my head
And depress me for the whole day,
I become nasty like a mean beast
Without meaning to do so.

Oh paper! I do not want to hide anything from you . . .
For as the only confidant, you know how to provide relief.

(Clermont Ferrand, Vichy France May 20, 1944)
Translated by the author.

The next day after breakfast we left the hotel with Mlle Anny and M. Raymond, two counselors I did not know, and took the train to Lyon. We spent the night in a filthy shelter in Lyon. I remember my revulsion because I had to sleep on a dirty mattress with scratchy blankets and a disgusting pillow. Early the next morning, a new counselor arrived. Her name was Marcelle, and she was not one of the regulars who had escorted me from one hiding place to another or hand-delivered mail from my mother. She took us back to the station where we took the train in the direction of St. Julien near the Swiss border.

At first all went as planned—that is until we got to Viry. It was a tiny train station and the train only stopped for three minutes, not long enough to let thirty youngsters get off. Half succeeded while the rest of us, including me, were stuck on the train. The fear I felt grew as each turn of the wheel took us farther away from Marcelle and the other children. Finally the train stopped, and we scrambled to get off.

We immediately walked away from the station's platform because we didn't want to attract attention. I didn't even bother to look at the name of the station, which must have been St. Julien. We briefly huddled to decide what to do. We had to get back to the previous station, but we thought that taking the road was too dangerous because we knew it would be patrolled. So, we chose to walk back on the railroad tracks. The ties on the tracks were not evenly spaced and we had to adjust our stride with every step. We had a five-year-old with us who had to be carried, and we had to carry our bags too. We walked as fast as we could. I walked, my mind filled with fear and questions. How far did we have to go to reach the previous station? Would the others wait for us? Could we be seen from the road? We walked in silence, stopping briefly to transfer the little boy from one older boy to another, while someone else carried his bag. After what seemed like an eternity, we got back to Viry in about two hours. The station was in the middle of nowhere, surrounded by fields. There was no sign of the group. Eventually, someone came to meet us, and he led us to Marcelle and the rest of the children who were waiting for us, crouched behind a hedge near an open field. The two *passeurs* (guides) who were to lead the way were already there and so, without taking time to rest, we continued toward the Swiss border.

At first the paths we took were relatively comfortable. We crossed open fields by running across one at a time, ducking all the way to avoid being seen. At one point, we heard patrols marching on the road and hid behind hedges and shrubbery. We realized we were all at the mercy of anyone coughing, sneezing, or making a sound. We resumed our journey once the patrol had passed. After more than an hour of walking, I recognized packages from our group lying on the ground. Some of the children had taken along too much stuff they could no longer carry, so they dropped things along the path. Like Hansel and Gretel, they left a trail. Our *passeurs* then realized that they had literally led us around in a circle.

We then took a different route through the underbrush. That presented a problem for the five-year-old. Several of the bigger boys took turns carrying him, but the branches were hitting his face and he would cry out from pain every time. So the guides assembled us and told us that they did not want to jeopardize everyone's life because of the boy. If he did not stop crying, we would have to leave him behind. None of us wanted that. It was all for one and one for all. Jacques Majerholc, one of the older boys, carried the five-year-old while Paulette, the boy's older sister, carried Jacques' bag. The other boys took turns carrying the five-year-old on their shoulders while another boy or girl would carry the bags. Two of us would walk on each side of the child. I remember holding the branches away from the little boy's face. Walking through dense underbrush, this was quite an undertaking. We progressed slowly.

It had rained and the ground was soaked. The shoes someone had bought for me were falling apart. They had soles made of wooden slats that were glued to an inner sole made of cardboard, and they were useless in the mud. By midday, the sun was warm and we were sweltering in our double layers of clothing—I had my winter coat on. As we all trekked through the underbrush, our handheld bags felt heavier by the hour.

We were pushed to exhaustion but kept going because our lives depended on it. After what seemed like an eternity, we came upon a huge coil of barbed wire stretched along the border. It must have been six feet high. By the time I got to the coil, the wires had been cut. Was it done by our guides or had it been cut previously by others fleeing the Nazis? I couldn't tell. By the time I reached the barbed wire, the opening was wide enough to let one person pass at a time. No one talked. I thought we must have entered no man's land because there was no sign of the Swiss border. I knew that we were still not safe, for the Germans were known to pursue people into no man's land and shoot them.

But at least we were walking in the right direction. Soon we came to a second coil of barbed wire, and beyond that we saw the Swiss side of the border—a tall fence strung straight across with barbed wire—and a Swiss soldier, his gun over his shoulder, staring at us as if we were a familiar sight. Fortunately, we had been warned that Swiss uniforms resembled those of the Germans, so we were not scared. The sight of him gave us renewed energy as we crawled under, climbed over, or squeezed between the razor sharp wires to get to the other side.

As I approached the fence, I saw a small group of adults farther down with one man on crutches. To my amazement, I recognized him as someone I had met in Nice at the synagogue. But now he was injured. I wondered what had happened to him. Had he been beaten or tortured? He had to lie down on the ground while one of the other people in the group pulled him under the barbed wire to the Swiss side of the border. I made no attempt to speak to him, as I was focused on getting myself to the other side of the fence, squeezing between barbed wires while trying not to tear my clothes.

To my deep regret and disbelief, Marcelle Colin, whose real name was Marianne Cohn, did not cross with us. When she stayed on the

Marianne Cohn, wartime name Marcelle Colin. Used with permission from the Mémorial de la Shoah in Paris.

French side of the barbed wire fence I asked her, "You are not going back to that hell, are you?" She didn't say anything, but nodded. Later I learned that, just one week after our crossing, she led a larger group of children to the border and she was caught, tortured, and killed. The children were saved thanks to the intervention of Jean Deffaugt, the Mayor of Annemasse, and Monsignor Raymond, the Cardinal of Nice. During a recent visit to the new Musée de la Résistance in Toulouse, I stumbled upon a terrible photo of Marianne, showing her mutilated body lying in a ditch. Today, Marianne is memorialized in France as a great heroine of the French Résistance. She was barely twenty-one years old.

❦

Several years ago, my friend—and former member of the Jewish underground—Frida Wattenberg organized a reunion in Paris at the Mémorial de la Shoah for the people living near Paris who had crossed into Switzerland together. We were reminiscing about our fateful crossing and

I had always wondered why the station master had given the signal for the train to pull out while we were still getting off the train in Viry. I thought he had rigidly followed the schedule for the town, but according to Simon Liverant, one of the boys in our group, we opened the train doors on the tracks side instead of on the platform side. Perhaps that's why the station master could not see that passengers were still getting off. Or perhaps Marcelle opened the doors on the wrong side intentionally in order not to attract attention to so many children getting off the train.

At one point during our reunion, an elderly, distinguished-looking gentleman with snow-white hair and a moustache introduced himself to me as the five year old. His name was Paul and he was the younger brother of Paulette and Bernard Goldstein.

A couple of months ago, I met Peter Feigl, another child survivor who crossed from France into Switzerland. While exchanging memories, we discovered with excitement that not only was he in Florac at the Christmas camp with me, but he was the lucky boy who sewed his real papers into his coat in Clermont Ferrand and traipsed through the woods with us on that dramatic day.

Switzerland

12. CLAPARÈDE

The Transit Camp

As soon as we were on the Swiss side of the fence, my joy was boundless. Many of us kissed the ground and exchanged true names. Once everyone had gathered, we were arrested around 1 p.m. and taken by Swiss border guards to the nearest border station called Pierre Grand, though I must admit that it did not feel like an arrest. Let's say we were taken into custody. We were questioned and I gave my name, date of birth, and my parents' names.

After that, we all walked to Claparède, the transit camp in Geneva run by the Swiss Army. We were given brief medical checks. At one point, the man in charge asked our group who was Polish. That seemed to me an unusual request. I was Austrian, but had a crush on Jacques Majerholc and he was Polish. Since I was afraid the Poles would be separated from the rest of us and I wanted to stay with him, I said, "My father was born in Poland. Does that make me Polish?" In lieu of an answer, I was directed to stand with the Poles. That's why my Swiss documents indicate Polish citizenship. I was questioned further and told them I didn't have any relatives in Switzerland, but I mentioned I knew a M. Steinmetz who was a refugee in Zurich. How I knew that remains a mystery because we could not correspond while I was in hiding.

The next day, we were interviewed more thoroughly. In my verbal interrogation with G.A. Geiger, I recounted my movements from Vienna to Cahors to Switzerland and gave him the false names of my escorts, as they were the only names I knew. I stated that my mother was still in Montlaur and that my father had been deported. I had come to Switzerland fearing German laws against Jews. I told him I had no financial support in Switzerland or resources abroad and the only items I had brought to Switzerland were toiletries. The final question on the interrogation form

Swiss identity card with the nationality listed as Polish.
Edith is wearing the blouse she made in Cahors, 1944.

Arrest document CH AEG Justice et Police EF/2 n°7586 from Claparède, dated
May 22, 1944, for crossing into Switzerland illegally. Original document
at the Archives de l'État de Genève. Reproduced with permission.

Eidgenössisches Justiz- und Polizeidepartement
Polizeiabteilung

Département fédéral de justice et police
Division de police

Dipartimento federale di giustizia e polizia
Divisione della polizia

Einvernahmeprotokoll
Procès-verbal d'interrogatoire
Verbale d'interrogatorio

7586

Genève den
le   23.5.44.
li

1. Name: Nom: Cognome:	MAYER	2. Vorname: Prénom: Nome:	Edith
3. Staatszugehörigkeit: Nationalité: Nazionalità:	Polonaise	4. Bei Staatenlosigkeit frühere Staatszugehörigkeit: Ancienne nationalité (en cas d'apatridie): Precedente nazionalità (per apolidi):	
5. Vorname des Vaters: Prénom du père: Nome del padre:	Schmil-Juda	6. Vor- und Geburtsname der Mutter: Prénom et nom de famille de la mère: Nome e cognome di nascita della madre:	Anna BUCHHOLZ
7. Geburtsdatum: Date de naissance: Data di nascita:	15.6.28	8. Geburtsort: Lieu de naissance: Luogo di nascita:	Vienne (Autriche)
9. Früherer Wohnort: Ancien domicile: Domicilio precedente:	Cahors (Lotte)	10. Beruf: Profession: Professione:	écolière
11. Zivilstand: État-civil: Stato civile:	célibataire	12. Konfession: Confession: Religione:	israélite
13. Begleitende Familienangehörige: Membres de la famille accompagnant l'intéressé: Congiunti che accompagnano l'interessato:			

14. Ausweispapiere:
Papiers d'identité: .... aucun
Documenti di legittimazione:

15. Militärische Einteilung:
Incorporation militaire:
Incorporazione militare:

16. Grund und Umstände der Flucht sowie eingeschlagener Weg:
Motifs et circonstances de la fuite ainsi que route suivie:
Motivi e circostanze della fuga come pure percorso seguito:

Née à Vienne, je suis restée dans cette ville jusqu'en 1937. J'y ai commencé mes classes que j'ai continuées en Italie à Gênes où je suis allée 2 ans. Après ce temps je suis venue en France à Nice jusqu'en 1942 puis de là Montlaur (Aude) à Castelnaudary (Aude) à Moissac- Mende-Pezenas et à Cahors où je suis restée jusqu'à ces derniers jours.

Ma mère est encore actuellement en France à Montlaur et mon père est déporté..

Je suis venue en Suisse de crainte des mesures allemandes contrelea israélites.

J'ai passé la frontière avec un convoi d'enfants organisé par une organisation israélite. De Cahors j'ai été accompagnée par une demoiselle Denise jusqu'à Clermont-Ferrand, de là par une demoiselle Anny et un monsieur Raymond jusqu'à Lyon. Puis de Lyon par une demoiselle Marcelle jusqu'à la frontière depuis Viry elle a été aidée par des passeurs.

Interrogation document CH AEG Justice et Police EF/2 n°7586, dated May 23, 1944. Original document at the Archives de l'État de Genève. Reproduced with permission. (Continued next page.)

17. Ort und Zeit des Grenzübertrittes: Pierre-Grand le 2.3.44. vers les 14h. Dès notre passage nous
    Lieu et date du passage de la frontière: avons été arrêtés et conduits un poste de douane.
    Località, data e ora dello sconfinamento:

18. Gesundheitszustand: visite effectuée
    État de santé:
    Condizioni di salute:

19. Verwandte und Bekannte in der Schweiz: una tante Mme. X à Zurich.
    Parents et connaissances en Suisse:
    Parenti o conoscenze nella Svizzera:

20. Allfällige Garanten in der Schweiz: aucune
    Répondants éventuels en Suisse:
    Eventuali garanti nella Svizzera:

21. Genaue Zusammenstellung der Vermögensmittel im In- und Ausland:
    Liste exacte des ressources à l'étranger et en Suisse:
    Specificazione esatta dei beni patrimoniali in Svizzera e all'estero:
                                              aucune

22. Mitgebrachte Effekten (summarisch):
    Liste sommaire des effets (objets) apportés par le réfugié:
    Elenco sommario degli effetti (oggetti) portati con sè dal rifugiato:

        divers objets de toilette

23. Vermerk ob Mitteilung über Verhalten der Flüchtlinge bekanntgegeben:
    L'« avis au réfugié » a-t-il été porté à la connaissance du réfugié?
    La « Comunicazione ai rifugiati » è stata portata a conoscenza dell'interessato?

Einvernommen durch: Der Flüchtling:
Interrogé par: Le réfugié:
Interrogato da: Il rifugiato:

        G.A. Geiger   Edith Mayer

asked if "the refugee [had] been given instructions on how to conduct herself in Switzerland." It was an odd question and Geiger left it blank.

As soon as I was on Swiss soil, I started to express my feelings in a poem. I had time to complete it in Claparède while waiting to be questioned:

LIBERTÉ

Mon rêve est réalité
Nous voilà en liberté!

Plus de cache-cache,
Plus de mensonges,
Plus de faux papiers,
Plus rien qui me ronge.

Je ne veux point penser au lendemain.
Pour aujourd'hui nous sommes tous réunis
Et ici on ne nous veut que du bien.

Est-ce vrai que je suis libre?
Il me semble que je suis ivre!
Je me laisse aller à ce délice
Car fini est le supplice
De sans cesse jouer la comédie
Sans jamais montrer son ennui.

Mais désormais tout cela est fini
Et j'aspire de nouveau aux douceurs de la vie.

Camp de Claparède, Suisse, Le 23 mai 1944.

FREEDOM

My dream has come true
We are free!

No more hiding
No more lying
No more false papers,
Nothing to trouble me.

I do not want to think about tomorrow.
For today we are all together
And here no one will harm us.

Is it true that I am free?
I think that I am drunk!
I let myself feel this delight
Because ended is the torture
Of always pretending
Without ever showing my true feelings.

But now all this is behind me.
And I yearn again for the sweetness of life.

Switzerland, May 23, 1944.
Translated from French by the author.

After I was processed, the Swiss asked me if I would stay in Claparède to work. That put me into a real quandary. After the thrill of being reunited with my peers, should I now be separated from them? At the same time, I was so grateful for the safety the Swiss provided that I said yes. I stayed while the others left for the quarantine camp of Le Bout du Monde—The End of the World—which was in the section of Geneva called Champel. At last I could keep a journal, something I had been unable to do while in hiding.

Claparède was a busy place with refugees streaming in daily. I did laundry, dishes, whatever I was asked to do, and I didn't complain about the work. We had a curfew and I was supposed to be in my room by 9 p.m. One night, I had lots of dishes to wash and laundry to fold, so I stayed in the kitchen to finish the job. I was reprimanded, but gently, because I was working. The next day, Chameau (George Hamel), the oldest chieftain from the scout camp in Florac, arrived in Claparède. Somehow he had managed to get into Switzerland. I was starved for news of the others as I knew only too well what dangers they faced daily. We sat in the dining area in plain sight to chat, so I went to bed late again and was reprimanded—this time more severely. I was angry about these reprimands because I worked hard from morning until night for no pay. I was not quite sixteen and was never thanked. In my mind I had done nothing wrong, except miss my exact curfew.

In my diary I vented my frustration:

Camp de Claparède
May 30, 1944

I am disgusted . . . I could pull out my hair. What is my mother
doing? My father? Is he alive? My brother? What will become
of me? What will become of us? Nothing but question marks.
With whom can I talk? Those who are here don't understand
anything . . . When I see the barbed wire so close and on the
other side people walking, free, free. Ah freedom, when will you
be mine completely? I have you, but only partially. True, it's a lot,
but [it's] not everything. It's been a long time, [I'm] always locked
up, and this time behind barbed wire. In the basement there is a
room enclosed with barbed wire. It's called the prison.

Here is what triggered this mood. One of the counselors who
had taken care of me in France arrived at the camp of Claparède.
He knows me and I was delighted to see him again. In the evening
I talked with him because I knew that I would not be able to do
so the next day. But, I should have gone to bed at 9 p.m. and I did
not go up to my room until 9:30 p.m.

You had to see how I got bawled out. It's useless to tell me that
they want to keep me and then [they] treat me like a workhorse.
To make things worse, they told me that, if that happened two or
three times, I would be sent back to France because it was as if I
had disobeyed an order, and an order is an order.

I should have asked for permission to stay downstairs longer
if I wanted to chat. But the night before, when I was supposed to
go to my room by 9 p.m., I finished the dishes instead and folded
laundry, they chided me a bit, but nicely, and they seemed pleased
to have everything done. So, to work like an idiot, what for? It's
depressing. And then again this morning, another incident. It
seems like nothing, but I have had enough . . .

So here I am, in fine shape. But I feel better now, a little re-
lieved. I will try to act cheerfully, and then there is something else
that sustains me, it comes from above.

Excerpt from diary, translated from French by the author.

The last straw came when I saw an Orthodox couple with two teenage
children—a boy and a girl—being loaded into a van. I knew that the Swiss

put refugees in a van, drove them across the border into Nazi-occupied France, and left them in the middle of the road. I knew this was a death sentence, so I protested vigorously. This was too much for the Swiss. I was told that there had been complaints about me, that this was not the first.

Camp de Claparède
June 1, 1944

I'm still here. Another incident. I am furious, I am boiling. You should have seen with what haughty tone I was spoken to. Fortunately I was not the only one to get bawled out. And then a soldier says, "If you want to stay here longer . . ." as if I had been the one who asked to stay. "Once, twice, three times, OK. But now it's every day and several times a day. This morning the CO told me there were complaints about you," etc. etc.

This is really too much. And what promises they had made to entice me to stay! Had I known it was going to be like this, I would not have stayed. I can't get over it. We are here to work, and then we are treated like prisoners and worse. Every day there are criticisms and with a manner . . . you can just imagine. I have not calmed down yet, but I am laughing anyway, because I don't care about anything anymore.

Excerpt from diary, translated from French by the author.

I was promptly shipped off to Champel after I had spent less than two weeks in Claparède. Looking back, I think the Swiss treated me like a soldier from whom blind obedience was expected, whereas I saw myself as an autonomous individual filled with gratitude and willing to work of my own free will in order to help out—two irreconcilable notions.

Despite my clashes with the Swiss border guards, I recognize that I was very lucky to make it into Switzerland. At the time, I did not know what the Swiss policy was in reference to Jews fleeing the Nazis, as it wasn't articulated until the end of 1942. Up until then, decisions were made by the cantons (like states in the US) since Switzerland is a federation. So, whether or not the Swiss guards granted entry depended on where a person crossed the border. After the mass deportations began in 1942 and desperate Jews tried to find safety, Switzerland developed a more cohesive policy, superseding the policies of the cantons. Switzerland was open to unaccompanied children under the age of sixteen—like my group—families with children under the age of six, pregnant women, and hardship cases—like the man on crutches from Nice.

13. GENEVA

Champel, Le Val Fleuri, Le Centre Henri Dunant

After only twelve days in Claparède, I was sent to Champel, a quarantine camp run by the Swiss Army. Normally we were to remain in the camp for three weeks; however, there were outbreaks of scarlet fever, diphtheria, and numerous cases of impetigo. I celebrated my not-so-sweet sixteenth birthday in this quarantine camp.

There were 117 people of various ages in the camp. We were housed in an old private residence with a large yard, and the estate was surrounded by barbed wire and guarded by armed soldiers. For washing, there were two troughs behind the building that had cold water trickling down through holes in a pipe. By mutual agreement, women and men washed during different set hours. I would strip down to my underwear, but never beyond that. Fortunately it was summertime so the situation was tolerable. The younger children who did not wash themselves came down with impetigo. They were frequently sent to the hospital to be scrubbed, and they came back looking as red as boiled lobsters.

I slept in a room with six other girls. Boards about seven or eight inches high were nailed to the floor to make walls that held the straw we slept on. Each of us was given a blanket, and at night, we all slept lined up side by side like sardines. There was a little path left along the edge to navigate around the room. Since we had only the clothes on our backs and few belongings, the lack of space did not present a problem. I don't remember any of us complaining about that. We bunched up our belongings into bundles, which we used as pillows. In the morning, we would neatly fold our blankets and roll them up, leaving the straw exposed.

When I left Claparède to rejoin the others in Champel, I was glad to be back with my peers, but life with teenagers who had nothing to do and no adult presence to guide them was not all sugar and spice. One interesting phenomenon was that there were two groups of young people: my group, mostly made up of those who had been to Florac and with whom I had crossed the border, and another group, the Zoot Suits, with whom we had little interaction.

My group always got together on Saturday night to have an *oneg*, to sing and talk and dream about what we would do when the war was over. These *onegs* tried to recapture the flavor of our Friday nights in Florac. We were very idealistic; we called ourselves the Maccabees, and we were going to work for a better world and build a Jewish homeland once the war was over. In the other group, the girls were dressed provocatively, the boys had trendy zoot suit hairstyles, and they held dances in their dorm room with one fellow bellowing out swing melodies through an improvised megaphone. None of the adults had anything to do with either group and no one took an interest in us. We were left to our own devices. Admittedly, the cohesiveness of our group began to fray after several weeks, though the two groups remained separate.

On Fridays a Jewish organization provided each of us with a brown paper bag that contained Shabbat treats, usually an apple or an orange, a small pack of raisins, canned cream of chestnuts, or a can of sardines. We would save most of it for our *oneg* on Saturday night. This showed much self-restraint on our part because when we got up from the dinner table, we were often still hungry and there were no second helpings.

Although books were not available, someone got his hands on a copy of *Cyrano de Bergerac* by Edmond Rostand. We lined up to read it. There were fifteen people ahead of me and when my turn came, I could not put the book down. I loved the story and thought it was the greatest. I even missed lunch because I kept reading. Such was our intellectual drought.

A few people in the camp managed to obtain cigarettes, and some of my peers encouraged me to try. Felix from Vienna offered me a cigarette, and I smoked without inhaling. He pointed out that I was not really smoking. So I inhaled and had a big coughing fit. That did it. I knew smoking was bad because Papa had gotten so sick from nicotine poisoning. I concluded smoking just wasn't worth it and never smoked again.

I continued to keep my diary where I put down my crushes and disappointments, all very adolescent stuff. Once I spoke to a soldier guarding us. He told me about his family problems and told me soldiers were forbidden to speak with us. There was one confrontation with the Swiss that I wrote down verbatim.

July 6, 1944

Now to the other adventure, still in room 9 [my room] . . . During the day, our dear Henri installed a fine lighting system to allow us to stay up after "lights out." He had a [blue] light bulb [hidden] in a closet during the day then took it out after the lights were turned off. This allowed us to spread our blankets out on what was left of our straw. This installation would have been superfluous if the gentlemen of room 15 did not always stay in our room until 10 p.m., when they were kicked out unceremoniously by some camp official.

That night we were supposed to inaugurate this fine installation, so we did not rush to prepare our "beds" on our yellow "mattresses." We wanted to have something interesting to do in the blue light. I forgot to mention that the blue light bulb had been taken from the toilet. In addition to that, we had broken the light bulb in our room, so we had to replace it as well. We found another light bulb, so here we are with one broken [bulb] and two replacements. I should add that the toilets had no lights, except for moonlight. To add insult to injury, our friend [told] us to ask Pierre for another light bulb since we broke ours. In the end he went and asked for one.

So here we are. [After] lights out we took our little blue bulb from the closet, we unscrewed the bulb from the ceiling, and everyone was delighted with the ingenuity of our friend. An unannounced visit from the head of the camp was a common occurrence, and this time was no exception. All of a sudden someone tried to open the door. [I was standing guard.] I pushed back long enough to allow us to flip the switch and put out the light, and then I opened it. It was the head of the camp with Pierre. "Since you know how to break light bulbs and how to replace them by swiping the ones from the hall or the toilets, you will have no light bulbs until further notice. By the way, Pierre, take their bulb right away."

Upon hearing this, Henri climbed on the bench to unscrew the light bulb. But the head of the camp flipped the switch and our famous blue installation was turned on. I was scared. I was still standing by the door badly shaken, with my legs threatening to collapse. But I managed to stand.

"Now, now," he said, "what is this? I see, one light bulb is not enough. Pierre, take this one as well. Who is the head of this room?" "It's me," said Moineau, [her scout name meaning sparrow]. "Well, you will spend four days in prison. That'll teach you for next time."

At that point I was so indignant that I said, "If she goes, I will go too." "Good, you will go as well, in fact the whole room will go," to which I replied, "if we have to," and he added, "and you will be sent back [to France] together," and I added, "if necessary." He slammed the door and left.

Now all the kids reproached me and told me I should not have said anything because it made everything worse, that I did the same thing the other boys had done with the fellow they put in prison, that I was wrong, etc. etc.

I was so shaken I could barely stand. But I will skip [this] because it is useless to talk about my feelings. The next morning all the girls were quiet, anxiously awaiting what would happen next. When I went down to get a broom and, as representative of our room, I was told that we were all stupid girls. At breakfast we got another official reprimand by the head of the camp. The end of the story was that room no. 9 had to clean all the windows of the building. This job was started, but not completed.

Excerpt from diary, translated from French by the author.

My story went viral (as we say today) and by morning, everyone knew about the incident. When I came down the next morning, one of the refugees in the camp greeted me with, "*mes hommages Mademoiselle*" (my compliments). I was so sure that she was mocking me that I answered her with a sassy remark, "*mes fromages, Madame.*" Offended, the poor woman left in a huff. Now I realize that perhaps she meant it as a real compliment because I had stood my ground in the face of threats.

Since I was very insecure, I accepted the opinions others had of me. Upon reading this passage, I saw a different girl: a spunky kid who stood up to the Swiss, not an easy feat. Later I also realized that by speaking up, I saved Moineau from four days in prison. My indignation stemmed from the recognition that Moineau, who was a little older than the rest of us and a sensible, mature young girl, had not been involved either in the planning or the execution of our scheme. I felt it was unfair that she should be the one to be punished. That's why I spoke up even in the face of threats to my own safety. Although the Swiss saved our lives by letting us in and caring for us, their constant threats to send us back to France and certain death over every minor infraction detracted from their generosity.

⚜

As the three weeks of quarantine stretched into months, the ambulance would come, sometimes as often as four times a day, to take people to the hospital. Finally, to control the spread of disease, the camp authorities took drastic measures: they burned all the straw we used as bedding and distributed a fresh supply. They asked us to stay outside until 4 p.m. and before we were allowed back into the building, they took everyone's temperature. Those with a temperature were shipped off to the hospital or to the nearby infirmary.

Toward the end of my stay, I began running a fever with a painful sore throat. It felt like diphtheria all over again, but I knew that you could not get it twice. I was sent to the infirmary in an adjacent building called Le Val Fleuri and vaccinated against diphtheria, in spite of my protestations since I had just had the disease. I spent a week recovering there from what must have been strep throat and then I was sent off to Le Centre Henri Dunant with a large group of young children.

The Centre, run by the International Red Cross, was named after the founder of the Swiss Red Cross. It was housed in the former Hotel Carlton, an elegant hotel across the street from the Palace of the League of Nations. On our way to the Centre, we carried our little bags and walked the length of Geneva from south to north for an hour or two on a hot summer day, past well-dressed people who stared at us. I was conscious of the fact that we looked like refugees and felt as though the word Jew was plastered on my forehead. I was tired of being a refugee and so much wanted to be like everyone else. For me, this walk was a humiliating experience.

When we got there, we were told to leave all our belongings in the front hall, and we were ushered into bathrooms where we were told to leave our clothes. Everything had to be cleaned and disinfected. Then we were washed. I objected strenuously when a middle-aged woman began to wash me since I was old enough to wash myself, but the woman insisted. Another humiliating experience. Then, wrapped in towels, we were sent to the next room to be deloused. I had short hair, but the other girls with long hair were given short haircuts and the boys had their heads shaved. Then we were given clothes from the Schweizerische Kinderhilfe (Swiss aid to children) and another week of quarantine followed. At last there were books to read and we slept in real beds with real sheets, all welcome changes. At some point we were examined by a physician. I was diagnosed with an active case of tuberculosis, though my case was milder than some. I spent two weeks at the Centre.

"Dear Madame, [I am] doing well. Have what I need. What is my mother doing? How is she? Think of you all the time. Tender kisses." Sent via the Red Cross' Tracing Services while at Centre Henri Dunant, August 15, 1944.

This was my first opportunity to see whether the Red Cross could help me find my family. I gave them what information I had, including the dates when my brother and father had crossed the demarcation line into German-occupied France. I also attempted to find out how my mother was doing by writing to Mme Niermans in Montlaur.

At the Centre, I met Dolly Citroen. She was a university student, young, very pretty, charming, and dynamic. I shared my frustration and my sense of humiliation with Dolly. She was very understanding and we became friends. To my great disappointment, she left after the first week.

In August I was off to Alpina in Chésières-Villars, a small ski resort town above Montreux, to recover.

14. CHÉSIÈRES-VILLARS

Alpina

I still remember my arrival in Alpina. We took the train to Montreux and from there, the cogwheel train up the mountain. I recall the scary train ride at the edge of the precipice. It was August 23, the day Paris was liberated by the Allies. The mountain peaks were covered with snow. When our group of twenty children got to Chésières, a small bus took us to the sanatorium. Alpina was a privately owned sanatorium for children with tuberculosis. The owner, Mme Rapa, had made her home available to the Red Cross during the war, and it was to be a transitional home for us where we could recuperate from our illnesses and hardships before being sent to homes, schools, or orphanages for Jewish refugee children.

The sanatorium was located in the picturesque ski resort of Chésières-Villars. The home was built on a slope, with all the windows facing south. It had five stories, and each floor was recessed to allow the full sun to shine on the terrace and reach into the rooms on the floor below. There was a terrace on each floor and, during peace time, they would put out small beds for sick children. The top floor had a game room with a ping-pong table. Out front was a playground with swings and a seesaw—I had never seen one before and wondered what it was.

By the time I got to Alpina, the forty or fifty children, mostly teenagers, had already gone on many outings together, so groups were formed and I felt like an outsider. Most of the girls my age were gossipy and I had little in common with them, so I didn't talk much and kept to myself. To my pleasant surprise, I found Dolly Citroen who was now working there, but she left after only one week to go back to university in Geneva. The rest of the staff consisted of *surveillantes* (supervisors)—as opposed to *moniteurs* (counselors)—who were more concerned with keeping us in line than with our emotional well-being. They were quite a contrast to the counselors who looked after us while we were in hiding. There was also a nurse called

Alpina in Chésières-Villars, 1944.

Soeur Helene (or Sister Helen). Some of the *surveillantes* were bossy and unpleasant like Mlle Icky, who would come around and punch us in the back while we were sitting, unsuspecting, eating our meals. It was her way of making us sit up straight.

Since many of us were run-down or sick, we had a daily siesta, and in the evenings, there was a curfew with lights off around 10 p.m. We had good washing and shower facilities, but hot water was only available once a week on Fridays. I was so tired of being dirty that I took cold showers every day. During the day, we often went on excursions to pick berries, get wood, or hike. Those who had money could also go to the movies in the nearby village, and we were free to visit other homes for refugee adolescents located nearby. I recall visiting Les Avants, a home for Orthodox Jewish children. One excursion I remember started at 2 a.m. We hiked through the forest, feeling our way in the dark, so we could reach the nearby mountain, Le Petit Chamossaire, by daybreak to watch the sunrise. The staff in charge made a big bonfire and we had breakfast on the mountaintop before returning to Alpina. I remember the awesome feeling of watching the sun rise from behind the mountains. I enjoyed that adventure tremendously.

Among the children in Alpina were six-and-a-half-year-old twin girls. I took them under my wing as if they were my little sisters. One Sunday, they expressed the wish to go to church, so I got them all dressed up and ready to go. That led to a major run-in with Soeur Helene who forbade me to take them to church for reasons that made no sense to me. She got very angry and yelled at me. I was very frustrated because I did not think I had done anything wrong, and I must have responded in kind. The next day, Soeur Helene came to my room and apologized, admitting that she had yelled at me first. In an effort to make up, she offered me books to read, but all she had were detective stories and I was not interested.

In fact, books were a scarce commodity in Alpina. When Dolly left for Geneva, she promised to send packages of books to me and two of the other teenage boys, Jacques Hepner and Leon Wodo, who shared my love of books. We would take turns reading them and then send them back to Dolly so we could get a new shipment. This common interest in books created a bond between us and fostered our friendship. Books were important and I read whatever was available. Among the ones I remember were *Fleuve* (River) by Thyde Monnier—a book that had a profound effect on me—Anatole France's *Les Dieux ont soif* (The Gods are Athirst), Pearle Buck's *The Good Earth*, Edmond About's *L'homme à l'oreille cassée* (The Man with the Broken Ear), *Romeo and Juliet*, and *Hamlet*. I wanted so much to have someone with whom to discuss these books and their ideas, but the adults in Alpina were not interested in our emotional welfare or our spiritual or intellectual growth. I do not recall discussing the books with Leon or Jacques.

Edith in Alpina, 1944, wearing the same skirt and blouse, and an ill-fitting jacket and shoes from a charity.

I had seen Jacques on the day of our arrival; he was leaning out of the second story window to look over the new kids. He had a white bandage around his neck, a common practice to treat a sore throat. I do not recall seeing Jacques around much except at mealtimes as he spent much of his time in his room, reading or sleeping. Were it not for our common interest in books and the fact that he was also a friend of Leon's, I probably would not have gotten to know him. As for Leon, he was one of the boys in the home who was always cheerful and joking around. We all had simple chores like setting and clearing the tables. Leon volunteered to work in the kitchen so he could scrape the pots and get a little more to eat. Since there were other boys with the same first name, we ended up calling him Leon Cuistot—the kitchen Leon. I liked him a lot; in fact, I had a major crush on him. But since he always seemed to flirt with all the girls and did not show any particular interest in me, I didn't think I could stand up to the competition.

Early in my stay Mme Rapa, usually a distant figure, decided to lecture us. She came into the dining room, surrounded by the staff. This lecture had a negative effect on me, which I described in my diary:

August 31, 1944

At breakfast, the *directrice* gave us a talk about the organization of the house, etc. She did this in an arrogant and not very courteous tone. We can recognize a Swiss person who has not suffered and who does not understand, in spite of all appearances, what it's like to be a refugee. You have to have experienced it in order to understand it. She boasts about how she and her fellow Swiss do good deeds of which we are the recipients and reminds us how grateful we should be. I thought she was making fun of us or that she didn't know what she was saying. I felt like laughing in her face, but . . . Orders were barked at us in an authoritarian tone. At the slightest comment, we are [called] impertinent, ungrateful, and I don't know what else. So be it. They all forget that that's not the best way to approach us. They won't have us this way. They think they're going to impress us with their orders that do not tolerate an answer? But they are making a mistake . . . As for me, I'm indifferent to everything. They leave me completely cold and they think this will be a way of improving the atmosphere of this house.

Translated from French by the author.

I wrote extensively in my diary, covering many pages, pouring out my heart. I expressed constant concern for my father, my mother, and my brother. I berated myself for having saved my own skin by going into hiding, leaving my mother alone in France—as if I could have done anything to help her. On Erev Rosh Hashanah 1944, the staff had prepared a nice dinner for us. I was getting ready to go to the dining room when I was handed a letter from the Red Cross. This letter informed me that both my father and brother had been sent to the transit camp of Drancy outside of Paris, and from there, to Auschwitz. At the time, I had no clue what Auschwitz meant. Once they were in German hands, I imagined that they were doing hard labor while exposed to the elements, hunger, ill treatment, and without medical care. I prayed for my family every day. I thought that, once the fighting was over, I would go and look for my father in the chaotic aftermath. I also thought that if my father survived, he would be sick and I would have to work to help support him. I was torn between the desire to find him and my duty toward my mother, who I imagined would not be able to travel with me.

Although I did not have access to radio or newspapers, news of the Allied advance was reaching us in real time. I also found out through letters from friends that two of the counselors from Florac—Giraffe (Raymond Winter) and Souris (Marcel Gradwohl)—had been caught in France and shot. I was completely devastated by the news. I followed news about the Allies, waiting to hear when Carcassonne would be liberated because that's where I assumed my mother would be. When I learned that the Allies were advancing at a pace of forty kilometers a day, I thought that the war would soon be over. Then in October, we learned that the Germans were organizing a strong counteroffensive. It would take more than six months before Germany's collapse.

In late September, children began to leave, either for school or to be placed with families or acquaintances. They were replaced by a bunch of rough boys from the rural areas of the Alsace-Lorraine region. These boys were different—vulgar and rude—and I had nothing in common with them, so I stayed as far away from them as I could. As the other children were leaving, Leon and I were among the handful of the *anciens* or old-timers who remained. That is where our friendship began. By then, I was working full time in the laundry and helping Mme Rapa by straightening out her room and washing her silk stockings daily. The washer woman, Mme Dufresne, was a simple Swiss peasant in her thirties, who had no teeth. Once, Leon and I were in the kitchen eating with her when she pointed to a cover girl on some magazine and told us that once upon a time, she had teeth like that. We looked at each other with a complicit smile. She was a very considerate woman though, with a big heart; when I worked with her in the laundry, she would not allow me to do some of the heavier work.

In October, Leon too left for Geneva. He would go to school while living in a home called Les Murailles, and we promised to write. My concern for my family, my loneliness, my uncertainty about the future, and my utter sense of abandonment led me to become deeply depressed. In my diary I wrote that "nothing gives me pleasure . . . and I don't even like to sing anymore," as singing was something I had always enjoyed. My bedroom faced the Massif du Mont Blanc and every morning, I could see the awesome sight of the sun rising over the snow-capped mountains, coloring them a tender pink. That sight saved my sanity. Although we could frequently hear the sound of gunfire, it was hard to imagine the war raging just on the other side of those magnificent peaks.

The Swiss authorities must have tried to find a place for me. There was talk about sending me to work as a seamstress in some workshop. I was sixteen years old, a good worker, and no one seemed to care about my education or my future. As for me, I was too dumb, ignorant, or downtrodden to make any demands, nor did I have much of a say in the decision. Because I had become very religious during my time in hiding, I now refused to eat non-kosher meat. As a result, the only request I made was to be placed into an observant home. In the end, the directors of an orphanage for refugee children needed a nanny for their newborn baby. I was told I would also have the opportunity to study, so I accepted.

Before I left, I went to visit Mme Dufresne in the modest chalet that she shared with her husband and two children. She treated me to a big omelet and gave me a man's handkerchief, saying, *"C'est un beau mouchoir"* (it's a beautiful handkerchief). This was a generous gift from her, since I knew she used rags for herself—I still have that handkerchief. Mme Dufresne taught me a huge lesson: kindness and compassion have nothing to do with education, wealth, or status in life. They can often be found among the humble. This woman was humble in a most unselfconscious way.

I left Chésières in November—the last of the old-timers to leave.

15. ULISBACH AND SPEICHER

The Nanny

In November 1944, I went to work as a nanny in Ulisbach, near Watwil via Winterthur, in the German-speaking part of Switzerland. Miriam and Henri Dybniz, called Dyb by his wife, were running a home for Jewish boys mostly between the ages of eight and fourteen. I took care of their new baby Monique. I fed her, bathed her, dressed her, and often took her for walks.

That's where I first ate Bircher muesli, a mix of oatmeal and fruit served with cold milk. To me, it tasted like manna from heaven. We were housed in cramped quarters. The house was a small chalet and, with about thirty children plus the staff, we were bursting at the seams. The downstairs common room, called *die Stube*, was the only heated room in the house. Once in bed, it usually took me one hour to warm up enough to fall asleep at night. In the morning, my bedroom window was covered with frost on the inside, and snow blew in through the cracks. The room was equipped with a large pitcher of water and a wash basin, and I often had to break the ice in the pitcher before pouring water into the basin—that's how cold the room was. Once out of bed, I was cold for the rest of the day.

I worked six days a week with only Saturdays off. I was on my feet all day: rising with Monique, changing her diapers, feeding her three or four times a day, and taking her out for walks. During her naps, I washed her diapers by hand, rinsing them in cold water and hanging them up to dry outdoors or indoors, depending on the season. Every evening I gave her a bath and put her to bed. After that, Miriam would give me additional work like scrubbing the wooden floor in her rooms by attaching steel wool to my shoes so I could shuffle around the room over and over again. She also had me clean the hair out of her hairbrush. I realized that Miriam liked to be waited on and she had aristocratic airs, something that took me by surprise, especially given our situation.

Monique and Edith, July 1945.

Meanwhile, I was losing another year of school and was desperate to get an education. I saw myself as young and healthy and thought that, after the war, I would need to work to help support my parents who might be sick, especially my father. I still had no idea what being sent to Auschwitz meant, so I hoped to see him and Kurt again. I pleaded with Miriam to let me learn how to type and take shorthand. I also wanted to learn English. Jacquot, a sixteen-year-old boy, was not working and was being tutored in math by M. Fuchs, one of the counselors. During her brief stay, my roommate Charlotte, who was my age and whose parents were friends of the Dybniz family, was sent to school. But for me, Miriam ignored her initial commitment to get me some schooling and showed no interest in my welfare. Upon my insistence, Miriam finally gave me a typing manual, pointed to a typewriter in her office, and said, "Here, go type." So I did, but not until the end of the day after putting in my usual ten-to-twelve hours and after putting Monique to bed. Miriam also gave me an old shorthand book, and I taught myself shorthand.

There was no one my age to talk to. I had no interaction with the boys, perhaps because I was treated like a servant. One entry in my diary reads, "If I don't get to be with kids my own age soon, I think I'll go nuts." On one of my walks with Monique, I passed by a house with a tennis court where two teenage boys were playing tennis. Oh how much I would have liked to do that!

My faith had become very important. I also read avidly, both secular and religious books, from the Bible to the Zohar. I had requested placement into an observant home, to the exclusion of more practical considerations, yet soon after my arrival in Ulisbach, I was already in despair. With the full workload and Miriam's constant put-downs, I became very depressed, as shown in my diary entries:

November 13, 1944

I have nothing to tell you because I no longer feel anything. I'm becoming a machine, a servant, who is learning not to be disgusted by anything. So be it. I'm lost. But stop, because with the little willpower I have left, I don't want to slide into another crisis, an easy thing if I continue.

Getting down to the facts, I must say that I am learning how to type all by myself. At least I'll have that. I really think that except for spelling and French, my brain is going to sleep and I fear that it will no longer be good for anything when the time comes to wake up . . .

I'm frustrated that Monique starts to cry as soon as she wakes up or when I put her to bed while I am typing. As a result, I waste a lot of time and since I decided to really learn how to type, my progress is slow. So be it.

I went to bed because I want to be up there [in the Dybniz' cramped quarters] as little as possible. Although I've only been here for four days, I'm already fed up.

November 16, 1944

All I can say is that I'm sad, so sad and sick of everything. Tonight, I put a question in the "question" box: "Is man at birth basically good or bad?" I must add that destiny is beginning to intrigue me. But all these ideas don't come from me. I don't have a shred of intelligence in my brain. Whatever I do, it does not come. It's because intelligence cannot be ordered, nor does it come by studying. Why am I so stupid? I keep thinking about my loneliness, my lack of affection, my character flaws, often about my family, then about myself again . . . Often I make excuses for my bad disposition and my actions. These are my thoughts. In the evening I almost always think about God. Then I tell myself, especially when I am sad, that the thought of God should cheer me up, sustain me, especially since I believe so strongly. I don't want to doubt my faith, but trust in God cannot be ordered. What to do?

Translated from French by the author.

⚜

After about three months in that chalet, we moved to Speicher near Trogen, four kilometers west of St. Gallen in the Appenzell. The building was on a hilltop with a 360-degree view of the surrounding area. From there you could look down on Lake Constance (the Bodensee) in Germany to the north, the Austrian Alps to the east, the Säntis mountain range to the south, and the city of St. Gallen to the west. It was a magnificent spot and the Swiss Army had an observation post nearby to keep an eye on Germany, for the Swiss were prepared to defend themselves in the event of a German invasion.

In Speicher we moved into a big four-story building made of wood, a real fire trap. It had once served as an orphanage for Swiss children, but the few Swiss children in it were moved to another orphanage and we got the run of the place. I assume the authorities must have made a deal with the Dybniz to educate the Jewish boys because all the children were schooled in-house. Dyb called the place Kinderheim Futura. The staff consisted exclusively of Jewish refugees with the exception of the nurse who was Swiss. They were all professional people who were competent to teach. On Fridays, classes would stop at noon, and in the afternoon the children themselves cleaned the building for Shabbat.

We had trouble getting a decent cook until we found an Austrian refugee, who once owned a restaurant in Vienna. He cooked delicious meals, although everything we ate was dairy since this was a kosher home and kosher meat was not available. We got our milk from the farmer next door. Our cook poured the milk into large shallow pans, let it stand overnight, and then skimmed off the fat to make butter; so we drank partially skimmed milk. I ate a lot and often went back for seconds. Sometimes I would even go to the kitchen between meals to get a snack. I was always hungry—perhaps I was making up for lost time. I was getting plump.

Miriam lacked kindness. Once I was told to get something in the cellar. I went downstairs and reached for the string to turn on the light when

Kinderheim Futura in Speicher. Miriam, back row on the right, is
yelling at one of the boys. She must have been loud because several
people are looking at her. Photo given to Edith, 1945.

I fell over a crate someone had carelessly left at the bottom of the steps, injuring my calf. I went back upstairs with a painful hematoma. Instead of giving me the usual ice compress to numb the pain and reduce the swelling, I was given a wet washcloth. I had been sitting for five or ten minutes with the washcloth when Miriam showed up. "That's enough," she said, "get back to work." So I did. Because this injury never healed properly, I was left with a permanent lump on my calf that caused me pain whenever I walked fast. Another time, I developed severe cramps in the calves of my legs. The doctor who examined me said that it was because of my footwear, which didn't provide any support. The whole time I was in Switzerland I wore sneakers or old shoes and clothes donated by the Schweizerische Kinderhilfe, a Swiss charity for children. So, Miriam bought me a pair of old lady shoes. Neither these shoes nor the clothes helped to improve my self-image. To make matters worse, Miriam criticized my appearance and told me that I looked and acted like an old woman.

I had a lot of initiative. Once, a little girl of about nine or ten came to the home after staying with a Swiss family for nine months. She told me they never washed her hair, so I washed her hair. When I was done, Miriam ordered me to wash her hair and I told her I already did. That, she approved of. But another little girl wanted a haircut, so I gave her one.

Miriam yelled at me with such emotion that you would think I had disfigured the child for life. Yet I remember that in spite of all this, I tried hard to please her. She knew that. Once, she told me "*sonst wärst du längst über alle Berge,*" that is [if I had not changed], I would have been sent packing a long time ago, as if *she* was the one doing me a favor by keeping me on.

Another episode stood out. A new boy had arrived who must have been about twelve. Always neatly dressed, he was watching longingly as a group of boys played soccer. I recognized the feeling of being excluded and so I encouraged him to go play with them and not worry so much about his clothes, which could always be washed. We spoke for quite a while. Unfortunately, the conversation took place under Miriam's open window. When I went back into the house, I got such a tongue-lashing, "What have you done? You have destroyed what his parents taught him. . . . You have to go back and tell him you were wrong." I was devastated. He was a nice boy and I had acted like a big sister. Now I had to go back on everything I said? This incident troubled me for a long time. Who was right, Miriam or I? The fact remained that Miriam destroyed what little self-confidence I had, as is reflected in my diary entries:

January 14, 1945

In general, I feel rather unhappy. I am no longer the light and cheerful Edith of the past. I think that's over. Miriam tells me I'm becoming an old woman, a grandmother . . .

January 21, 1945

I'm beginning to despair. But no one knows it. With whom should I talk? . . . Things can't go on like this with Miriam . . .

Translated from French by the author.

Miriam had become very cold and distant, not to mention hostile. She worked me hard and I was never paid, nor given any pocket money. I accepted all that. What was hard to take, though, was Miriam's constant criticism. She never left me alone. Whatever I did, she found fault. And yet she was the only adult in my life. The other counselors paid no attention to me and there were no other people my age I could talk to.

The biggest revelation came to me when I stumbled on a passage in my diary. After several months in the home, I was notified that a family willing to take me in had been found. It meant Miriam would lose her nanny. Suddenly, she became very nice and even gave me little gifts. In my diary I wrote, "She is so nice, how can I leave? And who will take care of Monique?" as if that was my responsibility. I was blind and naïve. As soon as I turned down the offer without even finding out more about it, she reverted to her old hypercritical and exploitative ways.

My strong faith had sustained me during those difficult times, so imagine my profound despair when, during a Shabbat service, I began doubting God and lost my faith. I needed answers and suddenly these prayers no longer made sense. It hit me so hard that I started to cry during the service. Afterward, Miriam asked me why I was crying. When I told her, she dismissed my profound despair with a wave of the hand as some adolescent foolishness. I was alone. I now had to carry on without the emotional and spiritual support of my faith.

After I pleaded with her for English lessons for six months, Miriam finally assigned M. Mandel to teach me English. He gave me a copy of *Englisch lernen ein Vergnügen*, a textbook for adults. I met with him for twenty minutes, three times a week. He would check my homework, listen to my memorization, and assign the next lesson. Six nights a week, from 8 to 10 p.m., I studied. That gave me twelve study hours and just one hour with M. Mandel each week. In three months, I finished the book. I knew the irregular verbs now, mastered basic grammar, and learned basic vocabulary.

M. Mandel also gave me André Gide's novel *La Porte Etroite* (The Narrow Gate) to read. It was the story of a young man and a young woman from the same upper-class milieu. They liked each other and were destined to marry. But she had spiritual aspirations and did not want physical intimacy, so the wedding never took place. I didn't care for the story, which left me frustrated because I felt they should have married since they loved each other. When I shared my thoughts with M. Mandel, instead of discussing the book with me, he dismissed my reaction in a way that made me feel stupid. After that, he didn't give me any more books to read. This only reinforced my negative self-image.

In April 1945, several of us went to the movies to see a comedy with Laurel and Hardy. It was the only time I went to the movies during my entire stay in Switzerland as the Swiss were very strict about not allowing anyone under seventeen at the movies. The program began with the newsreel, as it was customary to show the news in movie theaters before the feature film. This time, it showed the Allies marching into Germany and discovering the death camps. They showed the concentration camps, complete with gas chambers and crematoria. I was in a state of shock. It was the first time I learned what the Germans had done. I was sobbing so loudly that they had to take me out of the theatre. Without access to radio and newspapers, I wasn't able to learn much more about what had happened to my family and the rest of the Jews until much later.

On May 8, 1945, Germany signed the Unconditional Surrender. The war, or should I say the nightmare, was over. It was time to count the dead. Every day, news arrived at the home to tell the children that their relatives were dead. The boys sitting in their dorm rooms stared at the pictures of their parents and cried. My heart went out to them. What could I say? When neither parent survived, there was an active search to find relatives anywhere in the world who would take in these orphans. Children without relatives ended up in *maisons d'enfants* run by the OSE or by other Jewish organizations.

As for me, after watching that newsreel, I wasn't sure if any member of my family, including my mother, had survived. I realized that my thoughts of going to Germany to find my father were not realistic after I found out that Auschwitz was a death camp and that Germany's goal had been to kill all the Jews. I was not going back to Austria. There was nothing there for me. In France, I didn't have anyone either and so I thought that, if no one survived, I would go to what was then Palestine. What else was I to do? I was only sixteen and I had no education and no skills.

⚜

It took at least six weeks after the liberation of France for the mail to be re-established. On December 1, 1944, I received a message via the Red Cross that read as follows: "I am in good health. Try to find your brother . . . Let me hear from you soon." There was no "Dear Edith" or "Love Mom," so I wasn't even sure it was from her. Still, I planned to go back to France as soon as possible. Once mail contact was established, we were able to write to each other.

After continuing to work as a cook in Montlaur, my mother eventually got another job, still as a cook, working first in Anzème then in Guéret for the prefect of the Department of the Creuse, a hotbed of the Résistance. Officially, she remained an agricultural worker or farmhand as this was the only job open to foreigners. In Guéret, the *maquisards* (members of the Maquis) would walk around openly, their guns slung over their shoulders, stopping at the boulangerie to ask for bread. Whenever the prefect was notified that there would be a raid, he alerted all those in danger, including my mother, so they could hide in the woods during the night. By noon, he would send out the all-clear signal.

I always wondered how my mother managed to get that job and move from Montlaur. Since my mother never told me, I can only assume that the members of the underground who brought her my letters alerted her to the position with its sympathetic prefect who could protect her. Montlaur had become increasingly dangerous as the tribunal in Carcassonne hounded her for not showing up in court for the purpose of affixing a stamp on her papers with the word *Juif.* Under the circumstances, the position in Guéret turned out to be a godsend.

As soon as the south of France was liberated, my mother left her employer and moved to Toulouse, where she eventually reconnected with me. She knew where I was because someone had scribbled in the margin of my last letter to her, "Edith is in Switzerland." Both the International Red Cross and the OSE tracked me down. The OSE kept careful records for all the children with both their real names and their fake names. This was especially important for younger children who may not have remembered who they were. The OSE's goal was to find them and reunite them with their families whenever possible, or to find suitable homes where they could be adopted. If all else failed, there were a number of *maisons d'enfants* where the children were lovingly cared for while they continued to go to French schools.

In my letters to my mother, I described what I was doing, to which she replied that I was being treated like a servant. Of course I objected to that description, but not before sharing my mother's comments with Miriam. For instance, in my diary I discovered that all the children would go on interesting hikes on Saturdays and Sundays while I stayed home either to look after Monique on Sundays or alone in the empty building on Saturdays, my only day off. Or I would take long hikes all by myself, crossing dangerous ravines. Miriam began to treat me a little better after I shared my mother's comments, and I was finally included in outings with other children in the home. I remember how much I enjoyed my only excursion with the whole group—a hike to the Säntis with its mountain lake where we were offered goat milk either warm, straight from the goat, or chilled in the cold water of the lake.

Before I left, Miriam bought me a summer dress to go with my old lady shoes. She gave me twenty Swiss francs and encouraged me to buy

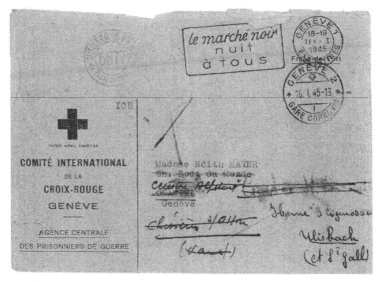

This letter from the Red Cross shows how difficult it was to track Edith down because she moved so often. Postmarked January 1945.

a useless bracelet. I was blind to Miriam's exploitation and I remained attached to her, even after my return to France, and I kept up a lively correspondence with her.

In July 1945, I returned to France to rejoin my mother. On my way, I stopped in Zurich to see Otto Steinmetz, Putzi's younger brother. He was a year older than I, and I saw that he had become a dedicated Communist while working in a Swiss labor camp. M. Steinmetz had managed to get his son and daughter into Switzerland, but my brother he sent to become a Prestataire. Then I stopped in Geneva and took one last swim in Lake Geneva at seven in the morning before taking the train to Toulouse.

⚕

During most of my time in Switzerland, I was very lonely and utterly miserable. Academically, it was a complete waste, except that I learned basic English and typing. At the same time, I appreciated the fact that I was alive and especially that I had been spared the concentration camp experience. Above all, I was now healthy and strong and able to face the rigors of the hard years that lay ahead.

Introduction to the Postwar Years

"Es irrt der Mensch, so lang' er strebt."
Johann Wolfgang von Goethe, *Faust*, "Prolog im Himmel" line 317
("While striving, Man is apt to err.")

Most people think that when the shooting stops, it's all over and everyone can go back to the way things were. But when a life is so disrupted, one has to start from minus zero, and it takes a very long time to pick up the pieces and put one's life back together.

For France, the war and subsequent occupation represented a hiatus during which all progress stopped; one might even say that there was economic regression. The goal for everyone was simply survival, the need to navigate the ever-present surveillance of the authorities to stay out of prison or worse while getting enough food to eat. After the war, France had to start with a new constitution for the Fourth Republic. Even with the American help of the Marshall Plan starting in 1947, France took years to rebuild her economy.

Those among us who had lost everything now had nothing: no country, no family, no home, no money, no education, and no help. In addition, we had to confront the inconceivable cruelty of Nazi Germany.

As I faced these issues, I searched for answers and for meaning while struggling to make ends meet and trying to catch up on lost schooling. This struggle to put one's life back together is not often talked about. And yet it is what we do with our freedom and, ultimately, with our opportunity that matters most, for during a crisis we have few choices.

Toulouse, France

16. A YEAR OF FLOUNDERING

Denise Lévy, the counselor I had known as Belette, met me at the railroad station in Toulouse on a hot day in July 1945. I was glad to see her again. She had often taken me from one hiding place to another and was with us in Florac. She brought me to the subsidized restaurant where my mother usually ate lunch. When we got there, my mother was overjoyed to see me, and the feeling was mutual.

After lunch, I picked up my little suitcase and we took the streetcar to the last stop and then walked a good half hour to her place on the Chemin des Sept Deniers. She had rented a small room with kitchen privileges from an older woman, a masseuse by profession. My mother slept on the bed and I slept on a box spring; I had removed my mattress which was covered with wool because summers in Toulouse were very hot.

I did not know if my mother was aware of Papa's and Kurt's deportation from Drancy to Auschwitz or that Auschwitz was a death camp. For many weeks, we tiptoed around the subject of Papa's and Kurt's fate, trying to break the news to each other gently. It was almost a relief when we discovered we both knew the awful truth. Though we still hoped they both survived and believed that Kurt at least had a chance, the bitter reality of their deaths sank in very slowly.

After a two-year separation, we had to get used to each other. Since I was no longer a child, my mother tried her best to be nice, albeit with less and less success. There were issues that needed to be addressed—my education, the matter of housing and of making ends meet, as well as the unspoken issue of how to deal with the recent trauma.

Since I did not go out unless I had a specific reason to do so, our lodgings became like a prison. I would go stir crazy in the tiny room I shared with my mother. I was used to working from morning until night, and in Toulouse there was nothing for me to do. I often sang all the songs I learned to get rid of my excess energy. My mother thought I was being cute. There were some girls in the neighborhood, but I didn't socialize with them because we had little in common. They would go dancing on weekends, and I never went with them. For one thing, I did not feel like dancing.

Adjusting to life in a big city did not come easily to me either. I was disoriented because I was used to being led around by counselors, so I frequently got lost and would sometimes take the streetcar in the wrong direction. Though I very much disliked living in a collective, it took me a while to get used to being on my own.

When the war ended, the

Edith and her mother, wearing clothes sent by Aunt Anny, Toulouse, 1945.

enormity of the horrors of the Holocaust became public for the first time. There were exhibits, publications with photographs, and books. In addition to the pictures shown during the newsreel before every film, the press was full of what the Germans and their collaborators had done. I went to the exhibits and I looked at the pictures with horror and disbelief. I had to know, yet the facts devastated me. My whole world crumbled. It seemed the good people were murdered while the evil ones survived. Life seemed meaningless, unfair, unjust, and not worth living.

I contemplated suicide, even after I had gone to so much trouble to stay alive. I had to decide. If I chose to live, what kind of life would I create for myself? Should I take the straight and narrow path, like a nun, and cut myself off from the world? I was used to poverty and was chaste, but could I take a vow of obedience? That was impossible. I had to be able to think for myself, make my own decisions. What if I lived a selfish life, doing whatever I wanted without regard for others? Those who did so seemed to prosper—Nazis who got away, collaborators, and traitors. No, I couldn't do that either. The strong moral values my parents had instilled in me prevented such a choice. But why bother to strive for a better life? Why not indulge in pleasure only? What was the point of being ethical? Any effort to lead a just and an ethical life, as far as I was concerned, seemed to be a waste of time. The daughter of one of the survivors, a tall, attractive young woman, became the mistress of a wealthy Frenchman much older than she. Frequently, she would stop at the café where her parents traded in the black market, wearing an expensive fur coat, often accompanied by her lover. Was she right?

In Switzerland I lost my faith in God that Shabbat morning, which was such a profound spiritual crisis for me. How could anyone contemplate the possibility of a benevolent, merciful God after Auschwitz? The bearded Jews with their pious manner and black market activities were nothing but hypocrites to me. I was very judgmental, confused, and my values and beliefs were foundering on the rocks of the war. I turned my back on traditional Judaism, but retained a strong sense of right and wrong.

To make matters worse, the mood among the French was no better. After four years of German occupation, France cried out for justice, and hatred and a desire for revenge flourished. We all knew that human justice could not redress the abominations the Germans and their collaborators had committed. I could not understand how a human being could be nice to his own child and then brutalize another child in front of its mother.

Some Jewish children my age thought only of having fun and catching up on lost time, but I could not. I needed answers. My quest was intense, to the exclusion of other more mundane pursuits. Insights came slowly and I did not find answers in Western thought. I did not discuss these struggles with my mother, but I expressed them in my diary.

In Toulouse, I joined the Mouvement de Jeunesse Sioniste (MJS), went to meetings, and participated in long discussions. My peers all had more education than I did, which continued to make me feel inferior. I had no understanding of political events. I objected to girls serving in the army in what was then Palestine. My mother was not thrilled with my attendance at these meetings. Her goal was to get us to America. Immediately after the war, she applied for our immigration to the United States. Because of the American quota system, there was a five-year wait for applicants born in Austria, but I was not about to sit idle and twiddle my thumbs while waiting for my number to come up, so I began to build a life in France.

In the postwar years, about one-third of the French people voted for the Communist Party. After the war, there was a clear political battle for the hearts and minds of men. The Communist Party rented a large storefront in the heart of town, diagonally opposite the United States Information Agency (USIA). While the Communist store windows were full of propaganda—with books, flags, and slogans—the USIA displayed posters showing life in America. There were pictures of houses for ordinary people with front yards enclosed by white picket fences. It looked too good to be true for, in my experience, only rich people lived like that. In my ignorance, I did not know what to believe. The Communist slogans sounded so idealistic: "From each according to his ability, to each according to his needs." Of course, I did not know the truth, but I had a gut feeling that all was not as rosy as the Communists would have us believe. Luckily, I withheld judgment. Had I joined the Party, I would not have been admitted to the United States.

Politics and philosophy aside, it was clear we needed to get out of the tiny room we shared, but housing was in very short supply. Then my mother learned through an acquaintance that a tiny apartment was available on the rue des Princes. The rent was affordable, just 500 French francs a month. But the tenants, a Jewish couple, wanted three times the monthly rent for key money—that is, for the privilege of giving us the keys to the apartment—an arrangement that had nothing to do with the landlady. Somehow my mother came up with 1,500 francs and we moved. The landlady continued to charge us the same low prewar rate. Later on, I spent more on my daily showers at public baths than we spent on rent, but even so, it was often difficult to come up with those 500 francs every month.

The neighborhood was safe with older houses for blue-collar families at the bottom of the street and gleaming new villas uphill in the newer section. Our neighbor Mme Rigal worked as a cleaning lady now and then, and her husband worked in a factory. An old, unwashed couple lived across the hall. The husband worked in a shoe factory. The fourth apartment had a high turnover rate with sometimes unsavory tenants.

The house was on a narrow and hilly street. The nearest streetcar stop was down the hill, about ten minutes away. I walked to town most of the time since the carfare was beyond our means. The house was built with mud and stones that were visible where the plaster was peeling. The exterior was cracked and broken stucco. After a rain I could see dampness creeping up on the interior walls.

Our apartment consisted of one small room and a tiny kitchen. There was no running water; the fountain, our source of water, was half a block away. Several times a day, I filled our pail and large pitcher and carried them back to the apartment. Every night I made sure the pitcher and bucket were full so there would be water to wash in the morning. The kitchen sink allowed water to drain into an open gutter. I washed clothes in the kitchen and went out to the fountain to rinse them. While this was

*The slum house Edith lived in from 1946 to 1952. There were
four two-room apartments. Photo taken in 1956.*

not bad in the summer, it was rough in the winter because the water was
so cold. The entire floor was covered with worn tiles that were cold in
winter, and there was a small wood-burning stove in the middle. Often
we couldn't afford to buy the wood needed for heating. We also had an old
three-burner cooktop provided by the gas company.

There was no toilet, only an outhouse, Turkish style, with a cement
floor and a hole in the middle. It was in the rear courtyard and was shared
by the four apartments. It was emptied once every nine months when a
sanitation truck would come by and pump out the contents of the hole.
The neighbors often missed the hole, and I got so disgusted that I cleaned
the place every week with an old broom and carbolic acid diluted in water.
I hoped the neighbors would get the hint and help by taking their turn to
clean the latrine. One neighbor, Mme Rigal, did it a few times, but the
others did not, so my mother forbade me to continue cleaning it.

A curtain separated the main room from the kitchen. My mother
slept on a box spring in the room that also held a large table she used for

The fountain at the end of the block where Edith went for water and laundry. Edith is pictured with her friend Huguette, 1956.

work, three chairs, and a small unpainted chest. All the furniture came from charitable organizations. She bought a used armoire from the previous tenant and, later, we were given a foot-operated sewing machine by Organisation Reconstruction Travail (ORT), a Jewish charity that promoted vocational training. I slept on a folding bed in the kitchen. The Rigals lent us a folding table, so during the day I folded the bed and pushed it against the wall. Then I would unfold the table where we ate our meals and where I did all my homework. At night I folded the table, put my books on a chair, and opened my bed. Next to the chair there was a small alcove with two shelves and a bar to hang clothes.

My mother had no marketable skills, so she ended up working in sweatshops in the burgeoning garment industry. At first she worked for a furrier, sewing on buttons and linings. That was hard work because with every stitch, she had to push the needle through leather. Later she worked as a presser. She frequently lost her job because she was often late for work and she also complained a lot.

I maintained contact with the Oeuvre de Secours aux Enfants (OSE). Marthe Levy, a member of the Sixième during the war, was a social worker with the OSE. She filled me in on the fate of some of my saviors. Her brother Souris had been killed, as had Giraffe. She bravely carried on. Marthe tried to help me. After my experience in Switzerland, I wanted to work with young children. After Marthe made all the arrangements for my training in Limoges at an early childhood center run by the OSE, my mother decided against it. Then I was interviewed by an OSE vocational guidance counselor who spent an hour and a half with me. She concluded that to do what I wanted I needed the *Baccalauréat*, something I already knew.

After my rejection of the Limoges training, the OSE dropped me. I tried correspondence courses that my mother paid for, but they were too difficult. I needed coaching under the direction of a teacher because I was so far behind. At seventeen, I was too old to go back to the equivalent of the seventh grade in a *lycée* and start from scratch. When my mother learned that I knew basic English, she wanted me to maintain it so she paid for private English lessons. The teacher, a nice lady, did not give me a book of grammar or exercises. She asked me to read and translate a novel, but I didn't have enough vocabulary so the work was tedious. The English lessons turned out to be a waste because I often poured my heart out to this lady about the constant aggravation caused by my mother—in French, of course.

Then I enrolled in a private business school part time. I asked to continue studying the old shorthand method I taught myself in Switzerland, and they said that was fine. I was also able to practice my typing. I went to classes in the morning and had a part-time office job in the afternoon.

Meanwhile, I told everyone I knew that I wanted to go back to school. In the subsidized restaurant I met two ladies, Frau Freund and her daughter, who were social workers. They suggested that I contact Mme Ginodman, a social worker in Moissac who had limited funds available for scholarships. I met Mme Ginodman in Toulouse. She offered me a one-year scholarship to complete the curriculum that students cover in six years of *lycée*, and to pass the test for the first *Baccalauréat*. I asked for more time, but I was not given a choice. It was one year or nothing. I accepted the challenge.

I was introduced to the Cours Noyon, a private school in Toulouse. My mother and Mme Ginodman accompanied me on my first interview with Mlle Noyon, a petite, middle-aged woman with an assertive manner. We were led into a comfortable but dark living room, and she and I argued over German grammar. She insisted that I learn it and I said I could not. The argument ended in a draw. Later she told me that this was her way of testing me. She took me on a trial basis for one month and made no promises of success given the amount of catching up I had to do. School started on October 1, but I was to start classes with her on September 1. I was happy and excited.

⚜

I met Françoise, who became my best friend, in the subsidized restaurant. She was six months older than I, tall, well-dressed, and slender, with shoulder-length black, curly hair, dark eyes, and a full, sensuous mouth accentuated by red lipstick. I thought she was strikingly beautiful. She went to the restaurant with her father. Both her mother and her little sister had been murdered. Françoise worked in a small film distribution agency, Filminter, and she helped me get a part-time job there.

In the office, Françoise and I worked well together, though we wasted time when our boss was not around. One time during a heavy downpour, we made little paper boats and threw them from our window into the gutter, watching them sail away. The office building we worked in was on the street leading to the Lycée de Garçons (secondary school for boys), and it was lined with bookstores. Boxes filled with secondhand books were put out on the sidewalk, and I always browsed through them. These books were incredibly cheap so that even I could afford to buy them. I picked up a number of classics that way. One book that left me puzzled was *Madame Bovary* by Gustave Flaubert. I could not understand that woman. She had a perfectly good husband and she was throwing him away, spent money well beyond her means, and above all, she neglected her child. How could she do that? Living through the experiences I had just gone through, Emma Bovary was incomprehensible to me.

After lunch, I was often late for work because it took more than an hour each way to get back and forth from our room on the Chemin des Sept Deniers to the office, and the idea of packing a sandwich had not yet crossed the Atlantic. The subsidized restaurant closed after a while and other eateries were prohibitively expensive, so I had to go home for lunch. I tried to walk fast, but the injury to my calf from Switzerland gave me painful cramps.

Françoise and I spent lots of time talking about the pain our parents inflicted on us. Her father was a difficult man, and life with my mother had become one of constant crises and emotional outbursts. On the rare occasions we went out with members of the opposite sex, Françoise got all the attention. At seventeen I still looked like a kid, was badly dressed

*Edith in Toulouse, 1946, wearing the coat
she had turned inside out in the hospital.*

in hand-me-downs, and makeup or lipstick were not part of my world. One day, Françoise's father and my mother decided to send the two of us to the opera to see *Così fan Tutte* by Mozart. The show was dazzling, but Françoise and I couldn't figure out what was going on because we didn't know the story and there were no surtitles. Still, it was exciting to be at the opera. That summer, Françoise and her father decided that she should go to Cheltenham, England, to live with her aunt. She would spend a year there and learn English. We parted tearfully and promised to write.

All this time, I had been corresponding with Miriam. Out of the blue, she sent me an invitation to come and visit her. She and her husband were running a *maison d'enfants* in Malmaison, a suburb of Paris. She offered to let me stay with her for a month. I jumped at the opportunity and, with my mother's blessing, I left for Paris at the beginning of August 1946. Monique did not remember me, so I had to curb my enthusiasm. She had grown up, and her mother had trained her in good table manners. The Dybniz also had a new baby boy who was cared for by a nanny. During my visit Miriam was very nice to me. She didn't criticize me and allowed me to spend my days as I wished.

I had a nice month. I visited Josephine de Beauharnais' castle in Malmaison. I went swimming in the Seine and came out covered with oil. It's a miracle I did not get sick! Leon was still in Switzerland, but I saw Otto Steinmetz and Jacques Hepner while I was there. Both of Jacques' parents had survived the persecution along with his twin sister, and they reclaimed their apartment in Paris. Jacques looked good in a stylish suit and modern rimless glasses. Leon, who had lost both parents and his two younger siblings, and I thought Jacques was a very lucky boy, but something must have been desperately wrong because he committed suicide several years later.

Otto's story was different. He was nineteen and worked at *Paris-Match*, the well-known picture magazine. He was a dedicated Communist who spent his nights putting up Communist posters. This was against the law and, if he were caught, it could have landed him in jail. He also didn't bother continuing his education. That, I thought, was a mistake, and I told him so, but he only had eyes for the Party. We met under the Arc de Triomphe on the Champs Elysées. He told me that the concierge's daughter was running after him, but he was not interested in her. He talked to me about free love. I encouraged him to get more schooling and work for his own future, and we promised to write.

As August came to an end and I made my preparations to leave, Miriam asked me to stay and take care of her little boy. So that's why she had invited me to Paris! I was surprised just the same. Didn't she realize I was going back to school? I had told her about it, but she didn't believe me and pooh-poohed the idea. She told me it was an impossible task and not even worth a try. I left Paris without her moral support.

While I resumed my secular education, my sex education was nonexistent. For my mother, sex was a dirty word. To be pregnant was embarrassing. When I asked her why, she said that it showed the whole world you had sex with your husband! To which I replied, "Of course you have sex with your husband." I was almost eighteen years old and needed to get the facts. I bought a book, *Au service de l'amour* (In the Service of Love), written by a doctor. It gave me anatomy, physiology, and words of advice. While I did not agree with everything, at least I felt informed and my curiosity was satisfied.

17. SCHOOL AT LAST

Starting in September 1946, I began preparing for the *Baccalauréat*. In the French system, the *Baccalauréat* is a rigorous exam graded by teachers who do not know you, always recruited from out of town. Grades during the year did not count and you had to demonstrate a solid understanding of the material. The *Baccalauréat* covered all the general education courses in science (physics, chemistry, biology, astronomy, botany, and psychology); math up to trigonometry; two required foreign languages; philosophy; world geography; European history; and composition, writing, and research skills. It was a year of enormous effort and single-mindedness. I did nothing but study: no dates, no movies, no outside jobs, no sports except on Sunday mornings when I went for a walk or a swim, and I got very little sleep. Fortunately, I was in good health and could handle the physical and mental rigors. I got up every morning at six, did my exercises to retain good posture, and walked to school where I spent the entire day except for the lunch hour. I studied at least until midnight, and this went on for seven days a week.

Three people gave me moral support: Denise Noyon, my current teacher, Mme Brun from Nice, and the English teacher from Mende. Mlle L was very supportive and thought that I could do it, even though almost no one else did. My mother did not realize what I was up against, but was willing to give me a chance. Everyone else thought I was facing an impossible task and would fail. But, I recalled the words of Pierre Curie: "*Il faut faire de la vie un rêve et faire d'un rêve une réalité*" (We must make of life a dream and then turn the dream into reality), so I went to work to make my own dreams come true.

I absorbed knowledge like a sponge. I was fluent in German, had some background in English, and could read, write, and spell French without mistakes. I wrote easily because of my extensive writing in my diary, so I could write half-page essays without difficulty, but I had to learn how to write literary research papers. This required knowledge of French literature, the history of ideas, and the ability to organize my thoughts and present them in a coherent fashion. I knew arithmetic and my multiplication tables, but I had to learn algebra, geometry, and three-dimensional geometry. I also had to improve my vocabulary and do more reading in French and English literature. In German I did not have to do much, but I was petrified that they would ask questions about German grammar. That's why I took English as my first language and German as my second language.

I started my studies bright and early on September 1. Because I was so far behind and had so much catching up to do, Mlle Noyon would not promise anything. That's why I had a trial month before the regular start of classes. My first assignment was to write a self-portrait. I had nothing good to say about myself. I thought I was unattractive, fat, stupid, and that I had *mauvais caractère* (a bad disposition). I was also convinced that I had a mental block for math. I only saw one positive trait and that was that I had a lot of good will. While thinking about myself, I discovered to my surprise that I had courage.

Unsure of my math ability, Mlle Noyon started me on Latin and loaded me up with reading assignments and algebra. One day she gave me seven pages of equations to complete in one night. I brought them back without a single mistake. While it was obvious that I understood the material, she also noted that my accomplishment showed tremendous powers of concentration. When she asked one of the other students whether this meant she should give me more or less homework, he said less, but she said I should get more. And so she did. Of course I never complained because I knew it was necessary. When the math went well, she dropped the Latin so I could concentrate on math and French literature while keeping up with my English.

Then came a bombshell.

For a whole year, I had been throwing up once a month, like clockwork. Each time, my mother found a way to blame me—it was something I ate away from home, or I went out with my coat unbuttoned and caught a cold in my stomach—she was full of *boobe mysehs* (grandmother's tales). Before I went to Paris to see Miriam in July, I had another episode. I did not want to see a doctor, and I asked my mother to get me a laxative. I was so insistent that she went to the pharmacist to buy one and told him why. He told her he would be glad to sell her one but, he said, if I had appendicitis, it could kill me. With that I had to yield and see a doctor.

Dr. Cohen came to the house. After I had come back from Switzerland, we had gone to see him because I wanted to lose weight. He said that he would have to give me injections and check my heart frequently because there was some danger. I had just gone through some serious illnesses and I was not about to jeopardize my health, so I said no. He was married, but Françoise told me he'd made a pass at her. I thought it was because she was so pretty, but then he tried the same thing with me. After that, I never went back alone, though I did not tell my mother about it. He examined my belly and said I had chronic appendicitis. He said there was no urgency, but the appendix should come out. I went to a public hospital for the exam where the surgeon was surrounded by medical students, some of whom I knew, and so I was embarrassed to lie there with my belly exposed. I was told that I had a choice of whether or not I wanted my appendix taken out, which left me confused. Even so, we tentatively scheduled the surgery for September.

Because of my academic workload, I did not want to take time off to have an appendectomy, especially since the surgeon was so iffy about it. So my mother went to see Mlle Noyon and asked her to prevail upon me to have it removed. I would have the surgery done as a public charity case. Before the surgery, Mlle Noyon loaded me up with a pile of books to read in the hospital.

The hospital was run by the Sisters of St. Vincent de Paul, who wore big, royal blue, woolen skirts and large, white, starched hats shaped like funnels, blocking their side vision. They led us in the *Pater Noster* prayer every morning and every evening. I was placed in a ward with twenty other patients. On the morning of the surgery, I was told to walk down to the operating room in my hospital gown and to be there by 10 a.m. The surgeons were running late, so I was waiting, standing in the doorframe in the chilly fall air. Around 11 a.m., a bloody accident victim arrived and he took precedence. Finally around noon, my turn came. They put me to sleep with ether, and the next thing I knew I was in my bed with an orderly slapping my cheeks to wake me up. By then it was 1 p.m. and visiting hours began. As soon as my mother showed up, the orderly left and I kept throwing up from the ether. I wanted to be a hero in front of my mother, but I had no control over my nausea.

For two days I received neither food nor water and no IV. For seven days after that, I was only allowed liquids. Moving my right leg was painful because they cut into muscle tissue. Coughing or laughing was painful.

After nine days, they took out my stitches and sent me home. I had lost ten pounds and looked nice. Best of all, I no longer had a bloated abdomen and my stomach was flat! So that's what it was! The surgeon later told me that my appendix was very inflamed and it was a good thing it had been removed.

After a few days at home, Mlle Noyon pleaded with me to return to school because she was holding up her math lessons until I came back. Two weeks after surgery, I was back in school, leaving my books at home to avoid carrying heavy things, and riding the streetcar instead of walking. By then, I had read only some of the books she had given me.

Now Mlle Noyon had a full complement of students, ranging in age from twelve to eighteen. We were an odd lot. There were two music majors studying at the Conservatoire for half a day and no public school could accommodate their schedules. Anne Marie and her sister came from a well-to-do family from Blagnac. Anne Marie was very bright and pretty, and her parents wanted to speed up her education. There were a couple of students who needed the special attention only a small school could provide. There was a girl like me who was preparing for her *Brevet Elémentaire*, an exam covering the first four years of *lycée*. She only needed to catch up on two years of schooling. Mme Ginodman also sent two nineteen-year-old Jewish boys who told us they wanted to write poetry and were interested in learning, but they did not study and were gone within a month.

And now the fun really began. The pressure was on and I was working full steam. I covered the first three years of *lycée* algebra quickly. Plane geometry was all right, but when algebra was combined with three-dimensional geometry, I slowed down. I was learning new stuff every day and doing equations and memorizing theorems every night. But as things got more difficult, I needed more time

Mlle Noyon and Edith, Toulouse, 1946.

to work with the material. Yet I had to keep moving forward and I began having difficulties solving problems. My mantra before going to sleep and before doing math was "*mon esprit est lucide*" (my mind is clear). I always told myself I could do it. I used the Coué method of autosuggestion.

If I told Mlle Noyon that I stayed up until 1 a.m. to work on my problems, she would say, "Then stay up till 2 a.m." Of course I always got up at 6 a.m., no matter when I went to bed. The neighbors complained that I woke them up when I pulled my bed over the tile floor, so I pulled it out earlier, but without opening it because then there would be no room for the table.

⚜

During the school year of 1946–1947, rationing was still the rule. One day, my mother asked me to go to the bakery to buy bread with rationing coupons that were about to expire. I forgot. This led to an incredibly angry explosion on her part. In my diary, I recount the episode in a detached, matter-of-fact entry of several pages, in the style of Cyrano de Bergerac's *Gazette*:

May 3, 1947

Latest news: this morning, at 8 a.m., my mother threw me out. It is with deep regret that I realize my mother is crazy. Sad, but true.

She started by beating me while screaming abominably, with the laughter of a Fury and an animal satisfaction in her eyes. Her face was lit up and I saw a sadist in front of me in the process of satisfying her instincts. As I defended myself, pinching her to make her let go of my hair that she was pulling hard, she started to hit me even harder, pinching me, twisting my mouth, my nose, and hitting my face.

I remained silent, my face closed, eyes dry, looking at her as a spectator, but with a feeling of deep sadness because I realized that my mother was crazy, her passions unleashed. I was the only person on whom she could vent her animal instincts, and she took advantage of that. Then she started to cry, her face congested, eyes red, and white saliva coming out of the corners of her mouth. It was horrible to see. I who love beauty, who want to see only beauty . . . Alas! My mother is crazy. What to do? I can't put her into an asylum.

From time to time she would let go, with screams that would break a heart of stone. I was not moved. I looked. I waited . . . for the end. Once she twisted the ring finger on my left hand which weakened my hand. Then she came back, twisting my face the way you twist laundry, beating me as if I were a carpet to get rid of its dust. I was a little handicapped because of my left hand, but I held on to her arms anyway. With her arms held and unable to do as she pleased, she found nothing better to do than to bite me. So be it. Finally she wanted to take away my keys, searching in my schoolbag, my pockets, in all my things, but unable to find them. In the process she took away some vitamins that were in my bag. Fortunately they only cost four francs. So I'll be able to replace that. I feared that she would find the seventy francs I had saved by economizing on a thousand little things and that I will need now.

Finally she allowed me to look for the keys by myself. But I didn't remember where they were. I heard her scream, swearing that I would not put a foot outside the door before handing her the keys. Maybe I was wrong. I don't know myself. But there was no other solution. And when I finally found the keys, I gave them to her without hesitation. I managed to stop her from shoving me when I left and I walked out with my usual greeting and a "see you later."

At one point she had tried to drag me out of the apartment by pulling my sweater, and she tore it in the process. During the entire assault, I remained calm. At the beginning I was perfectly calm, although my hands were trembling. I think I was breathing faster. That's all. But I did not cry, did not feel like crying, I just looked. Once outside, I could not hold back a few tears. It was the reaction. I walked slowly, arriving at the edge of the canal. I tried to get hold of myself. It was difficult. I was thinking of the previous night when my mother had come home at 10:30 p.m.

I had started to study in bed, everyone was asleep. Then she started to talk to me. She spoke for at least a half an hour, in a monologue, sometimes raising her voice, always insulting me, swearing, promising me lots of unpleasant things, sometimes stopping to catch her breath, but only to start up again with more vigor. At first I tried to study in spite of her, but since she kept going, I closed my books and notebooks and crawled under the quilt, stuffing my ears. Since I could hear her anyway, I began to talk to myself, repeating always the same thing in a low voice, so as not to hear what she was saying, "*tu me casses les pieds*" (you bug me, you bug me, you bug me). Then I got upset. I began to cry. Finally I prayed for help. When she had enough, she stopped and I, very calm, fell asleep. My only regret was that I had not studied.

Translated from French by the author.

I went to school with my books. When I came back in the evening, she was not home and the door was locked. I waited on the back porch until 10 p.m. I was locked out. I did not know what to do as I had no idea where she was, nor when she would be back. And I had not eaten. There was a home for Jewish children in town, so I went there and asked to spend the night. It wasn't too far from our house and I was sure they would take me in. They gave me supper, but I could not study. The place was filled with noisy younger children, and there was no room set aside for study.

The next morning I went back to school, unprepared for class. During the day my mother showed up, angry. She accused Mme Ginodman and Mlle Noyon of wanting to take away her child. My mother dragged me and the social worker to the police station. The *commissaire* (police commissioner) listened first to my mother's complaints; then he questioned the social worker. When my turn came, he asked me what I wanted. I told him I just wanted to be left alone in order to study. I don't know whether he expected me to be some kind of juvenile delinquent, but he looked puzzled and dismissed us with a wave of his hand.

My mother had frequent emotional outbursts, always at the tenth decibel, wherein she criticized and blamed me for everything that wasn't right in the world. Initially, I shouted back, but Mlle Noyon advised me to stop responding. When her shouting was too much for me, I learned to leave the apartment and wait at the entrance of the house for her rage to subside. This could take more than half an hour. Then I would go back in. She remained a constant source of pain and anguish during all the years we lived together.

During that time, I also kept up my correspondence with friends from Switzerland including Leon, Jacques, and Otto. My mother was in the habit of opening all my mail, even mail from my former teacher, Mme

Brun. I recalled that she had done the same thing to my brother in Genoa. When she discovered that Otto was talking to me about free love, she went ballistic and forbade me from corresponding with him, as though anything could have happened between us with me in Toulouse and him in Paris. No matter. Mail was very important for me, so I followed Kurt's example by having my letters sent care of *poste restante* (general delivery) and I would stop at the post office several times a week to see whether I had mail. A letter from a friend could make my day. In those years I had no close friends in Toulouse. When Françoise came back from her year in England, she commented on how much I had changed while she was the same. This was true. We parted as friends, since there was no reason we couldn't stay on good terms even though we'd drifted apart.

During my year at the Cours Noyon, my mother lost her job. My scholarship covered my tuition and gave me a tiny subsidy, so my mother had to keep working. She found piecework with a different furrier sewing linings into fur coats and putting on buttons. This was work she could do at home. Every morning I carried two fur coats along with my books and dropped them off at the furrier on my way to school. I picked up two more coats after school. This job was not enough to cover our living expenses, but she did it for quite some time until she found another job.

I thought my mother was old, but in 1946, she was only forty-three. She was in her prime, but she acted old. She walked slowly, had me do all the cleaning, laundry, carrying water from the fountain, heavy work around the house, and had me carry her bags in addition to my book-filled schoolbag. She gained back all the weight she had lost during the lean war years. She was a large woman who weighed about 200 pounds.

I tried to make up for what my mother had lost. I understood that losing a husband and son in the Holocaust must have been unbearably painful. In the immediate postwar years and for the rest of her life, she focused on their pain. If she woke up during the night, she would dwell on their anguish. When she ate something good, she had trouble enjoying it. She mourned her son more than she did her husband. Once I took her to see an operetta in Toulouse and she felt guilty for having a nice evening "when . . ." She surrounded herself with books on the Holocaust and tried to make me feel guilty by declaring that I did not remember Papa and Kurt.

For a long time I tried to make up for her losses as best I could, until I realized that no one replaces anyone else, nor was it healthy for me to try. Over the years, she compared me to my poor dead brother, insisting that he would have been the good child. It was futile to compete with the dead. She could be cruel and once she blamed me for his death. What twisted thinking caused her to arrive at that conclusion was beyond me. Fortunately for my sanity, I rejected her views.

But, I made allowances for her behavior. I was raised on the "Honor thy father and mother," until one day the wisdom of the Ten Commandments struck me: it did not say, "Thou shalt love thy father and mother," only honor. That I could do. This realization removed the guilt I felt for no longer loving her. And yet love was what she craved more than anything else.

On top of everything else, my mother was very bossy and treated me like a young child. During a visit to another doctor, the physician told her I was growing up and she should give me more independence. When I heard that, I whispered, *"Mir aus der Seele gesprochen"* (my feelings precisely). My mother got very angry and left in a huff. It must have been pretty obvious for him to notice it in the course of a brief visit.

She never shared her concerns with me and I was never part of her decision-making process. There were a couple of Jewish widows and a widower nearby, and she spent her evenings and weekends talking to them. I never questioned this at the time, but now that I have grown children, I find this strange.

Edith and her mother in Toulouse, 1946, wearing coats sent by Aunt Anny from New York.

As for me, the events of World War II presented many challenges: confronting the horrors of the Holocaust, dealing with my mother, learning to accept and get used to the loss of my father and brother, getting an education, and coming to terms with life as I saw it. In the immediate aftermath of the war, no one seemed to address the profound moral, spiritual, and philosophical implications raised by the Germans' behavior toward the Jews and others, and the complicity of the Western democracies and of the Vatican through their silence and inaction. There seemed to be no interest in exploring deeper, spiritual concerns. But I needed answers if I was to go forth and lead a constructive life.

Given the horrors we had just experienced, Judaism's basic tenets provided neither answers nor explanations. I only saw needless suffering. As a child, I saw my very observant parents—my father's daily prayers with *tallis* and *t'fillin*, the kosher home, observance of Shabbat and holidays, my mother's monthly trip to the mikvah, and so forth. My father truly lived his religious faith. While I was in hiding and through most of my stay in Switzerland, I became very religious, falling back on the faith of my childhood. I prayed every night for my father and brother, I recited the *Mode Ani* in the morning and the *Shema* at night. My loss of faith in Switzerland was a major blow because God had been such a source of strength for me. It had been my rock to which I turned at all times. And then? Nothing. I was alone. There were moments of profound despair. The kind of Judaism I was raised with did not explain anything for me. It emphasized obedience to God and the moral precepts of the Torah. But in the aftermath of the Shoah, the questions raised were not dealt with. Everyone, Jews and Holocaust survivors included, was eager to get back to work, back to normalcy, back to rebuilding their lives.

Since Judaism was not helpful, I kept searching because I somehow had to come to terms with the Holocaust and the absolute evil it represented. After the war, the bookstores were filled with new editions of Franz Kafka, Heinrich Heine, and Bertolt Brecht along with André Maurois, Jean-Paul Sartre, Albert Camus, and many other authors suppressed during the German occupation. Among the books on display in the store windows were many on Eastern thought. Books on Hinduism and Buddhism sat side by side with existentialism. I read voraciously, seeking answers from different sources.

Christianity, through my limited knowledge of those beliefs, fared no better than Judaism. While not denying the importance of faith, neither the divinity of Jesus nor the redemption of man's sins through the crucifixion and the suffering of Jesus made sense to me, nor could Christianity explain the depth of evil and depravity we had just witnessed, at the hands of Christians no less. While the Hindu gods could be confusing to a Western mind raised in monotheism, the idea of reincarnation appealed to me. It provided new avenues of thought for the inexplicable. Given the enormity of the crimes committed and of the suffering caused, no human justice could redress the balance. The one assumption I made was that life had to make sense, and that what I saw of it only represented the tip of the iceberg.

Another important insight came from the novella *Colomba* by Prosper Mérimée. *Colomba* took place in Corsica and described an ongoing feud or vendetta between two families: the della Rebbias and the Barricinis. To avenge the death of his father allegedly at the hands of the Barricinis, the head of the della Rebbia family was obligated to kill the head of the Barricini family to defend his family's honor. The Barricinis in turn were honor bound to kill the head of the della Rebbia family. Like a ping-pong ball, the hatred went back and forth between the families over generations. I saw where hatred and revenge led and decided that I had the power to stop the hatred with me: I did not have to return hatred with hatred.

That insight, coupled with my conviction that life had to make sense, allowed me to let go of hatred and leave it to the universe to somehow restore the balance. The need to bring perpetrators to justice, however imperfect, remained because we need to live in an orderly civil society under the rule of law. But I was fully aware that even the death penalty for perpetrators would not restore the balance for all the suffering they had caused.

My reading also led me to eighteenth-century thinkers. I concluded that we did not need rules issued by a divine authority. We could follow the humanism of the eighteenth-century philosophers as a guide to ethical behavior. This freed us from rules that no longer made any sense. Only it was not enough, so I continued to search. It was a slow process and there were moments of profound despair, but I had to find answers and I had to find meaning because what I saw of life was unfair and unjust. In the end, it was my studies that contributed to opening my eyes. The order and vastness of the universe, the parallel between the microcosm and the macrocosm, the continuum of life from mineral to plant, from plant to animal, and from animal to human led me to see intelligence at work, a nurturing of life in all its forms, an infinity that I, who had trouble with simple math problems, could not begin to fathom.

What was I to make of this universe subject to immutable laws? There seemed to be an intelligent order, but what was its source? I began to recognize a divine force manifesting throughout the universe. My understanding of the divine began to shift away from my childlike view. Just like the sun shines on the good and the bad, just like the rain falls on the fields of the good and the bad, so this nonjudgmental creative energy was the same for everyone. This kind of life-sustaining force was universal; it was the creative source of all life. What differed was our understanding of this divine energy. But there was no separate creative force for Christians, Jews, Muslims, or Buddhists, good men and evil ones. It was the same divine intelligence, the same creative source of all life for every man, and that made us all brothers.

As I grappled with these profound spiritual and philosophical ideas, I began to develop my own *Weltanschauung* or worldview. My idea of a divine presence was that of a benevolent, life-sustaining, intelligent force that does not judge us. We judge ourselves. I must do my best in my own sphere while continuing to strive to grow, understand, and improve myself. If we create peace, harmony, understanding, and love in our own little world, we will have increased peace and love in the whole world. Still, I kept my ideas to myself because my views were at odds with those of people around me. Given my mother's ideas and temperament, I learned early on not to share my thoughts with her. Nor was anyone even interested in addressing spiritual concerns as people were focused on solving current social problems. As for the survivors of the Shoah, most of us were busy picking up the pieces and rebuilding our lives, and we didn't have much time to search for answers. Nor did we receive any psychological help to deal with the horrors.

⚜

As we got closer to the exam, Mlle Noyon pinned our hopes on the literary dissertation. For an entire month, I wrote a composition every day under exam conditions: I was given a topic, blank sheets of paper, and three hours. The French routinely published the dissertation topics given at the *Baccalauréat* in previous years, so there was an ample supply of topics available. I recall a few of them. One was, "History justifies anything we want, according to Voltaire." Another topic was a paragraph from a sermon by Bossuet wherein he vigorously defended the absolute monarchy by divine right of King Louis XIV. Did Bossuet defend the absolute monarchy so strongly because he could see that it was on its way out? Of course you could not simply give your own ideas. After restating the topic, you had to provide the pros and cons of the issue by citing various authors, either literally from the many texts we were required to memorize or by referring to their writings. In the end, you could give your own conclusion based on the previously quoted material. By the time exam day arrived, writing a paper had become second nature. The written tests took two days. Three hours were for writing the composition, three hours for math, three hours to translate a piece about an antediluvian animal from English to French, and three hours of German translation. I did well, except for the math problems, but I passed.

Once you passed the written exam, you faced orals in French, English, math, history, and geography. There was no time to study history that year and I managed to get a medical deferment to take the oral exam in the fall. I was truly exhausted and the excuse was not faked. It gave me the summer to bone up on history.

⚕

Vacations for young people in those days were segregated by social status: workers went on their vacations and students went through the Office of University Tourism. Since I had left-leaning views, I idealized blue-collar workers and chose to go to an inexpensive camp for young workers for two weeks. Though I was poorer than most of my fellow campers, they rejected me, to my surprise, because I was preparing for the *Baccalauréat*. There was only one other student in the camp, and I ended up spending most of my time with him talking or playing ping-pong.

When I got back to Toulouse, Mlle Noyon gave me a massive tongue-lashing for taking off those two weeks. After that, I buckled down. At the oral in September, I did well in English—they thought I had a good pronunciation. I boned up on my math theorems and did a competent *explication de texte* (analysis of a text). My history results were poor compared to my other grades. Most of the material was new to me, so my knowledge was flat so to speak, because I couldn't distinguish between important events or major trends and secondary ones. I remembered details without understanding the whole picture.

But, happily, I passed. I had achieved the seemingly impossible. Mme Brun shared in my triumph and remained very encouraging. I happily wrote to Miriam about my success. Her response was acid, "It's not passing the exams that counts, but only what you absorb." After that, I stopped corresponding with her. I wrote to Mlle L to share my news, but by that time she had moved to Caen, the city in Normandy that had been heavily damaged during the Allied landings. That was just like her. She knew there would be much work to do and a great need for healing the physical as well as the emotional scars of the war. After she moved, I lost track of her. The following year I went to the Lycée de Jeunes Filles in Toulouse to prepare for the second *Baccalauréat*.

Although I had passed the exam, I realized that I did not have the same depth of knowledge as someone who had completed six years of *lycée*. But I had acquired skills and the ability to think things through. It was as though someone had pried my head open and inserted a wealth of knowledge and ideas. Best of all was that I felt I had learned to think more rigorously and I could now figure things out for myself. I finally stopped having the sense of being buffeted by others, and it felt wonderful. Above all, perhaps I was not as dumb as I thought because I knew that getting my *Baccalauréat* was quite an achievement.

⚜

Denise Noyon became the dominant figure in my life and I idolized her. She changed my life by taking on the challenge of helping me earn my degree under incredibly adverse circumstances. When it was all over, she said she would never again help anyone make up six years of schooling in one—only two or three years at most. She knew she had pushed me to the limit and beyond. She also helped me cope with my mother. She told me I was intelligent, that I was to accomplish important things, and that to do so, I had to isolate myself and stay away from people. This advice was constant and runs like a theme through my diary. I accepted everything she said as if it were gospel truth.

Mlle Noyon came from a very conservative, French Catholic family from Lille. She said her family had aristocratic roots, but they had dropped the *particule*, the "*de*" that denotes aristocracy. She lived with her parents in a house where two rooms had been set aside for her school. In order to earn enough money, she did bookkeeping on the side. She never married. When my mother threw me out, I went to school without breakfast, so Mlle Noyon sat me down in her little yard and brought me coffee and some bread. She asked me to speak in a low voice so that her parents wouldn't hear. She was feeding me behind their backs; I thought that was strange and later, I wondered whether it was because I was Jewish.

She also said she was clairvoyant and into psychic phenomena. To enhance my ability to perform academically, she would frequently hypnotize me. I always remained conscious of what she was doing, she never made any suggestions that I was not comfortable with, and I always remembered what she said. She would have me relax on her bed. To speed things up, she would apply pressure under my brow bone near the bridge of the nose. I was never out. She calmed me down and relaxed me, especially to help me cope with my mother. She also fed me suggestions via the Coué method to help me with my schoolwork. I used her ideas for my own autosuggestion, especially for solving math problems.

Some of her contributions to my life were less beneficial. As a clairvoyant, she said that she helped physicians diagnose illnesses. (In those days we could not look inside the body as we can today.) Now that I understand a bit more about clairvoyance, I know that it is not one hundred percent foolproof. But at the time, I was led to believe that it was as clear as normal vision. A series of incidents should have opened my eyes. Once, upon arriving at school, she told me she heard that I had made a flippant remark to some people in the outdoor market about my Jewishness. This was untrue and totally out of character for me. After years of persecution, the last thing I would have done would be to assert my Jewishness. But instead of asking where she got this information, I assumed that someone had badmouthed me. In fact it must have been something she had "seen" or "picked up," possibly given her own anti-Jewish sentiments. Another day she told me that some Jewish students had sent a fire truck to her house; on a different occasion, it was an ambulance. This frightened her elderly parents half to death. I believed that, too. There were more stories along the same line. She expressed a great deal of anger and hostility toward the Jewish students she accused of doing this to her. I questioned some of the students she was accusing and they had not done anything of the sort. Now I realize she must have imagined all that. She was probably not lying, but she was playing with visions. She may have seen images that corresponded to her preconceived notions.

She fed me the lives of saints. I read the story of St. Teresa of Avila. I did not relate to her strict asceticism, nor could I ever accept the idea that the suffering of one person could relieve the suffering of another. St. Teresa would walk and inflict pain on herself in order to relieve the suffering of the missionaries in Africa. That did not make sense to me. She also gave me a biography of St. John Vianney, who was *Curé d'Ars*, a parish priest who experienced poltergeists and other supernatural phenomena.

*Edith and Mlle Noyon. This photo was taken in 1956
when Edith visited Mlle Noyon in Lille.*

He taught that dancing was sinful and I, who so loved to dance, refrained from doing so for a long time. Once, my mother dragged me to a Purim ball where I met an old friend. He invited me to dance. While I did not refuse, I purposely was so stiff that he asked me if something was wrong.

Finally she gave me *The Rosicrucian Cosmo-Conception* by Max Heindel. This book was outside the teachings of the major Christian churches. It was for initiates and dealt with esoteric teachings and mystical Christianity. The book was written at the end of the nineteenth century and drew on Christian mysticism from the medieval period. I discovered for the first time that Christians accused Jews of killing their Savior. It also reflected the racist ideas that led to discrimination against Blacks and Jews. Needless to say, Jews were presented in a bad light. The book had a negative impact on me. I was not equipped to deal with these accusations and it was certainly not what I needed at the time. It made me feel guilty and I even apologized mentally, though I had no idea whether these accusations were true or false, nor did it make sense to me to punish people for things that happened two thousand years ago.

At the time, however, my devotion to her was absolute. In my eyes she could do no wrong. She had done so much for me; she had turned my whole life around, mostly for the better. Besides, there was no one else to talk to or to provide a counterweight to her influence.

18. THE SECOND BACCALAURÉAT

I was accepted at the Lycée de Jeunes Filles in Toulouse. I was nineteen years old, barely one or two years older than most of my classmates who were nice girls, mostly middle to upper-middle class, many from well-to-do families. France's secular public schools were reputed to be better than the parochial schools, so they attracted good students. The first *Baccalauréat* weeded out the weaker students. Several girls were repeating this class because they had flunked the second *Baccalauréat*, something that was not uncommon.

I did not get the philosophy professor I wanted. The woman I ended up with was conscientious, but uninspiring. She had a reputation of doing a good job preparing students for the *Baccalauréat*. In her mind, her job was simply to get us to pass the exam, and so most of the time she lectured and did not allow for much discussion. During breaks she did not want to talk in order to save her voice. I expected that, as a student of philosophy, she would have made some of the insights her own instead of just teaching us who said what without delving more deeply into the subject. She was our most important instructor because we spent eleven hours with her every week. We studied philosophy, psychology, ethics, logic, sociology, and metaphysics. She viewed her own religion as a crutch and a weakness. To me, philosophy was an attempt to explain and understand the mystery of life, so I did not think this admission spoke well of her. We read Descartes' *Discourse of the Method*, Plato's *Phaedo*, and Auguste Comte's discourse on Positivism. The philosophers who came up with systems and answers to explain the riddle of our existence fascinated me, and I was disappointed every time critics found flaws in their worldviews. To me, the philosophy course was more than a required subject—it was a search for answers to my burning questions about the meaning of life. I threw myself into the subject and received good grades on the twice-monthly dissertations we had to submit. I won second prize in the subject.

In math we did calculus and astronomy. I was fascinated by astronomy since it opened up the immensity of the universe and gave me a new perspective of life on earth. Botany and biology were equally fascinating and became subjects I came to love. I loved biology so much that I thought of studying medicine, but even I realized that was an unattainable goal. Our finances simply did not permit that. We covered botany and human anatomy and physiology, but without touching on the reproductive system, even though most girls were between the ages of seventeen and twenty and should have been informed. Instead, on Thursday mornings they offered us a class in childcare where we were taught how to bathe an infant—a class that no one took seriously. We took physics and chemistry, my first exposure to both subjects. Those too were fascinating. We had lab work in biology, and I was so excited when I looked through a microscope for the first time and saw the individual cells of a thin layer of onion skin. It was from my biology class that I learned about proper nutrition. It was part of learning about the human body and its needs, and as a result I became more selective in what I ate. We also kept up with French literature and with English.

Our professor of history and geography was a short, stocky woman in her thirties with a pug nose and large, horn-rimmed glasses. The students made fun of her and she was unable to maintain discipline. The girls threw spitballs in her presence or they brought their silk stockings to mend during class. But she was an excellent teacher and I used to sit up front so I could hear her lecture. In geography we covered the great economic powers including the United States, the British Empire, and the USSR. I discovered a real love for history, and at the end of the year, I tied for first or second place in that subject. I also received two lesser awards, one for English and one for physics. Imagine my surprise when I flunked my second *Baccalauréat*. I went to talk to my philosophy professor, but she said there was nothing anyone could do. Grades received during the school year did not count. I planned to take the exam again in the fall, a common fallback.

Financially that year had been tough. Though my scholarship was extended for a second year, it was not increased in spite of France's raging inflation. To make matters worse, my mother was frequently out of work. At one point we had nothing to eat and I went to school hungry. It finally occurred to me that I could stop at the Jewish children's home for lunch.

*Classe de Philosophie, Lycée de Jeunes Filles, 1947. Edith is in
the back, far right. Her professor is in the front, center.*

I left the food in the CARE packages we received from Aunt Anny for
my mother.

A word here about Aunt Anny. After the Anschluss, she and her husband, Alfred, had fled Vienna for Paris where Alfred continued to work for
a subsidiary of Standard Oil. When France fell in 1940, they escaped to
Lisbon and boarded the last ship for Cuba where they waited for two years
for their quota before immigrating to New York City in 1942. While not
as wealthy as in Vienna, Alfred had developed an import/export business
and they were comfortable. After contact was reestablished, Aunt Anny
frequently sent CARE packages. Initially, these consisted of army surplus.
Later, she would send us clothes and some food items.

Fearful of flunking the *Bac* again, I did not allow myself to go anywhere that summer. The possibility of failing the tests was so threatening
that I stayed home and studied twelve hours a day from 8 a.m. to noon,
from 2 till 6 p.m., and from 8 p.m. to midnight. In Toulouse the weather
could get very hot and humid. That summer I started to get headaches.
Did I stop studying? No. Instead I put a wet washcloth on my forehead
and continued with my books. Of course, I flunked again. Faced with an

empty page and four hours to write a philosophical dissertation, my mind went blank. I was exhausted.

This was a disaster. Now what? I wanted to continue and try again the following spring, but my scholarship was not renewed. My mother did not know what to do. She went to see Mlle Noyon who told her that I should be allowed to try again. My teacher agreed to take me on for free, every day for half a day. The other half of the day I worked for a Spanish woman as a seamstress apprentice. My mother was concerned I should have some skills to earn a living, so she thought that working with a seamstress would be a good idea. I received no pay and she wasn't teaching me to make garments either. I took up many hems and sewed on lots of buttons. What the seamstress did was to make some clothes for us during the off-season at no charge.

It would be another tough year under Mlle Noyon's influence. She pushed me to befriend Anne-Marie and again encouraged me to stay away from other people in order to realize my potential. My diary is full of her exhortations. Anne-Marie, nicknamed Maïtou, was four years younger than I. She was very pretty, always well-dressed, and from a well-to-do family. She was very bright and we enjoyed talking with each other, but our life experiences were miles apart. Once, we were asked to sing something in class. She sang a cute little song about a girl who was a disappointment to her family because they already had two daughters and they had hoped for a boy, but her little cousin made up for that. Maïtou was praised to the skies. When my turn came, I sang "Ode to Joy." Mlle Noyon's reaction? "Yes, you sing to pitch." That's all I got. With the power she had over me, that was the end of my singing.

I finally passed the written and oral exams in June 1949. I still remember the topic of my paper. We had to discuss the rights of the city or community versus the rights of the individual. The proper approach was of course to debate the views of famous philosophers before reaching a conclusion. Many of us were concerned that the professors who graded our papers might be Communists, so we had to tread lightly, at least we thought so. After that painful experience, I never again flunked an exam. I became very disciplined and organized, often denying myself even simple pleasures in order to be prepared. Above all, I learned to walk into an exam fresh, alert, and fully rested.

By the summer of 1949, my mother and I were desperate. She was working, but her earnings were not enough for the two of us and I could not find any work. France's economy had not recovered from the war and jobs were scarce. I went to M. Levy, a member of the Consistoire (the Jewish community organization) in Toulouse. He told me a young rabbi from North Africa and his wife had just had a baby, and she needed someone to help her around the house. When I went to see her, she refused to give me a job because, she said, she could not order me to scrub the floor since I had the *Baccalauréat*. I pleaded with her, but to no avail. She would not hire me.

I went back to M. Levy who told me about a Jewish merchant who needed a sales girl. M. Finkel traveled to the *foires*, the outdoor markets, and every day he would be in a different town. It was a very low-status job, totally unsuitable for a young lady, but we were desperate. It was a choice between starvation or this job, so I took the job. It was backbreaking work. Every morning we left Toulouse between 5 and 6 a.m. and traveled for one-and-a-half or two hours to our destination. Then we unpacked the van, set up our table, pitched the overhead tent, laid out our wares, and were ready for business by 9 a.m.

I was on my feet all day, except for a brief twenty- or thirty-minute rest at lunch. We had a wicker trunk and M. Finkel would sit on it, but I was almost never allowed to sit on it. "The trunk cannot support two people." Or, "It's better not to sit because, if you then get up, that chases the customer away." So I was on my feet for twelve hours every day. On the heavy days of my period, it was murder. Around 6 p.m. we packed up our stuff and loaded the van. This usually took two hours, and then it was time for the trip home. I rarely got home before 10 p.m., and more often it was 11 p.m. I would fall into bed exhausted only to start all over again the next day.

My first day at work was the day after I had my math oral for the second *Baccalauréat*. I was in Cahors at the market when the math professor who had tested me the day before walked by. He stared at me, absolutely incredulous. "This could not possibly be the same girl who demonstrated the theorem about sines and cosines the day before," was clearly written across his face. He did not stop and I did not say anything.

On occasion we would go to a more distant town where there were only one or two big market days every year. Then we had to stay in a local hotel. The shepherds wearing black smocks and broad-brimmed hats would come down from the Pyrénées, walking all night with their herds of sheep.

They sold their animals at 4 or 5 a.m., ate breakfast, and by 8 a.m. were ready to shop for clothes, tools, and other necessities. These market days were similar to our county fairs except that there was real merchandise available in addition to farm products and, rarely, amusement park rides.

One time, M. Finkel neglected to reserve two rooms for us and there was no other room available. So he took the room for himself while I slept in the back of a truck filled with hardware. Only a canvas separated me from the street. There were revelers in the street, and at one point a street fight broke out. I did not dare stick my head out. Nor did I sleep much that night.

M. Finkel considered Sundays a half-day. I worked from 7 a.m. until 1 or 2 p.m. in Toulouse, at the Place St. Sernin. The problem was that there was no public transportation because the streetcar did not run on Sundays. I had a one-hour walk to get to the square and another hour walk back uphill in the hot summer heat to get home. By the time I got home, I was too exhausted to do anything but sleep. During the entire summer I did not crack a book or go out, nor is there a single entry in my diary during those three months.

M. Finkel never picked me up at home. Instead he asked me to wait for him on a bridge at a crossroad near the canal, about twenty minutes walking distance from my house. One time he was very late. It was 6 a.m. and I was getting chilly, so I put on the sweater I carried in my bag along with a handkerchief and my identity card. As I took off my jacket to put on the sweater, a policeman approached and rudely asked me what I was

Edith working on the foires *with M. Finkel, summer 1949.*

doing. I told him about my sweater. Still rude, he asked for my profession. He looked incredulous when I told him I was a student. By then I had figured out that he took me for a prostitute. "Do you have ID?" he asked. I pulled out my card that showed that I was a student. His demeanor softened. "What are you doing here?" he wanted to know. I explained that I was waiting for my *patron*, my boss, who was late and I was pacing because I was cold. He left, satisfied, but not without keeping an eye on me.

In 1949 there were still a lot of Germans in France. They were POWs working in France as part of World War II reparations. After four or five years they were allowed to go home. Before leaving France, they would shop. By 1949, goods were abundant in France and even the quality was improving. My knowledge of German came in handy. One day a German POW came to buy some underwear from our stand. By the time he left, I

Edith's carte d'identité.

had sold him two shirts, a sweater, and a suit in addition to his underwear. M. Finkel was very pleased. My bonus? A box of pastries.

My mother was heavily criticized for allowing me to work at this kind of a job. "For this you let her study?" her friends asked. At that time in France, nice girls did not do this work. I told her the fable from La Fontaine about the miller, his son, and the donkey. In the story, the miller rode the donkey while his boy walked alongside. People they met criticized the father for his lack of kindness toward his child, so the father let the boy ride the donkey, but people found fault because the young boy let his old father walk while he rode. Then both father and son got on the donkey, but people criticized the men for cruelly burdening the poor animal. Finally, both father and son walked. Sure enough, people called them stupid for walking when they could ride the donkey. It was my way of telling her that people will always find fault. The story made her feel better.

Throughout all this time, my mother was pushing me to get married. I was twenty-one years old. My goal was to continue my education, so marriage was the last thing on my mind. In my diary, I discovered that one of her motivations was to help me find a man of some means so that she wouldn't have to work. She clearly did not have my best interest at heart, especially since she knew that I sacrificed so much in order to study.

M. Finkel didn't start out as a *forain*. He had an engineering degree in agronomy. Before the war, he represented Massey-Harris (the precursor of Massey-Ferguson) and sold agricultural machinery. But the war turned everyone's life upside down, so there he was trying to get back on his feet. And he was not alone. The *foires* attracted a motley assortment of people.

I must have been good at selling because at the end of the summer, M. Finkel offered to equip me with a van and merchandise to go out and sell on the markets by myself on his behalf, but I said no. I was determined to go to university. Also, M. Finkel was anything but generous. He paid me *FF* 7,000. When I left to go to school, he paid my replacement *FF* 12,000. That hurt. When I asked him why, he answered, "Because you live with your mother." Didn't he know that we were in dire financial straits? In my naïveté, I did not think that anyone would take advantage of me to such an extent. He had a wife and a teenage son, who never helped his father out, but he exploited me mercilessly. Toward the end of the summer, he made a pass at me. I was not interested. Instead, I made fun of his big hands. He was hurt and that was the end of that.

19. FACULTÉ DE LETTRES

When I found out that I had passed the second *Baccalauréat*, I was over-joyed. I immediately applied to the Faculté de Lettres and was accepted. During my first visit to the school that summer, I ran up and down the empty hallways, noticing the names of the classrooms, inhaling the smell of the old building, and checking out the large amphitheater. I was like a kid in a candy store. It was a dream come true.

I looked forward to the start of school. There was a formal solemn return to classes for the *Académie*—or all the schools of the University of Toulouse. It was marked by a ceremony called *commencement*, literally meaning beginning, which was held in a large, modern amphitheater and was comparable to American convocation ceremonies with distinguished speakers. At the ceremony, three honorary doctorates were awarded. The recipients were Charles Morgan, an English author popular in France whose novels I had read in translation and whom I admired a great deal, an Italian scientist, and a Belgian economist. In my diary I refer to it as one of the most beautiful days of my life, and I was supremely happy being in an intellectual atmosphere. At the ceremony I chatted with a sophisticated young woman who sat next to me. Her name was Aline Berger and we became close friends throughout my student years. She was a philosophy major and we often exchanged notes in our search for the meaning of life.

Finances continued to be a major problem. There was no help from the university's social agency. Luckily, I did not have to pay the usual fees except for a library and an infirmary fee. By 1949, the French government had accepted some responsibility for the deportations, and I became *une pupille de la nation*, a ward of the nation, as if my father had been killed on the battlefield. I applied for and received a very modest scholarship from the French government of *FF* 6,000, definitely not enough to live on. To make matters worse, it was not paid out until February and classes began in early November. So I would hang out at the social services office to beg for jobs or for an advance of coupons for the discounted student restaurant. I had given my mother all the money I had earned at the *foires*. For books, streetcar fare, and personal expenses, I relied on the little money I earned from tutoring.

I tutored everyone and everything. Denise Noyon had me come to her school to teach German. I prepared a girl for her entrance exam to the Post Office. We did mostly arithmetic and geography. I taught German to Vietnamese students who were preparing for the entrance exam to one of the *Grandes Écoles*, the equivalent of our Ivy League schools. I tutored a neighbor girl who was preparing the *Certificat d'Études*, even though she was a hopeless case. I remember doing a translation from German to French on schizophrenia. I did whatever work I could find and never turned down an honest job.

When school started, we were told that we had to buy *des dictionnaires de Licence*, that is English and German dictionaries for that level, in addition to other books. I did not have the money to buy these expensive books, especially since I had given my mother all the money I earned in the summer. My mother was still working in a sweatshop in the garment industry in Toulouse. To earn the needed money, I decided to do piecework. Every day she brought home two suit jackets that had to be hand-finished: collar, lining, button holes, buttons. It would take me at least two hours for each coat. This lasted for about six or eight weeks until I earned enough money to buy the dictionaries. I never missed classes, but I did not do much studying during that period or get enough sleep. Healthy or sick, I had to keep at it because once I took on the responsibility of doing the work, the suit jackets had to be ready by the following morning.

In school I had to work twice as hard as the others; given the speed with which I had rushed through the classics, I had often only read a summary of the works and not the full text. That and my jobs left no time for a social life. My mother warned me that I had to choose between going to the university or clothes. Of course I chose school, which meant that I had no money for clothes. Coming up with the money for shoes was particularly challenging. Once I was invited to a Christmas party. All the women wore dressy cocktail outfits while I wore my navy blue skirt, a blouse, and a navy sweater, the same clothes I wore to school every day. At the beginning of our first year, the students organized an outing. We rented a bus, packed a picnic lunch, and took off for the nearby Pyrénées.

*Photo of Edith on a Sunday morning outing on the
Garonne, Toulouse, 1948. Taken by a fellow student.*

We had so much fun that a second outing was planned. I remember staying
home for the second trip because I needed to study. I often think about
that sacrifice because I wanted so much to go, yet I felt duty bound to stay
behind and study. Nor was there time or money for sports. I still took my
breaks on Sunday mornings with a walk, a swim, or a canoe trip in the
Garonne, usually alone. Later when the river became polluted, I paid to
swim at a pool.

The French university system was very different from American col-
leges and universities. It was a cross between American graduate schools
and independent study. Lectures were given in the large amphitheater
that held one to two hundred students, and there was little opportunity
to meet the professors except in your major. Assignments were published
in a monthly bulletin we bought at special bookstores that catered to the
needs of university students. At that time, the French started to experi-
ment with the curriculum. They introduced a preparatory year called the
Propédeutique. Instead of plunging into our major, we all had to take additional general courses covering the eighteenth and nineteenth centuries
in depth. We studied literature, history, art, music, and architecture—we
looked at those two centuries from every angle. The courses were taught
by professors from different disciplines. It was a lot of work, but it was
also very exciting because for the first time, the whole picture began to

emerge. All those little facts we committed to memory for the *Baccalauréat* fell into place like the pieces of a giant jigsaw puzzle. Suddenly, I could see the sweep of history.

I was thrilled to be in school. I had a difficult time narrowing down my choice of major. My first love was psychology, so in my first year at the Faculté I attended both my required courses and psychology classes. I could not keep it up though and besides, certain classes were reserved for majors. I found out early on that I could not have gotten a degree in psychology without spending a year in Paris because experimental psychology was not offered in Toulouse. I knew that this was beyond our means and so I dropped it. My second love was history. I took a lot of history classes and did well. One of my professors urged me to choose it as my major. When I told him about my plan to major in German, he advised me to first get a degree in history and then I could do the other stuff. That too was out of the question since I didn't have the necessary financial resources to stay in school that long.

In addition to the *Propédeutique*, we had to pass four exams to earn our degree. The material for the exams, which included in-depth knowledge of specific books, authors, and periods, was always taught over two years assuming that each student would take one test every year. With the requirements of the *Propédeutique*, that meant five years in school. Many students took longer but I couldn't afford to for we were starving, our living conditions were primitive and degrading, and life with my mother was more than stressful. To get a degree in a foreign language, the school required an additional one-year stay in the country of the target language; but I knew I could avoid that requirement since I already had native fluency in German, so I chose German with English as a second language and a French literature minor. That shaved one year off my course of study. Assuming I could pass two major exams each year instead of one every year, I could theoretically earn my degree in three years.

Our social lives, housing, and emotional or spiritual needs were of no concern to the *Académie*. There was no football team or other collegiate sports. The dean of the Faculté de Lettres was a professor with a reduced workload. He was assisted by two secretaries. That was it. The small social services office was in a separate location and served the needs of all the schools in the area: medicine, pharmacy, engineering, letters, law, and so on. Students were left to their own devices. There were no *in loco parentis* concerns. You were free to attend classes or not. Classes for each course were given once a week, not three times a week, putting greater responsibility on the student for independent study. You had to hand in monthly research papers for each subject in addition to the lengthy translations in the language departments. Exams were held only once, at the end of the year, so in theory, you could goof off most of the time, then cram at the end. To succeed in this system, you needed a great deal of self-discipline.

There were often requests to share our class notes with fellow students who lived far from the school and could not attend classes. I typed lecture summaries in the school's office, using my own notes and those of a fellow student. The office mimeographed them and I sent them out. I spent lots of time doing that—for free of course. Because of this work, I developed friendships with two young men: one was a would-be military career officer who was in Spain at the time, the other was in Tunisia. I never met either one, but we corresponded.

For me, the university provided the first casual interaction with members of the opposite sex. While I did not date, we often did things as a group, especially in the German department. One of us would volunteer to buy tickets to a Wagnerian opera or a concert for the whole group, and we would all go together. We also had a social event every year where the professor briefly honored us with his presence. I was elected treasurer of the German language club. I somehow knew who had money and who didn't, and this was kept quiet when it came to paying dues. For our annual party there was money for champagne for the professor, with wine, soft drinks, and cookies for everyone else.

At the student restaurant, I met students from North Africa. I was friendly with several Muslim students from Algeria, something that my fellow Jewish students from that country held against me. It was the time after Israel's struggle for independence and the subsequent expulsion of Jews from North Africa. Of course I should have been better informed, but I was totally absorbed in my studies. My friends were not practicing Muslims: they ate during Ramadan, consumed alcohol, and enjoyed casual interaction with French girls, well aware that they would have to give this up once they were back home. They expressed their concerns to me about that.

I also met a student from India, nicknamed Maxi. He was from Pondicherry, a one-time French town on the southeast coast of India. He was Catholic and he made fun of my interest in Eastern religions. I thought he was a brilliant young man. He studied both law and Latin, and he could get away with preparing his exams in just the last few months of the school year. It was a purely platonic friendship, but we were very close, walking together, sharing our dreams and aspirations, and exchanging long letters when he was in Paris.

My love life was nonexistent. Except for the casual contacts at school, in the student restaurant, and at the library, I did not date. There are long monologues in my diary about that. I wanted male companionship, perhaps even more than just companionship, and then I would berate myself for wanting that. But with the pressure to study for the exams in order to pass them at the first try, plus work, there was no time for romance. I should add that my appearance was probably not very attractive to young men. In 1949, I looked like a kid, wore no makeup or even lipstick, and I was badly dressed. My mother had received a small amount of money from someplace: Germany, Austria, or France, I really don't know. What did she do with that money? Instead of buying me something nice to wear, she went out and bought third-rate kitchen towels for my dowry! The quality was inferior, stiff, and nonabsorbent, as fabrics had yet to reach prewar quality, but her concern was that I did not have a bridal trousseau. Such were her priorities.

In the spring of 1950, one of my classmates, Huguette Desprats, lost her father. Her mother had died when she was three and her grandparents helped raise her. I had much empathy for her as I too had lost my father. We ended up becoming close friends. Huguette benefited greatly from our friendship because I helped her with her papers. I would proofread her German translations and monthly dissertations and make needed corrections. After her father died, her grandparents did not allow her to spend the week in Toulouse, where she had a room in a boarding house run by nuns. She now had to live at home and traveled to Toulouse only once a week for classes.

Every summer I was invited to visit Huguette's home in Cahors and also her grandparents' country house. She was very wealthy, yet she complained of boredom. I found that incomprehensible because I always had more books to read than I had time. For me those two summer weeks in Cahors were a novel experience. I ate very well and I did not have to work. Her grandparents had a full-time maid and the dinner table conversations were interesting. I was introduced to her extended family, characters all.

Her family had taken over the estate of French aristocrats at the time of the French Revolution. It was my introduction to what we called *la vieille France*.

Throughout my student days, I was wrestling with the trauma from war and persecution, searching for the meaning of life and for what I could do to help create a better world. I would bring up current problems, share my interest in culture, and talk about great men. I was rebelling against the status quo, rejecting all tradition, including my own, and seeking an understanding of the divine and the absolute. Huguette was a good Catholic and did not question anything, even though she had experienced her own personal tragedy with the loss of both parents. Instead, her goal was to live a quiet and peaceful life with few demands placed upon her. She told me, "*tu vas te casser le nez,*" that I aimed too high and risked falling down with a crash.

Huguette and Edith, university students, spring 1952.

Huguette was raised by her grandparents in a Victorian manner. With the family's daily five- or six-course lunches that lasted for two hours, Huguette became overweight and was not very active. She was very attached to her wealth, to her social position, to the pleasures of the table, and to her comfort. I concluded that trying to interest her in the pursuit of other goals was a waste of time, so I decided not to bring up my concerns and my dreams, and to limit myself to more superficial exchanges. I had responded to her initial invitation to visit her in Cahors with the idea of coaching her in German, getting some exercise, and maybe even having a party. None of this materialized. In addition to that, I was a vegetarian at that time and I avoided alcohol. So at every meal, her grandmother gave me grief. In spite of all that, we remained friends.

Mail continued to be important for me. I got letters from Jacques, fewer from Leon. Leon was working as a counselor in a home for Jewish orphans. I found out later that he had a girlfriend and he didn't write often because of the many demands on his time. While it is true that he was not preparing his future—the job he had was a dead-end job—his life was pleasant and carefree: he was a big hero to the children and his love life was fulfilling. Once he asked me in a letter whether I was happy. I had to think before answering. My studies were the fulfillment of a dream, but life with my mother continued to be a major source of stress.

After my first year at the Faculté, I worked again on the *foires* with a different employer. M. Miednik paid a little better, *FF* 12,000, allowed me to sit, but he was unpleasant. He was a chemical engineer, originally from Russia. He was married to an attractive French woman and they had three children. He too was trying to get back on his feet after the disruption of the war. Like M. Finkel, he was Jewish, though his wife was not. On the *foires*, the work was so exhausting that, again, I did not crack a book all summer, nor is there a single entry in my diary.

The social services office referred me to the local branch of a well-known bookseller, the Librairie Joseph Gibert, to help out for three weeks in the fall. Since classes in the *lycées* started about five weeks before the university, I had time to do that job after the job on the *foires* ended. The store was mobbed with long lines as all the students had to buy their textbooks for the year. I would start at 8 a.m. and work until 8 p.m. with one hour off for lunch. I remember that I needed to rest my feet at lunchtime, but I could not afford a restaurant, so I went to a newly opened ice cream parlor called the Igloo where I had a *café liégeois*, cold coffee with coffee ice cream topped with whipped cream. That was my lunch. I knew it was not a healthy diet, but I got to sit down and it was all I could afford.

One day M. Crouzet, one of my professors, walked into the bookstore. I still remember the incredulous look on his face when he saw me. He asked, "What are you doing here, Mlle Mayer?" I felt like answering, "What does it look like?" but I didn't. The fact was that, at that time, university students did not take jobs below their status. For my second year at the Faculté, my scholarship was increased to *FF* 8,000. However, that money continued to go to my mother. The money I earned from tutoring and from the bookstore allowed me to buy my books and also some badly needed clothing.

At the Faculté, my choice of studies was partly motivated by my desire to gain an understanding of what happened during the war. By studying German, I hoped to find an explanation as to how that country, that culture, which was partly my own, could sink so low. But my professors were of little help. There were two: Mlle Runacher and M. Boyer. She had been a high school teacher and her methods were geared to the *lycée*. Her lectures lacked depth, and I got little out of her class. M. Boyer was a Germanophile. He was old, loved music (the title of his doctoral thesis was "The Romanticism of Beethoven"), and he discussed neither the subject of anti-Semitism in German literature nor the horrors of Nazi Germany. There was a brief mention of Father Jahn's rabid anti-Semitism in his *Burschenschaften* (fraternal gymnastic associations) at the beginning of the nineteenth century, but that was it. The virulent anti-Semitism of the German Romantics and the long red thread of anti-Semitism throughout German history—starting with Luther and culminating with the racist ideas of the nineteenth century—were things I learned much later on my own. The arduous study of German philology, especially the sound shifts during the eighth and twelfth centuries, seemed a dry esoteric discipline that demanded much time and effort for little reward.

M. Boyer was not helpful in my academic studies either. While I received above-average grades in his classes, he denied me the top grades. There was another girl in our class whose father had been a diplomat in Switzerland during the war. She had received the benefit of first-rate schooling and she had an excellent command of German. She got the French equivalent of As. She was arrogant and well aware of her privileged status. Once as we climbed the stairs to the amphitheater side by side for our lecture class, we walked on either side of a handrail in the middle of the stairs. She turned to me and said, "There is more than this handrail separating us." At the time I didn't even realize what she was talking about, such was my naïveté.

In his tests, M. Boyer tried to "catch" you instead of using them as a learning device by giving students ample notice as to what the test would cover. Toward the end of my studies at the Faculté, still insecure and unsure of my abilities, I asked him whether he thought I was good enough to try for the *agrégation*, the top diploma for those in the teaching profession.

He wouldn't tell me. All he said was, "We'll see." Later on, I wrote to him that my employers considered me an expert in German. He wrote back, "I should hope so." It would have been nice had he encouraged me at the time.

At home, my situation—with the disgusting outhouse, the lack of running water, the obnoxious neighbors, and the lack of privacy—was still very demeaning. I recall going to school, clenching my teeth, and muttering under my breath, "I will not live like this. . . . I will not live like this." The irony was that one of my neighbors, a blue-collar worker, was jealous of me. He told me, "I too would like to push the pen." What did he know of my struggles and sacrifices? The housing situation also made studying very difficult. When my mother was home, she loved to talk, which prevented me from studying. She resented me for telling her, "Pretend that I am not home," but what was I to do? During the day, I went to the university library, with its old-fashioned green lampshades and dark wood paneling. In the evening, I went to the municipal library.

The municipal library was a new building, well-lit, warm in winter, with large tables where you could spread out your books and papers. While there was much traffic during the day, evenings were quiet as the library was filled with students. The drawback was that I had to walk home, alone, late at night. I usually took back streets to get home more quickly. It was a brisk forty-minute walk. I always walked fast, well aware that the deserted streets were not the safest place to be. The libraries worked for studying, reading, and taking notes, but not for writing research papers or preparing oral reports. For that I had to wait for the house to settle down and for my mother to go to bed, usually around 11 p.m. Then I would start working. That was the only way I could achieve full concentration and stay focused without interruptions. It meant staying up until the wee hours of the morning with the help of at least two cups of strong coffee.

On weekends it was my job to wash the floor in our tiny apartment. My mother would not even do the dishes. She let them pile up in the sink for me to wash. Ditto for sheets and towels. In general, I was the man around the house doing the heavy lifting, painting the kitchen buffet, and doing all the chores. Laundry was left for breaks in the school year. But that was the least of my concerns. My mother continually pushed me to get married. Whenever I passed a difficult exam, instead of sharing in my triumph, all she could say was, "You should only get married." In reading my diary, I discovered that she became cold and distant because I did not turn out to be the daughter she wanted. I was not like her. That was my

Edith with her mother in Toulouse, 1952.

biggest sin. So there was more rejection. However, my life was so full between my studies and my jobs that her coldness left me surprised but not troubled. My mistake was that I still tried to please her and to make excuses for her behavior.

That summer, I worked again on the *foires* and at the Librarie Joseph Gibert. My manager at the Librarie told me that I was a good salesgirl. When I expressed surprise, he said, "Didn't anyone tell you that?" Well, no one had. I should have guessed, though, because both of my previous employers had offered to set me up with a van and merchandise if I would go out and sell for them on the *foires*.

Since I passed all of my exams and because of galloping inflation, my scholarship was increased again to *FF* 12,000. Because that money continued to go to my mother, I got a job teaching German in a private school. One of my fellow students, who was Protestant, recommended me for the position. Le Collège de Ligny was a Protestant boarding school for high school students. It was my first contact with Protestants, having always lived in Catholic countries. I was so used to being discriminated against that, during my interview, I asked the director whether the fact that I was Jewish would disqualify me for the job. He shrugged his shoulders and said, "Of course not."

I spent Sunday afternoons and evenings preparing for classes. Monday morning I caught a bus at 7 a.m. After two hours, I got off in Ligny and taught until 5 p.m. The bus brought me back to Toulouse at 7 p.m. I taught classes all day with a one-hour lunch break. The faculty was made up mostly of young couples with little children. I don't think they were paid very well, but out in the country living conditions were pleasant. They were a very likeable bunch. I prepared for my classes and had a good academic year with the children. It also gave me practice in preparing lesson plans, something I had already done in the course of all the tutoring.

The headaches I had experienced during the summer spent preparing for the second *Baccalauréat* came back while I was studying for my final exams during the second year, but I was able to work through them and pass the exams. However, during my third year, the headaches started in February. I still had a great deal of material to cover and I knew that with these headaches, studying was impossible. After getting checked out by my physician friend to make sure there was nothing medically wrong with me, I designed my own prescription. Every morning I went swimming and for two weeks I did not study or even read, although I continued to attend classes. The treatment worked and my headaches went away completely. Then I started studying again for one hour at a time, then two, until I slowly worked up to seven hours. It was a far cry from the twelve hours I had spent studying previously, but I was able to keep the headaches at bay. I also learned to stay very focused in order to make every minute count.

At home, my lack of privacy continued to be a serious problem. I had to hide my books, my diary, and my correspondence from my mother. As a result I carried all these treasures around in my briefcase. I continued to read and study the *Rosicrucian Cosmo-Conception*. Some of their suggestions were useful. One involved a daily five-minute meditation exercise in the morning and the other a review of the day in the evening. One Sunday Huguette stopped for a visit. My books and notes were lying on the table. When my mother discovered them, she went ballistic. Our efforts to calm her down were in vain. Eventually, Huguette left. My mother continued to carry on, screaming I should give her all my "Christian" books. I lied and told her I had given everything to Huguette. In fact, my stuff was still lying open on the little table in plain sight where I had barely rearranged the papers. She carried on for hours. Eventually, she collapsed and went to bed. But the screaming, the threats, and the insults left me in a terrible state, my stomach churning, my head spinning and ready to explode. I had had enough. I could not take her anymore. After all my efforts for years to stay calm, to be nice to her, to be compassionate, it all seemed for naught.

The next day I went to Ligny for my usual Monday classes. I feared that, during my absence, she would rummage through my things. I was twenty-three years old, yet I had no privacy. I took all my notes with me, along with the letters from my close friends. In those letters we had shared our dreams and our insecurities, explored the meaning of life and the future. My correspondence was very important to me as these friends were close to my heart. During my lunch hour at school, I went to the kitchen, walked over to the stove, removed the cover and, one by one, burned my notes and letters from my friends. With each flame, a part of me went up in smoke. It was a searing, devastating experience. I was badly shaken. That's when I realized that anyone can lose his mind and be driven mad if enough pressure is put on him. I left the kitchen totally drained.

After that, I was ready to leave home. I could take my scholarship money and I was earning a little money on the side. I knew that financially I could manage on my own. What stopped me? It was the spring of 1952, a few months before finals. As was my habit, I had taped my class schedule to the wall in the kitchen, next to my bed. One evening, I was studying at the municipal library. At one point I was whispering to a friend sitting next to me and showing him some photos I had taken. When I looked up, guess who was standing behind me? My mother. "So that's what you do at the library?" she cracked. I remember feeling humiliated. I knew that if I left home, she would do the same thing and shame me in school. Being so close to my goal, I was not about to interrupt my education again, determined as I was not to leave Toulouse without a diploma. I stayed, counting the days to my freedom, and planning to leave as soon as feasible after the exams.

After that episode, only my determination to finish school kept me going. I put on blinders to my personal life and focused completely on my studies. Happily I passed the two remaining exams—one for French and the other for German literature—and so earned my *Licence ès Lettres* in record time. Instead of the usual four, five, or even six years, I did it in three, taking two major exams each year. I was overjoyed. Passing all my tests gave me a wonderful feeling. At that time, only five percent of French youth had earned this diploma. I must admit that I felt proud because I knew I had achieved a lot against great odds. My mother did not seem to share in my joy since her thoughts and words were always about me getting married while my focus was on completing my education. With the need to keep on working to earn some money while preparing for my emigration from France, there was no time to rest on my laurels.

One of my professors, M. Ferran, must have known that I needed to work and he recommended me for a substitute office job because the regular secretary wanted to take a month-long vacation. I ended up working for six weeks at an affiliate of Westinghouse called Schneider-Westinghouse. While there, I had an interesting experience with one coworker, a young man from a Catholic family of modest means. He was the oldest of nine children. He had his *Baccalauréat*, but his family needed the income from his job, so his dream of going on to the university was shattered. He looked up to me because I had just earned my degree and we became friends. One day in the course of our conversation, he mentioned that anyone who is not baptized goes to hell. That took me by surprise. I looked at him and told him that I was not baptized. His face sank. Finally, he managed to say in a low voice, "But you are much too nice to go to hell."

During the summer, I prepared my documents for my immigration to America. The whole process was very time-consuming. When we first applied for immigration, Aunt Anny had to provide us with an Affidavit of Support, a document required by the United States to ensure that she could support us financially and we would not be a burden on the American taxpayer. Then we were told we had to wait for our quota to come up. I was on the Austrian quota and my mother was on the Romanian. Because so much time had elapsed since we first applied, Aunt Anny had to send a second Affidavit of Support. There were many forms to fill out and questions to answer. It was during the Cold War between the United States and the Soviet Union, so when my turn came, I was carefully vetted. I had to travel back and forth to the nearest American Consulate, which was in Bordeaux. I was asked whether I had ever been a Communist or a member of the Communist Party, whether I had ever been a Nazi, or whether I'd ever been arrested. They asked me if there was any history of mental illness and I had to get a physical from a doctor approved by the Consulate to show that I was healthy. I even had to completely strip to show I didn't have any blemishes on my body. The American authorities also wanted to know all the addresses where I had lived in France. We heard from our friends in Montlaur that they had been questioned about us. Finally, I had to organize my trip to America, including passage on a ship from Le Havre to New York.

Summers were long in the south of France and I was always self-conscious to be seen in the same hand-me-down pink dress from Aunt Anny. It wasn't a bad-looking dress, but I hated pink and I hated polka dots, so I went out and bought some fabric and made myself two simple dresses. After my job ended in August I went to a two-week summer camp for students on La Côte d'Argent (Silver Coast) in Hossegor near Bayonne. It consisted of a tent city behind the dunes facing the Atlantic Ocean. I met students who only wanted to sleep with me; I was not interested. I still

Edith in the dress she made,
Bayonne, summer 1952.

believed in romantic love. I bought a ticket for the bus to Bayonne for a solo visit. With the little money I had, I bought a pound of apples at the market as food for the day and took lots of pictures including the one of myself in front of the ocean. On the way back I hitchhiked as I had no money left.

The most valuable experience I had in Hossegor was meeting a German law student, Franz G. We talked a lot. He was extremely nice and we were able to touch on the difficult subject of the Nazi period and my personal experience. He later sent me books for the thesis I had planned to write. With the books, he enclosed a card that said, "As a token, to make up a little for what cannot be made up for." I never forgot him and reconnected with him recently on a visit to Germany.

Aside from my correspondence with the Rosicrucians, I was obviously surrounded by Christians and by Christianity. I had been looking for meaning after the long years of religious persecution and found it nowhere. As mentioned earlier, I read books on Hinduism and Buddhism. I read *Vie de Jésus*, the biography of Jesus written by Ernest Renan, who was a free thinker. That book was not in line with traditional Christian thinking. All this was part of exploring life and its meaning. I also hated being Jewish, not because of its teachings, but because I hated being persecuted. Even today I don't think that a merciful God wants those who believe in Him to be gassed—for *kiddush hashem* (for the sanctification of His name). That does not make sense to me. I believe in freedom and ethics and goodness. Today, after looking at other religions, I feel that Judaism can stand up to any faith. But at the time, I did not see it that way.

Rereading my diary I came across comments made on this subject by people who were my friends. Aline said to me once that my being Jewish will cause people to *prendre un recul*—or step away—and another time she said that being Jewish was *une tare*—a blemish. This from a friend! Surrounded as I was by Christianity and Catholicism in particular, its mysticism and spirituality appealed to me. One of my good friends became a Carmelite nun. I recognized that there were subtle and not-so-subtle pressures to convert. Of course my mother's presence put a stop to those ideas. But I was not sure what I would do once I got away from her.

I corresponded with a fellow student who was a priest. Abbé Schildt was much older than the rest of us, having been a chaplain in the French Army during the war. He graduated before I did and went off to Ireland to teach at St. Patrick's College in Dublin. I was able to express my reservations to him. There was much I could not accept in Catholicism from the Immaculate Conception to the Ascension and more. The exchange with Abbé Schildt was helpful in clarifying my own ideas and he agreed that, under the circumstances, it was better for me to stay where I was. I am very glad I did not convert. The truth is that it has taken me a very long time to accept myself. I think the damage done to my self-esteem early in life left lasting marks. This becomes particularly obvious to me when I speak to American Jews who show a degree of self-assurance that I will never have.

❧

My mother helped me get ready for my immigration to the United States. She sewed on buttons and mended my clothes. Her motivation was not because she wanted me to look nice. No. She lived for the gallery. She said, "I don't want Aunt Anny to say that I sent you to her with torn clothes."

I left for the United States in November 1952. I stopped in Paris for a couple of days to say goodbye to old friends, especially Jacques, who was not doing well by then. I said goodbye to Leon and to another friend, Jean Jacques, who promised to follow me to America. That left me confused as to his intentions and I ended up writing to him *"pour en avoir le coeur net."* I needed to know whether he was serious about me. He was not.

Edith, the university graduate, in Toulouse, 1952.

The well-known French poet Edmond Haraucourt wrote, *"partir, c'est mourir un peu"* (to leave is to die a little). As my ship left Le Havre on November 14, I felt a piece of me stayed in France. I had become a French citizen, I had a French education, and although I had experienced much suffering and persecution in that country, I felt French. Now I saw myself as a wandering Jew all over again.

These thoughts tempered my sense of adventure. With my mother still in France because her Romanian quota was slower than my Austrian quota, with my thesis topic in my pocket, and with the right to more scholarship money, I was likely to come back to France once I mastered English and got to see America with my own eyes. At the same time, I was ready to date and to think about the next phase of my life—marriage and children.

America

20. AMERICA

The Immigrant

The crossing was stormy and most people got seasick; I did not. I went out on deck as long as the weather and the ship's crew allowed, and I welcomed the fierce wind and the movement of the boat. It was a strange sensation to be out in the middle of the ocean, waves crashing on deck, and the ship, a large ocean liner with three smokestacks, tossed about like a walnut shell at the mercy of unleashed elements. I took a photograph of the clouded sky pierced by rays of light that illuminated a speck of ocean. It was an awesome spectacle, almost biblical.

Among the passengers consisting mostly of immigrants and their families were a couple of young men who were medical students returning from Spain to their native Puerto Rico for Christmas break. I made friends with one of them, Octavio Hernandez, and we spent all our time together. During the trip, he brought out the Spanish version of *Reader's Digest* to teach me Spanish pronunciation. In spite of the rotten weather, his companionship made the crossing enjoyable and I have fond memories.

View from SS Liberté *in the middle of the Atlantic during stormy crossing. Photo taken by Edith, 1952.*

The ship that carried us across the Atlantic was a German ocean liner originally called the *SS Europa*. It had been given to France as part of post-World War II reparations and was now renamed the *SS Liberté*. The ship pulled into New York Harbor on

November 20, 1952. I had planned to rise early to greet the Statue of Liberty, but I overslept. As it turned out, that morning was so foggy that the tug boats pulling us into the Hudson River needed the help of foghorns.

We did not go through Ellis Island. American citizens and permanent residents were allowed off the ship upon arrival while I, along with the other immigrants, had to wait until officials from the Immigration and Naturalization Service boarded the ship. They asked to see my documents and my chest X-ray proving I did not have tuberculosis. Three hours after our arrival, I was finally allowed off the boat.

Aunt Anny was waiting for me at the pier of the French Line. The last time I had seen her, I was nine years old, but we had exchanged photographs. She also said she would carry a red book under her arm. That's how we managed to find each other on that crowded pier. Octavio waited for me to get off the boat, and he would not leave until he made sure that I connected with my relatives. He came over to say goodbye and took his leave of us. I did not have much luggage: one suitcase for my personal belongings—I didn't have many clothes—and one carton for my favorite books—Shakespeare, Goethe, French poets, and, of course, my precious dictionaries. I had left most of my other books in France with Aline. I could not leave them with my mother as they were "forbidden books."

I did not have a clear idea as to what to expect from Aunt Anny, especially since all our correspondence had been handled by my mother. For me, she was the wealthy relative who had always been kind to us. She had paid for my crossing. I was hoping to continue my education while working part-time as I had done in France, but Aunt Anny had other ideas. She told me the story of an immigrant who was not picked up with a taxi like me, but had to walk all night to get to Brooklyn where the family showed him a place to sleep. When he woke up, they handed him a newspaper with the want ads and told him to get a job. I got the message. To be fair, Aunt Anny was in no position to send me to school. The Freudenheim's financial situation was not comparable to what it had been in Vienna. She was also a bit leery lest I become a burden, and she made that quite clear to me. There were many horror stories of orphaned children brought to America by kind relatives where the relationship turned sour. She was also concerned that after my frequent moves, I would be unable to settle down, whereas my dream was the exact opposite: to lead a quieter, more normal life.

I spent a week in Aunt Anny's comfortable but small apartment on West End Avenue and 72nd Street. I shared her bedroom, sleeping on a borrowed folding bed. Alfred slept in the living room where the couch converted into a bed. She gave me little tasks to do like wiping the dust off her beautiful plants. When I repaired the lining in one of Alfred's coats, she admired my sewing skills. I had caught a cold during the crossing and she filled me with orange juice and grapefruit. The climate change from southern France to New York in late November proved a major challenge, especially since I did not have suitable clothes for American conditions. I had brought along a couple of sweaters that were too warm for America's heated homes and offices, and my overcoat was better suited to southern France where the thermometer rarely dropped below freezing. The bitter cold caught me by surprise and the icy winds from the Hudson River took my breath away.

During that week, I visited Frau Genia who lived in Washington Heights in Manhattan, then a popular neighborhood for German Jews. She and her daughter, Fritzi, and her old father had managed to leave Vienna right after the Anschluss to rejoin her brother and sister who were already in New York. My mother had taken the precaution of having us memorize their New York address so that we could find each other after the war, should we become separated. When I finally found them, I rang the bell at the apartment. Frau Genia opened the door just a crack and looked at me suspiciously. When I said, "Frau Genia," she replied in German, "*Wer sind Sie?*" (Who are you?). I enjoyed the moment before saying "Edith." She then flung the door wide open and said, "*Du hast dich nicht geändert.*" (You have not changed.) It was a happy reunion.

I also walked from 72nd Street to 116th Street to Columbia University where I had hoped to study and where I looked for a job, but the best they could offer was work in their library for $25 per week, which was below minimum wage. I could not live on that. Through her friends and acquaintances, Aunt Anny helped me find a furnished room on the Upper West Side of Manhattan on 96th Street off Central Park West. Two weeks after landing, I had a job as a file clerk working for EBASCO (Electric Bond and Share Company), a large engineering company that built power plants all over the United States. It was minimum wage, $1 per hour, and I got the job through Uncle Alfred. This was quite a letdown for me after I had worked so hard to earn my academic credentials, but I accepted it.

During the week in Aunt Anny's apartment, I must have gained ten pounds because she was a wonderful cook and gave me seconds whenever I said something was good. After I started working, I would grab a sandwich at the Automat for lunch, or I would pack a sandwich and an apple and eat them in nearby Battery Park where I could watch the ocean liners sail up the Hudson River or admire the Statue of Liberty on Bedloe Island. But dinner was always at her home. Eventually, I began to skip lunches to get my weight down again and I caught the wonderful lunchtime concerts of baroque music at Trinity Church near my office on Wall Street. It was an almost spiritual experience away from the hustle and bustle of the area, and it always left me refreshed.

Anna Freudenheim in New York.

At work, I could not understand American English as we were taught British pronunciation in France. It took me about six weeks to get used to it. In February, I signed up for an English course for foreigners at Hunter College. The instructor placed me in the advanced group in spite of my protestations because I did not think my knowledge of English was that good. In the end, he proved to be right and I benefited greatly from the class. I mastered the finer points of English grammar and worked on my pronunciation.

In general, I made no effort to meet people from the old country because I wanted to learn English as fast as possible. This was hard because my knowledge of American spoken English was not adequate to carry on a sophisticated conversation, and I missed that. I also entertained the idea of returning to

Alfred Freudenheim in New York, ca. 1950.

France within one or two years to use the scholarship and prepare more advanced degrees. When I mentioned that to Aunt Anny, her response was that I had achieved enough. She did not encourage me to work toward a PhD.

In spite of that I continued my preparation. My job was not mentally demanding and I felt that after seven-and-a-half hours at work, I still had a lot of energy to work on my projects. I lined up the books I needed to read. My plan was to work on the Czech-Austrian Jewish writer Franz Werfel. He had fled Vienna, gone to France, and managed to go to the United States. He married Alma Mahler, the widow of Gustav Mahler, who was living in Beverly Hills, California, at the time. Werfel wrote a number of books, including *The Song of Bernadette* about the young girl from Lourdes who had visions of the Virgin Mary—it was made into a Hollywood movie. He also wrote *The 40 Days of Mossadagh* about Iran. My professor M. Boyer had approved this project before I left Toulouse. Based on my diary, I also read avidly—books on America, the New Deal (which I did not fully understand), the American labor movement, philosophy, and more.

I continued to struggle with my religious identity. Some aspects of Christianity appealed to me, while the profusion of Protestant churches in the United States was incomprehensible, coming as I did from almost exclusively Catholic countries. I had no quarrel with the values that were inculcated in me from my Jewish heritage, but I'd had enough with the persecution. I kept these doubts to myself. I certainly could not discuss them with the Freudenheims who were attached to their Jewish heritage and identity. I had also toyed with the idea of going to California to the ashram run by Paramhansa Yogananda. I had read his book *The Autobiography of a Yogi* and his teaching appealed to me. Unfortunately, he died just as I arrived in America. Besides, I did not have the means to go to California, so that remained a pipe dream.

⚜

In late December, the Freudenheims left New York for Lakewood, New Jersey, and I was left alone in this big city where I did not know a soul. Not being able to communicate comfortably increased my isolation. It was very hard and I cried myself to sleep every night for months. The holidays were especially tough. I was the only one out on that snowy New Year's morning in 1953 making footprints in the fresh snow in Central Park while watching the squirrels chase each other.

With my first paycheck in my pocket, I went to Carnegie Hall and bought a ticket to a Sunday matinee concert. The kindly doorman allowed me into a dress rehearsal. I felt better after that. On Sunday, I put on my best clothes and had lunch at the famous Russian Tea Room on 57th Street, ordering the cheapest item on the menu, when who should walk in with his pencil mustache upturned at both ends—unmistakably, Salvador Dali. I also recognized his wife from his paintings, as she was his favorite model. That was exciting. Afterward, I went to Carnegie Hall to hear Bruno Walter conduct the New York Philharmonic in a performance of Mozart's Symphony No. 35 and Mahler's Symphony No. 4. I went home in high spirits.

I spent much time writing letters to my friends in France describing my impressions of New York and of America. One of the first things that struck me was that every child from every social class was wearing a snowsuit and was toasty warm. This impressed me greatly because I had always suffered so much from the cold. In general, I felt that the standard of living of the average American was closer to that of the wealthy in postwar France: everyone had indoor plumbing, central heating, and other amenities that were still not common in France at the time, even in urban areas. Another thing that came across was a sense of trust, from walking freely into stores to look at merchandise to circulating in the library stacks. Everywhere I felt an attitude of service without the pressure to buy. Finally, and this was the most important, the values were the same on both sides of the Atlantic, even if some of the customs were different. That, together with indoor plumbing and central heating, made it easy to adjust to American life. Above all, I appreciated the respect accorded to those who did honest work of any kind. In France, even my temporary job as a salesgirl in the bookstore was not considered suitable for a university student, not to mention my jobs at the *foires*. I loved the American attitude that there was no such thing as a dirty job. I loved the respect accorded to the self-made man, no matter how humble his origins.

The spring semester at Hunter College started in early February, and I developed a routine. I had classes three nights a week; going directly from work, I would grab a date nut and cream cheese sandwich at Chock Full o'Nuts before class. On Saturdays I studied English grammar, worked on my composition, tidied my room, did laundry, and ran errands to buy food

Battery Park and the Wall Street area at the tip of Manhattan.
Photo taken by Edith from a sightseeing boat, 1953.

for breakfast and lunch. Sundays were reserved for sightseeing in New York City, exploring a different area every week.

One Sunday I decided to visit Rockefeller Center. It was a gray winter day, so not many people took the tour. There might have been about nine or ten people in the large elevator when the tour guide suggested that we introduce ourselves to one another and share where we came from. Among the tourists were three young men from Germany. Since I was born in Vienna, we immediately switched to German and we spent the rest of the tour more or less together.

After visiting the rooftop with its magnificent views of Manhattan, the four of us decided to stop at the exclusive Rainbow Room on one of the upper floors. Our respective budgets did not permit us to dine at that pricey spot, so we limited ourselves to a drink. The conversation flowed freely. I learned that all three had been sent to the United States to learn about American-style banking and they worked as interns in two different banks. Since all three were in their late twenties, I assumed that they had served in the Wehrmacht—the German Army—during World War II. I don't recall the details of what I said, but it was probably limited to my recent arrival in the United States after the completion of my studies in France. They did not ask any questions and I did not volunteer additional information except that I was originally from Vienna.

It was early when we left the Rainbow Room. Having shared our interest in classical music, we decided to walk to Carnegie Hall and get tickets to a concert for the following Sunday matinee. After that, we ambled to a nearby restaurant on West 55th Street. I had been to Larre's once before and I remembered it as an excellent French restaurant with affordable prices. Everyone was pleased with the choice and we spent a very pleasant time together.

Since the evening was still young, we agreed that there was time for a movie. We ended up selecting a silly but charming movie, part of what became known as the "road pictures," with Bob Hope, Bing Crosby, and Dorothy Lamour. In the movie, the two men were explorers somewhere in the South Pacific. Both men naturally fell in love with the chief's beautiful daughter who could not decide which one she should marry. The story was set in Tahiti where everyone, including the chief, wore grass skirts and lived in grass huts with thatched roofs.

At one point Dorothy Lamour, the daughter, burst into her father's hut, exclaiming, "Daddy, Daddy, I know which one I will marry," to which the father replied, "Mazel tov!" It brought the house down. The incongruous setting juxtaposed with an expression familiar to New York audiences brought on massive laughter for everyone—except my German neighbors. They sat there, quiet and puzzled, and they asked me what that meant. At first I was reluctant to answer, fearful of what might follow. They asked me again. At that point I had to explain that it was a Hebrew expression meaning congratulations.

That's when the sky fell down. You would think that I had suddenly been stricken by the plague. Upon leaving the theater two of the young men left immediately, barely saying goodbye. The third escorted me to the subway and left. The following Sunday, someone else showed up at Carnegie Hall to make use of the tickets. I never saw any of them again.

I was deeply hurt. I had worked through the agony of the relentless persecution of the Nazi years, the horrible suffering and death of both my father and brother. I had made peace with mankind and with Germans. I was ready to view every human being as equal, created by the same life force. I had transcended hatred and I met these young men with good will, without any mental reservation, but it was to no avail. They were still brainwashed. Mentally they never left Nazi Germany. They probably forgot about this incident, but I feel the sting to this day.

⚜

The Freudenheims maintained their Viennese lifestyle. Alfred had opened an office in the Wall Street area for his import/export business and his employees were old acquaintances from Vienna. Their social circle consisted of the same friends, all well-off, who had managed to leave Vienna at the time of the Anschluss. They belonged to the Austrian Congregation on 95th Street west of Broadway, which was founded by Austrian refugees, and they had subscriptions to the Metropolitan Opera and New York Philharmonic. Aunt Anny would meet her friends for tea in the afternoon. In the summer, she went back to Bad Gastein—a resort in the Salzburg region—and later to Saratoga in upstate New York. I was initially included in the dinner parties with their circle of friends, but I must admit that I did not care for them. I found the women manipulative. Some were condescending toward me because I had no money. Fortunately, I had little to do with them and I had enough self-respect not to be affected by their judgment. Having witnessed the terrible loss of wealth and status by so many during the Nazi years, I learned early on the fleeting value of money. I learned that what mattered was not the size of one's bank account, but character and what was in one's head. I felt that my education was worth a lot more than money in the bank. At the same time, I could not count on this milieu to make friends, although one young man I met through them invited me to the Metropolitan Opera to see *Porgy and Bess*. That opera left me baffled, as I knew little about the African American experience. I wrote a review of the opera for my English class and got an A.

⚜

By the spring of 1953, my mother's quota was up and she planned to join me. I was not overjoyed at the prospect since I hoped my mother would stay in France. Her arrival in the United States put an end to the idea of returning to France as I felt that with her in the US, my ties to France were now severed. Huguette, who kept visiting her after I left, wrote that my mother could not live alone. I had no choice. I now had to find larger housing. Through acquaintances, I found a furnished apartment in a walk-up on Amsterdam Avenue and 88th Street. My mother arrived in May. She came on the Holland America line, and Aunt Anny and I picked her up in Hoboken, New Jersey. I paid for the taxi with money I had saved, and I think that impressed Aunt Anny, who had offered to pay for the cab. My mother soon noticed the closeness that had developed between Aunt Anny and me, and she became insanely jealous.

The apartment proved adequate for the two of us. One bedroom was used by the old landlady who spent her days in her daughter's apartment one floor below. We had the kitchen to ourselves and we each had a bedroom. Since my minimum wage income was not enough to pay rent and support the two of us, my mother needed to get a job. She was fifty years old. She found distant cousins who were well-off and they hired her as a cook. Since she lived with them most of the time, things were peaceful at home. Unfortunately, that did not last as she lost her job after a couple of months.

⚜

In my English class, I met interesting people. One was an anti-Nazi German who had left Germany and immigrated to America where he joined the army. He introduced me to his two favorite organizations: the Americans for Democratic Action (ADA) and the American Ethical Society. He invited me to an ADA meeting where I met a young man who took me out on several dates and after the third date, I decided to break it off. He invited me to an outing sponsored by the Young Members group

Baptism in the Passaic River. Photo taken by Edith, 1953.

Canoeing on the Passaic. Steven Cord is second from the left wearing a white shirt and sunglasses. Photo taken by Edith, August 16, 1953.

of the New York Ethical Society and I decided that since this was to be a group outing, it was OK to go. I planned to tell him at the end of the day that I did not want to go out with him again.

We took the bus to Passaic, New Jersey, and went to the Passaic River for canoeing, swimming, and a picnic. From my canoe, I saw a group of people being dunked in the river for a baptism. Since I had never witnessed such a baptism, I stayed behind to take pictures. When I caught up with the rest of our group, they looked so photogenic that I snapped another picture.

It was a fine day and I enjoyed it very much. As we got ready to leave, my date stepped on broken glass that some idiot had carelessly left on the river bank. Back in Manhattan he wanted to take me home, but I insisted that he go home and take care of his foot. Besides, I wanted to stay with the others. Those of us who lived on the west side of Manhattan decided to stop for a pizza. After that, it was time to call it a day. Steven Cord took the same bus I did and we talked a lot. At his stop he did not get off, but continued instead with me. We got to my home at 10 p.m. An hour later, we were still standing there, talking. I learned all about his hay fever and about his interest in Henry George. I had taken a course in post-Civil War US history while still in France, so I knew who Henry George was and that impressed him. He suggested I join the Young Members group for other social activities. The following Saturday, we went to see an off-Broadway show and Steve invited me to join him the next morning for a photo shoot in Central Park. That's how it all began.

Our courtship was brief. He was twenty-five, so was I, and we were both working. Once we decided to get married, there was no reason to delay the wedding. When Steve came to tell my mother that he wanted to marry me, she told him that I had no dowry. Of course he already knew that, but such was her concern. She gave us her blessing, especially since she had her wish: her daughter was marrying a Jew. After that, things deteriorated.

My mother wanted to delay the wedding until she found a job and was able to save enough money to pay for it. That would have meant a delay of months, if not years. Meanwhile my future in-laws invited us over to plan the wedding. On the way to their house, my mother informed me that she was not going to discuss it. That's when I decided to take matters into my own hands. I sat down with Steve and my future mother-in-law in the bedroom while my mother watched TV with my future father-in-law in the living room.

Engagement photo, 1953.

After that Aunt Anny, who offered to pay for the wedding, got in touch with my future mother-in-law and called my mother to report back to her. Well, that did it! My mother accused her of stealing her child—echoes of Toulouse. My mother's passionate love for Aunt Anny turned into equally passionate hatred.

Preparations for our wedding did not go smoothly. For starters, Steve received a notice from the draft board. After an initial deferral for hay fever, stomach problems, and I don't know what else, he was now called up. We decided to go ahead with the wedding anyway because as a wife, I would have certain rights should he end up in the army. Another impediment was Steve's jury duty. He was a juror on a case that went on for six long weeks. It was Steve's brother Stanley who helped us get organized by drawing up a list with over sixty items we had to do.

Meanwhile, my mother was going through menopause and acted as though she were dying. Her outbursts were unbearable. One night at 2 a.m., she woke me up by throwing a shoe at the glass door separating our two rooms. I was so frazzled I lost several pounds in the week before the wedding and I told Steve that I could not take it anymore. He reminded me that it was just one more week.

*Edith and her mother
walking down the aisle,
February 21, 1954.*

*From left to right. Front:
Steve's parents, Edith with
Steve, Edith's mother. Back:
Steve's brother, Stanley, with
his wife, Ruth, Aunt Anny
with Alfred, Steve's sister,
Rita, with her husband, Alex.*

*Front from left to right:
Frau Genia, Dora Klapholz,
Finny Seider (Genia's sister),
Steve's aunts and uncles.*

After the wedding, my mother asked me to swear that I would never see my mother-in-law again. I said that was unacceptable, she was my husband's mother, and that was that. So my mother made me swear never to see Aunt Anny again. She would not allow us to leave her apartment until I did. After squirming, hemming, and hawing for a while, I finally gave in but continued to see Aunt Anny anyway. I was uncomfortable, though, for an oath was an oath. I ended up writing about this dilemma to Abbé Schildt, my friend from school. He wrote back, "An oath is only valid if it is freely given. An oath given under duress is meaningless." I felt much better after that.

My mother continued to cause me lots of grief. During my first year of married life, her harassment gave me a bad case of the boils. I was working for a piano company on West 57th Street. At lunchtime, I was the switchboard relief operator and I called my mother every day; she would rant and rave the whole time about how Aunt Anny had stolen her daughter. Then one day, I was in the upstairs office when an employee came up to tell me that someone in the downstairs showroom wanted to see me. I put on my coat and went down. To my horror, I discovered that it was my mother, drunk. My mother, who never drank more than a glass of wine on Shabbat or holy days, pulled out a bottle of whiskey from her pocket. Her nose was red and she said, "Do you like me like this?" After that incident I stopped calling her and stopped seeing her. When I changed jobs, I did not give her my work information, only my home address.

Her Viennese gynecologist said her behavior was due to menopause and recommended dilation and curettage (D&C), a procedure that scrapes out the lining of the uterus. Of course nothing changed after the procedure, so he referred her to a psychiatrist. The psychiatrist said that if we put her in an institution, it would be the end of her and that since she was not suicidal, she really didn't need to be institutionalized. Steve and I agreed. The fact remained that my mother needed help to cope and she would have benefited from therapy. Antidepressants and talk therapy would have been appropriate, but this was the 1950s and these drugs were not widely used. My mother might also have refused to go to a shrink because in her view shrinks were only for crazy people, and she was not crazy.

At some point my mother moved to Boston. There she joined an Orthodox synagogue and resumed a more traditional observance of Judaism. She trained as a licensed baby nurse and supported herself that way until she was sixty-one. That year she had surgery for a detached retina and was no longer allowed to bend or lift. She managed to get by on social security, a small pension from the French government (she retained her French citizenship), and financial support from Steve and me.

Years later, we had resumed contact when shortly before Yom Kippur—the Day of Atonement, a time when Jews are supposed to forgive those who wronged them before they can ask for God's mercy—I suggested in a phone conversation that since they were both getting on in years, she and Aunt Anny should reconcile as it was time to make peace. Her response was to ask me if I was seeing Aunt Anny. I lied and said no. She never reconciled with Aunt Anny. Later, she invited my children to spend time with her and I said no. When they were older, they themselves limited their relationship with her. My mother died in Boston at the age of eighty-seven, a lonely, bitter woman. On her deathbed, her next to last words to me were, "*Du hast mich nie lieb gehabt.*" (You never loved me). Of course this was not so. The truth was that she had destroyed that love. She wanted love more than anything else, but never realized how she pushed everyone away.

For our honeymoon, Steve chose Williamsburg, Virginia. It was my first time on a plane and I was as excited as a kid, singing "I can fly" from the *Peter Pan* musical. Williamsburg seemed funny to me, the way the Cloisters in New York City was funny. The Cloisters was a reconstructed monastery in Fort Tryon Park in northern Manhattan. The medieval structure was imported mostly from France and rebuilt stone by stone. It had glass enclosures, central heating, and piped-in Gregorian chant. After seeing the old weather-exposed cloisters in Moissac and Cahors, the idea of a cloister with central heating and recorded chant struck me as incongruous. As for Williamsburg, what Americans considered antiques were items used every day in European homes.

When I met Steve, he was working as a technical sales representative for the Boston Gear Works. He didn't like his job, so on the way back from our honeymoon, we stopped in Washington, DC, to look into possible careers and check statistics at the Labor Department. He had been teaching adult education classes at the Henry George School in New York as a volunteer and he thought he would like teaching as a career. Steve only had a bachelor's degree from the Bernard M. Baruch Business School, part of City College of New York. He had rushed through high school because he was gifted, graduating at fifteen, and through college, earning his bachelor's at nineteen. After we came back from our trip, he applied to Teachers College at Columbia University where he was accepted with the proviso that he make up an undergraduate deficiency in American history, so he took the two history courses during the summer while working. Then he gave up his job to attend school full-time while I worked. He paid tuition from his savings and from a small inheritance from his Uncle Louis while our living expenses were covered by my earnings.

Steve's parents were very opposed to this. After a nice Shabbat dinner at their house, we told them about our plans and they took turns telling Steve why going back to school was a bad idea—all the money he would lose by not working, the cost of tuition, and more. As a young bride, I was intimidated and I let Steve handle his parents while I kept my mouth shut. With my financial and emotional support, Steve was able to pursue his dream. We moved into a furnished graduate student apartment on Amsterdam Avenue and 120th Street in a building called The Poinciana. It was very modest, but it was something we could afford.

My job at the piano company was not very satisfying. Barely earning above minimum wage, I did not care for most of my coworkers whose lifestyles were very different from mine. By this time I had achieved fluency in English and I had taken a course in speedwriting to prepare for an office job that required shorthand. With Steve's help, I applied for a number of jobs and ended up at an employment agency that sent me for interviews to two pharmaceutical companies, Merck and Vick Chemical Company.

For my interview at Vicks, I brought diplomas and references to the personnel office. After looking them over, the interviewer put me to the test. She placed me in a room with a record player, paper, pencil, and a typewriter. Now I was to take down a letter and then type it. Of course I knew correct business formatting and I produced a satisfactory letter. When I showed it to the interviewer, she said, "You indicated that you know French, yes? Please translate the letter into French and type it up." And so I did. I also knew correct French business style from my business courses and my jobs in Toulouse. When I handed the French version to her, she said she didn't know French, but she sent me to a secretary who was a native speaker. Of course my French letter was good, but this lady felt the need to pick on something she would have worded differently. I was hired that day in the international division of the company.

Soon after I started, the division was reorganized and I was assigned to Bill Coyne, a graduate of the University of Rochester who had spent a semester at Oxford. He was a cultured, wonderful man who always gave me glowing evaluations. He would show them to me and I was surprised because I did not think I was so great. We worked very well together and we became friends. The female support staff in the division was comprised of lovely young women, collegial and well-mannered, quite a contrast to my previous coworkers. Most were products of Catholic high schools with one or two additional years of business school. It was a friendly and pleasant environment. The division received awards for productivity. After three years, my boss and the whole division were transferred to Paris and I was offered a junior executive position in the international section of the media department. This would have been quite a promotion because at that time, all the management positions were staffed by men. But by then I was planning to start a family, so I declined. Today I probably would have accepted, but at the time pregnant women were not included in offices. Times have changed.

Steve and Edith chaperoning a dance at the High School of Commerce in Yonkers, New York, 1958.

Steve earned his master's degree in 1955 and got a job teaching high school at Hastings-on-Hudson. We moved to Yonkers and rented three rooms on the second floor of an old house. I was still working for the Vick Chemical Company in Manhattan and commuted by train. We bought furniture, a car, and we saved our money for a trip to Europe. Steve had never been abroad and I was eager to share my own background.

In hindsight I should have encouraged Steve to work part time so that I too could continue my studies toward a PhD. But I was not that familiar with the American system and on top of that, my struggle to study while working was fresh in my mind. Besides, at that time women stayed home as soon as the babies arrived while husbands were the main breadwinners. That meant it was important to boost the man's earning power. Hence my personal goals were put on the back burner. I continued to take undergraduate courses in American and English history with an eventual PhD in mind. Teachers College was not very helpful either. In fact, the French department chair was quite callous, saying I had to take fifteen credits to earn a master's even though I knew the material because they had to pay their electric bills.

❧

In the summer of 1956 we went to Europe, again over the objections of my in-laws who thought we should save our money for a down payment on a house. Going to Europe in those days was still a great adventure. We went by boat and everyone came to see us off. With history as his field of study, Steve enjoyed the trip very much as the past came alive for him. We started in London where we stayed with a family we found through Servas, a nonprofit organization founded after World War II for the purpose of promoting peace by bringing people together. We spent a week visiting the usual sights, going to the theatre, meeting teachers, and visiting a school with the help of our hosts.

Then it was off to Paris where we went straight to Jean Jacques' house in Malakoff. Since he was at work, we stored our luggage in his shed and I took Steve to the Champs Elysées for coffee and peanuts at a sidewalk café while we watched the world go by. Steve enjoyed it immensely. I saw my old friends Otto, Jacques Hepner, and Leon, who was particularly keen on hearing my impressions since he too wanted to immigrate to the United States. After the usual tourist circuit in Paris, we went to Cahors for a brief visit with Huguette who drove us to Toulouse where we took pictures of my old neighborhood. She found me too Americanized and was disappointed that we didn't stay longer, but our time was limited and there was so much more I wanted to show Steve. Huguette had not yet married. We kept up our correspondence until 1966 when I informed her I was coming to France and wanted to see her. She responded that she didn't want to see me and that she had disposed of the books my mother had left with her. In 1999, I learned from neighbors that she married late, had only one daughter—who was forty years old and single—and was widowed. I attempted to reconnect with her, but was unsuccessful. We spent a day with Aline and her husband in Albi. Since I was the interpreter for Steve,

I did not have enough heart-to-heart talks with Aline, something I deeply regretted.

From there we went to Nice where I bumped into an old friend, a fellow student from Syria who had just finished his studies. From Nice we took the train to Rome, sitting up all night. A fellow passenger suggested a *pensione* in Rome. With brazen confidence I took a taxi to the *pensione* where the host received us in his robe. It was early in the morning. Since a room would not be ready until later, we left our luggage and I took Steve to a café for a cappuccino. Steve had studied Latin, and our visits to the Forum and all the other antiquities were very meaningful to him. From there it was on to Basel where we had a lovely experience with a Swiss couple whom we also met through Servas.

It was again through Servas that we stayed with a German couple in Ludwigshafen. That was a big step for me, as I wanted to challenge my discomfort about setting foot in Germany. The family received us cordially, but we did not touch on the subject of the recent past or my own history. The man had only one eye, so he was spared military service. He was a chemical engineer working for IG Farben. At the time I did not know that the chemical manufacturing giant was involved in the production of the very poison gas that killed my family along with everyone else, nor did I know about their shameful use of slave labor, forcing people to work under the most inhumane conditions until they dropped dead.

On the way back, we stopped in Amsterdam and made a visit to what is now a place of pilgrimage: the Anne Frank House. We also spent a day in Lille to visit my former teacher, Denise Noyon, who had moved back to her hometown. She gave me a gold ring with four small diamonds as payment for a small amount of money I had sent to her when she was having financial difficulties. I had thought of that money as repayment for the 1948–1949 academic year when she took me on halftime without tuition, but it was a generous gift and I treasured the ring. Eventually she married an old friend from her youth who had become a widower, and that was the last letter I got from her. Her tone was upbeat and she seemed happy. On a subsequent visit to Toulouse I ran into Michele, one of the other students she had been very close to after I left her school. To my great surprise, Michele did not speak highly of her. She indicated that Mlle Noyon did not have all her marbles. Gradually it dawned on me that she may have been right.

Steve and Edith in London in front of Tower Bridge, 1956.

Edith with Aline Berger and her husband, André Mianes, 1956.

Edith in Cahors at the Cloister, 1956.

From left to right: Otto Steinmetz, Leon Vermont (né Wodowski), Jacques Hepner, and Edith in Paris, 1956.

Steve and Edith in London at the home of Servas hosts, 1956.

Our return trip home on the *SS Flandre* was pleasant with the ocean as smooth as a mirror, quite a contrast to my initial crossing. The whole trip was a wonderful experience for both of us and we have fond memories, but for Steve, it was a major eye-opener. We've been back to Europe many times since, but even though that first trip was on a shoestring budget and we had to rough it at times, it was the best experience. When we got back to the United States, we were ready to start a family.

⚜

I worked for the Vick Chemical Company until the end of my second trimester. That gave me three months to prepare for the baby, and to complete the paperwork for my American citizenship. I studied the brochure about American government, much of which I already knew from my studies in France. For the test I was escorted by Aunt Anny, who had long since become an American citizen, and by my mother-in-law. Of course I answered the questions with ease. The official also checked to see whether I was literate, which made me smile. He made me write a simple sentence. I could not be sworn in until after the November election due to a law that forbade the swearing in of new citizens in the weeks before an election.

My daughter Emily Paula was born on October 1, 1957. We needed to get out of the inexpensive apartment especially because our landlord, who was from Syria, got drunk every weekend—something we were unaware of before the baby because Steve and I went out every Friday and Saturday night to see plays, movies, or to attend concerts and ballet performances. There was screaming and yelling until 2 a.m. every weekend and we were scared. Steve slept with a kitchen knife under his pillow and what was worse was that we couldn't even lock the doors to our rooms. I felt particularly vulnerable with an infant.

The house was in a residential area and, without a car, I was completely isolated for days and weeks once the snow kept us homebound. That was very hard on me. Steve was back in school to take courses toward his doctorate, so he was gone not only during the week, but also on Saturdays and several evenings every week. On top of that, I had no outside help and I was afraid I would turn into a vegetable for lack of adult company and mental stimulation.

Finding suitable housing proved difficult because we could not afford market rental costs on Steve's high school teacher salary. With the help of Steve's cousin Alice, we found a middle-income co-op in Riverdale off Kappock Street. Before being accepted, we were thoroughly screened not only on our ability to pay, but also on our character. The Knolls, as the co-op was called, was built through section 213 of the New York State code for middle-income households. We paid $2,500 for a modern but modest two-bedroom apartment with our savings, and the monthly rent for utilities and upkeep was within our means. Our daughter Louise Judith was born on November 7, 1959.

Most residents at the Knolls were young couples with children, and their educational level was high. Like me, most women stayed home to care for the children, quite a change from my lonely days at Odell Avenue in Yonkers. The place was run by the residents with committees for everything from maintenance and the co-op nursery school to social events. As chairman of the adult education committee, I organized a lecture on nuclear war during the height of the Cold War with the Soviet Union, which convinced me that nuclear war was unthinkable. I organized a course on nineteenth-century Russian literature with a professor from a nearby university. We also had dance and exercise classes for women, and we planned activities for the children, especially during the winter months. Steve and I made friends and we socialized mostly in the evening after we all had put our children to bed. The women helped each other with occasional babysitting. Sometimes we would visit each other or arrange for a playdate for the children, a new concept for me. From 1961–1962, I served as chairman of the co-op's nursery school. Besides my activities on various committees, I also tried to remain current on recent publications from France and Germany. I read *The Tin Drum* by Gunther Grass, a book that, although it won a literary prize, did not impress me at all. Even so I had little leisure to pursue my interests since all of my time was spent caring for my two young daughters.

During all that time, Steve was continuing his coursework with a view toward a PhD. His master's thesis had been on the Yellow Peril and he wanted to continue with the same topic, but that work had already been done, so he chose Henry George. For two summers in 1960 and 1961 in order to escape New York's oppressive heat—before air-conditioning was commonplace—we rented a cottage in a bungalow colony in the Catskills. Steve was working on his thesis and he would bring me his typed notes for review. At the end of the summer of 1961, his work was done, but his chairman insisted that he become a full-time student if he wanted to get his degree. In spite of Steve's protestations that he had a wife and two children and needed to work, his chairman was adamant. Again, it was a matter for Columbia Teacher's College to pay their bills, for as a full-time student, Steve would pay higher tuition fees. Steve agreed to quit his job in January 1962, and we lived on the money that he had contributed to his pension fund during his six-and-a-half years of teaching. Steve's chairman also denied him a PhD because, he said, Steve only had one foreign language, Spanish. So he earned an EdD.

We knew that the American Historical Association held its annual meeting in December of every year and Steve had planned to go to Washington, DC, to look for job opportunities. The night before he was to leave, he went to bed at the usual time. I asked whether he was packed. That's when he told me that he was not planning to go. *What?* He explained to me that it would cost money for the train to DC, that he would have to pay for the hotel, and that he had papers to grade. I told him that after all the money he had poured into his degree, a few hundred dollars was nothing. As for the student papers, I told him to take them along so he could grade them on the train or in the hotel. So, upon my urging, he got up and packed his bag.

He came back from the conference with two job offers: one in Vermont and one in Pennsylvania. Upon the suggestion of his chairman, he chose Pennsylvania because it was a four-year school and the Vermont job was not. So we moved from New York City to a small town west of the Appalachian Mountains. During Steve's interview on a bitter cold day in January 1962, I asked the history department chair at the school whether there might be an opening in the language department. The head of the language department said I should come over. And so I did. Dr. Bieghler conducted the interview in English; after a while he switched to French, a test I passed easily. Then he sent me to his colleague who was a native speaker from Germany. We chatted a while and he said he would support my candidacy. And that's how I was hired as a part-time professor teaching both French and German language and literature. Since I had only accompanied Steve, I had brought no credentials with me. It was my fluency that won the day, especially since Dr. Bieghler was keen on hiring native speakers.

We moved in July 1962, but Steve had to return to New York to complete his degree requirements. By then our resources were totally depleted. The $2,000 we received from selling our apartment back to the co-op went for the down payment on a new but modest house. We had to buy because there were no apartment buildings and people were reluctant to rent to us because we had young children. This would eventually be held against Steve because in academia, it was not considered proper to buy a house before being granted tenure. But we did not know that. For living expenses we borrowed $3,000 from my brother-in-law Alex.

PENNSYLVANIA

After five years as a full-time mom including the last four spent at the Knolls, I was ready to go back to work. Moving away from New York, from family and friends, to a small town with a population of 12,000 was a big step. There were fifty Protestant churches of different denominations, one Catholic church, and a small synagogue built after World War II. During our interviews, we met the librarian who told us that people from east of the Appalachians did not adapt well to this area. I was determined that this would not apply to us. Having lived in so many places and done so many things, I felt I could adapt to anything. And our two jobs meant that for the first time in my life, I would be financially comfortable.

After spending the summer getting settled, I looked forward to being back at work with a job for which my education had prepared me. At that time, teaching eleven or even twelve classes was considered part time. The American college system seemed more like secondary school to me with classes three times a week, textbooks, and daily homework assignments. It was a far cry from the French university system, but I adapted.

There were other surprises. During the spring semester of 1963, my mother had to have major eye surgery. She panicked, telling me that she was going blind. She had a detached retina that required surgical repair. I needed to be in Boston with her and I had to miss my Friday and Monday classes in intermediate French. Since this was my first year of teaching, I did not want to impose on a colleague. Instead, I told my students that they owed me two hours for the missed classes, plus four hours of homework, which was a lot more than they expected. My assignment for them was to write a comparison between the French and the American Revolutions. I said that since they already knew the American Revolution, they only had to research the French Revolution. When I said that they already knew the American Revolution, there were a lot of heads shaking to indicate this was not so. Well, I got the papers alright, but no one except one student wrote something that showed any understanding or that addressed the topic. I clearly had to tone down my expectations.

I encouraged my students to go and see Europe for themselves. This was the time of the Cold War, and some faculty had pro-Soviet views, blaming the Cold War on Truman and the American government. The chairman put me in charge of all the work-study travel programs available at the time. Most students came from families of modest means. I would sit down with them individually and help them plan their trip, also giving them information on Servas, which allowed them to stay with families at no cost.

In addition the chairman put me in charge of the Modern Language Club. I developed programs each semester, working with the students as faculty adviser. We had an informal fall get-together where students returning from summer travel or exchange programs in Spain and elsewhere would share their impressions. Each semester I had a foreign film, a lecture or panel discussion, and a formal—the Christmas party in December and a banquet in the spring where the new officers were elected. In the spring we also had a *Fasching* or carnival. I often led the singing of Christmas carols in French and in German. For the lectures there were two topics I remember vividly. One dealt with the causes of anticlericalism in France, Spain, and Latin America. Since this could have been a controversial topic, my chairman sent me to the priest who ran the Newman Center. On his

Edith, 35, with fellow faculty members, 1963.

recommendation, I got the monsignor of the nearby diocese to give the talk. The other one that stands out was a debate by two professors as to whether there was such a thing as national character. These lectures were well-attended and attracted people from across the campus.

The 1960s were the time when the civil rights movement went into high gear. In our town, housing was segregated and there were other signs of discrimination. Together with colleagues and members of the Unitarian Fellowship, Steve and I organized a Human Relations Committee. With our sociologist friend Esko Newhill and his wife, Ruth, I organized a scholarship fund for post-high school training to be used by local African American high school graduates. I also organized a Speakers Bureau that touched on sensitive topics like race, history, and discrimination. I went around the campus and asked colleagues to pick a topic and donate their time for free. Those who invited speakers had to make a donation to the scholarship fund, so the Speakers Bureau fed the scholarship fund. Steve and others were working on integrating the one and only local swimming pool. Steve went around to the churches asking the ministers to collect signatures from their parishioners to integrate the pool. Not every minister was willing to do that.

In 1964 after the Selma, Alabama, murders, we participated in a march on Main Street, taking our two young daughters along. They were only four-and-a-half and six-and-a-half, but both still remember that march. We had received a permit to close Main Street to traffic for a walk down the three blocks from the library to the old courthouse. The storekeepers came out and stared at us. It was uncomfortable and it took some courage to proceed. We had a good turnout and the faculty was well-represented. At the steps of the courthouse, there were speeches followed by singing, and then we all disbanded. We memorialized the four young men who were killed, and we stood up for our values when it mattered.

As for the swimming pool, the students eventually got involved and threatened to boycott the local merchants. It took a sustained effort over several years but in the end, the pool was integrated and so was housing. We also started an After School Study Center for children from first to fourth grade where we arranged for one-on-one tutoring. It was a massive effort, spearheaded mostly by faculty and the local Unitarian Fellowship, a group we joined. We did not join the Jewish community until much later. At that time I also joined Hadassah, the Jewish women's organization that focuses mostly on medical work.

In 1968 our son, Daniel Alfred, was born and I took a one-year leave of absence without pay. Steve was offered a sabbatical for 1970. With permission from my new department chair I took another leave without pay. We decided to take a full year at half pay for Steve, using our savings and a small inheritance from Aunt Anny, who died in 1969, to cover expenses for a trip to France. I jumped at the opportunity to expose my children to France. I chose Nice, a city I was familiar with. Both of my daughters went to public schools while I tutored them in French and helped with their homework every night. They learned French and benefited greatly from the whole experience.

Steve spent his time working on a book. I explored opportunities for our students to study abroad at the University of Nice. On weekends we visited the surrounding areas. I signed my daughters up with the local Jewish youth group with which they spent time on weekends and on a ski trip during Christmas vacation. We connected with the local Mensa group where we met interesting people and made friends. For Christmas we hosted an officer from the Sixth Fleet, which had docked in nearby Villefranche. Although we had no Christmas tree, he was happy to be with an American family with children as that made him feel closer to home. He in turn invited us to visit his ship, an exciting experience for all of us, but especially for our children. On the way home we stopped in Paris and traveled back via Copenhagen where we spent three wonderful days.

The Cord family (from left to right: Steven, Daniel, Emily, Edith, and Louise) on the SS France *on the way to Europe, August 1970.*

From left to right: Daniel, Emily, and Louise at the
Tivoli Gardens in Copenhagen, June 1971.

Unsure as to whether I would have a part-time or a full-time load upon returning, I brought back a young French high school graduate to stay with us as an au pair to take care of our three-year-old son. I had a good year of teaching. At the end of it, my chairman asked me to prepare a reception for our graduates, something we had never done before so there were no established procedures. I had no idea whether there was a budget and no chance to ask him any questions because he skipped town. I did the best I could, asking colleagues to prepare some goodies for the reception. We all paid for everything out of our own pockets. We had a nice reception and things ran smoothly.

That summer, we left for a month to visit people we had met in France. Before leaving I did not get my new contract for the following year. When I asked my chairman about it, he said it was probably late and not to worry. When we got back, there still was no contract. Denying any responsibility, my chairman sent me to the dean who was the kind of man who could talk for an hour without saying anything. After an hour of listening to him, I just wanted to get out of there. The truth was I had no job. That hit me much harder than I had expected. The newly formed faculty union was no help. After trying unsuccessfully to find out what had happened, I ended up hiring a lawyer. Together we went to see the provost and, thanks to the newly passed Freedom of Information Act, I was able to see my file. That's when I found out the truth. My chairman lied to me. He had written to the dean to ask whether he had to take me back after we got back from Steve's sabbatical, not because I was not a good teacher, but because I often "asked for special favors because of my children." Since I was teaching part time, I had asked to have my classes grouped in three days instead of being spread out over five days and I asked for 9 a.m. classes instead of 8 a.m. classes so that I could get my children off to school. That was the extent of his grievance. I should add that the chairman had previously been my friend. We had often been to each other's house for dinner parties and he had been our guest for Thanksgiving as he was single. Compared to Steve's history department where most professors were married with children, my department consisted mostly of single faculty or couples without children, so it was not kid-friendly.

After vain efforts to get justice from the school or from the union, we decided to contact the state's attorney general in Harrisburg, the state capital. I prepared a brief. Among other things, I indicated that I had been promoted to assistant professor, that I had sat on tenure committees, and so forth. It was a long list and my lawyer seemed very satisfied. After examining my brief, he told me I should have been a lawyer. In Harrisburg we met a lovely lady who was the assistant district attorney. She took up my case, went to the school to get more information from my colleagues, and after two years, I was reinstated with full seniority. But I must admit that for me, the bloom was off. I had gone into teaching with stars in my eyes. Having worked in the private sector where the pressure of competition and the need to show a profit was strong, I had thought that in academia, things would be different. From my experience and from many other sources as well, I have since learned otherwise.

During that two-year hiatus, the department had split into two between Romance languages on one side and German and Russian as a separate department. Even though I had always taught both French and German, I was assigned to German and Russian because some colleagues in the French department were afraid that I would take away their jobs since I now had more seniority than they did. As a result, I often ended up with small German classes while the French classes were bursting at the seams because my French colleagues were afraid to let me teach French.

In the last few years of teaching, I had a new wonderful dean, Dr. Joseph Gallanar, who was very supportive of faculty. I had always been given the literature classes in the German department because my colleagues were trained in how to teach and had less interest in literature. I put together a course on post-World War II German literature and another one on fairy tales—both the folk tales and the romantic or gothic stories. I also had the idea of doing a vertical study of the Faust theme, but that course was later sabotaged by colleagues.

In 1976, I became chairman of the German and Russian department. This was also the year for our evaluation to be accredited by the mid-Atlantic states. I had a nice relationship with the interviewers and we easily got the coveted accreditation. I learned a lot as chairman about the budgeting process and I had access to the SAT scores of incoming students. This was a time when the state put pressure on schools to accept students with low SAT scores. We prepared special summer courses for them to help them catch up on basic English and math that they did not learn in high school. These catch-up courses were taught by college professors, which I thought was a mistake. I felt they should have been taught by high school teachers who were better qualified to teach at that level and would also have been less costly. But no one asked me and I had no say in the matter.

In the course of my tenure as chair, things deteriorated. 1976 was a very bad year with lots of illness, something unusual for me. I began to think about a career change. The following spring, the Faculty Union had arranged for brokers to visit the campus in order to help us with retirement planning, specifically 403(b) plans available to employees of non-profits. While Steve made the appointment, I ended up working with the broker, Peter Ward, and we became friends. He was impressed by the fact that I had some savings for my children's education and no debt, aside from the mortgage. Eventually he asked me whether I would like to work with him. I was surprised and asked him what he had in mind, part-time or full-time. He said whichever I wanted. I was intrigued.

Foreign languages were one of the most unpopular graduation requirements on campus. Every year like spring fever, the requirement became a topic of discussion in the School of Arts and Sciences. My colleagues were worried about losing their jobs if the language requirement was dropped and they put pressure on me to give easier grades, something I would not do. With the uncertainty of the language requirement and the bitter disappointment about my colleagues' lack of integrity, I had started to look for another position away from the university. Having previous outside work experience in the private sector, I never felt that teaching was the only thing in the world that I could do.

Taking up the invitation to work with Peter, I spent the summer of 1977 studying on my own for my insurance exam and my Series 6 broker's license. I passed both tests in the fall. During the following school year I helped Peter by setting up appointments and providing him with the school calendar. The following summer I tried my hand at talking to colleagues, and I was successful. The need for personal savings to supplement pension and social security benefits in old age was catching on, and the tax advantages of 403(b) plans similar to today's IRAs or 401k plans made them attractive. In 1979 I took an unpaid leave of absence, afraid to cut my ties completely with the university, and I took the plunge. And a plunge it was. I had no idea whether I would be successful as this was a completely new field.

With their negative attitudes toward anything having to do with business, my colleagues were convinced that my motive was money. That could not have been further from the truth. For a long time, I made less than I would have made teaching. Additionally, I worked twelve not nine months a year, plus all the overhead costs for travel, office expenses, fees, and continuing education came out of my pocket. My motivation was to escape the aggravation of departmental politics. I was never afraid of work, but I don't do aggravation. When I learned about the College for Financial Planning, I took the coursework, and in 1983 I earned the Certified Financial Planner designation.

MARYLAND

In 1984 I moved to Columbia, Maryland, where I taught evening classes and gave talks on money management and investing to become better known locally and build a client base. I also took the Series 7 test, which I passed on the first try. This career shift represented a lot of personal growth for me because its demands differed greatly from those of teaching. When I stood behind that desk, the students had to come to me and I had a certain amount of authority. Also my paycheck came in whether I had a good day or a bad one, whether I did a good job that day or not. With this job, I had to meet the public and provide a service. I changed my wardrobe to look more professional. At the same time I loved being self-employed. While I worked harder than in my previous job—including working weekends and evenings because the job had to get done and papers processed in a timely manner—having control over my time was invaluable. It allowed me to

Edith's family at Daniel's wedding, May 1999. Back row, left to right: Steven Cord, Daniel Cord, Edith Cord. Front row, left to right: Emily Cord-DuThinh, Louise Cord Guiot.

From left to right: Edith, Ted Brenig, Leon Vermont (Wodowski), California, 2011. Leon and Edith had been friends since they met in Alpina, Chésières-Villars in Switzerland during the war. Ted was Leon's roommate in Switzerland. They got together every year.

help my daughters on occasion with child care and gave me the freedom to organize my own life. Of course there was no secure paycheck. My income depended on my efforts.

I enjoyed my work as a financial adviser, especially after I joined Commonwealth Financial Network, a Boston firm with high ethical

Edith speaking at Howard Community College
in Columbia, Maryland, 2016.

standards and a very supportive back office. I found my work gratifying because I could put order into people's financial affairs and help them through difficult life transitions while providing for future needs. I did this for twenty-eight years until my retirement at age seventy-eight when I stopped in order to work on my book. Today I continue to write and speak about my experiences to share the bitter lessons of the past with the hope of building a better future.

21. REFLECTIONS

»Wie es auch sei, das Leben, es ist gut.«
(In spite of everything, life is good.)

—Johann Wolfgang von Goethe from *"Der Bräutigam"*

I viewed the traumatic experiences of my formative years as a burden that I did not want to pass on to my children. In this connection, I thought it was good that my husband did not share my experiences. Steve had a normal childhood as the youngest of three children in a stable, middle-class Jewish family with both parents born in America. By the time I became a parent in 1957, I had worked through the trauma, as much as one possibly can, and I made a conscious effort not to burden my children. It would have been impossible to hide my European background, so they always knew about the war and the deaths. I told them little stories about changing countries and learning new languages, so my daughter Emily thought I had all these exciting adventures. The horrors of the Nazi persecution were something they found out later, on their own, in their teens, but not from me. My goal was to let them grow up free to chart their own lives without burdening them with the pain from my past.

My children, Emily, Louise, and Daniel, received an excellent education. All went to graduate school and all had the opportunity to travel abroad during their formative years when these experiences could be incorporated into their lives. Above all, I am proud of the fact that all three are good and caring people. All three married, have children, and are following the straight and narrow path as productive adults making positive contributions to society. Sadly, Daniel died in 2012 of glioblastoma, leaving his widow with two young children. Thanks to my caring and capable daughter-in-law, Leigh, and the support of family and friends, the children are doing well.

✤

As for my ideas, they changed over time. In France I was influenced by the socialist ideas prevalent in Europe during the postwar years. France had started to move toward the welfare state so that, when I came to America, it felt like sink or swim. I was on my own. When we moved to Pennsylvania, I was told that there had been a Klan in town and that there was discrimination in housing against anyone with dark skin. Having been at the receiving end of discrimination for many long years, that certainly did not fit my thinking. Our friends and colleagues at the university were all liberals. As mentioned previously, my husband and I did get involved in the civil rights movement at the local level, working for what I hoped would be a colorblind America. At the time these ideas were not yet widely accepted, and we were met with some hostility. It took courage and persistence to take a stand against the status quo. When President Johnson started the Great Society, my reaction was: this is very nice, but can we afford it? What did I know? I was busy working while raising a family and had little leisure for nonessential pursuits.

Today my ideas about the economy and politics are better informed and I have given a great deal of thought to the role of government. Having experienced the heavy hand of a totalitarian state and its anonymous bureaucracy, I favor a smaller, less intrusive government. Even though privacy seems to be a thing of the past because of modern technology, it nevertheless remains a desirable goal. To help the disadvantaged, we as a society want to provide a safety net. We also want to level the playing field as much as possible and provide opportunities to all. But the postwar British motto of "security from the cradle to the grave" does not seem to me to be a desirable goal. It takes away incentives, it makes us more dependent on an already powerful state, and when taxes do not suffice to pay for this "security," we borrow and raise our national debt to dangerous levels, thereby weakening our national security. But most of all, I do not believe it is conducive to the development of the citizens. Ideally the goal of the state in a free society is to foster not only economic and political freedom and security, but also to enable each individual to develop and reach his full potential, for that, I believe, is the ultimate destiny of mankind.

✤

I frequently attend reunions of survivors of the Holocaust, meetings that now include our descendants. A major concern deals with remembering the mass murder of Jews. I see the memorials and the museums, I go to the annual commemorations of these horrific events, and I think: it's not enough. The thought of my father dying alone, after being dehumanized, crying out to a silent God for justice and mercy continues to haunt me. But, is it enough to remember?

No. Remembrance for its own sake is not enough if we do not apply the lessons of these experiences. Sadly, there have been other religious and ethnic persecutions since then. As far as the Jewish people are concerned, Jews have learned a few things. The Holocaust happened in the country with the most assimilated Jewish population. Jews were well-integrated into German society, adopting its language and culture while contributing to their host country in every field of endeavor. So assimilation wasn't enough to make us fully accepted. Jews have also learned that they can only rely on themselves and that they must be able to defend themselves. Never again will we allow ourselves to be so degraded and helpless. I think of my nineteen-year-old brother who suffered the same fate. Somehow I would have felt better if he had died standing up for what he believed in, defending himself and basic human values, instead of being enslaved and starved before being marched into the gas chamber. That's why Jews must have a state of their own in their ancestral homeland.

Although I now understand better how the Holocaust happened and what historic trends led up to it, I don't have an answer as to why it happened, any more than I understand the killing fields of Cambodia, the butchery of Yugoslavia, or today's unspeakable barbarism in the Middle East, Africa, and Asia. The question I ask myself is whether the world has learned these lessons. Less than eighty years after the mass murder of Europe's Jews, anti-Semitism has again reared its ugly head. I am deeply distressed by its latest incarnation, cloaked as anti-Zionism, because it is a sentiment that I had hoped was lost and buried for good after the Holocaust.

The focus on Israel is a fascination that leads many well-intentioned people to the ambitious goal of making peace. But peace starts with ideas: as long as there is hatred and incitement to violence, as long as the people surrounding Israel refuse to acknowledge that Israel is here to stay, all the treaties and good will of outsiders are useless. If we could all be one happy human family focused on raising happy, healthy, and productive children, creating freedom and prosperity for all people, sharing resources and trading in a peaceful manner, there would be no need for borders anywhere. But since that is not the case, and since discrimination and anti-Semitism continue, the survival of Israel as a Jewish homeland is a necessity.

Finally, while the oppression in Germany was initially aimed at its Jewish population, it did not stop there. Recall the famous words of Pastor Martin Niemöller: "First they came for the Socialists, and I did not speak out—because I was not a Socialist. Then they came for the Trade Unionists, and I did not speak out—because I was not a Trade Unionist. Then they came for the Jews, and I did not speak out—because I was not a Jew. When they came for me—there was no one left to speak for me." In the same way, we see Christians and other minorities persecuted throughout the Middle East with the burning of churches, the enslavement of women, book burnings, and beheadings. We see continued political oppression in many other countries with barely a peep of condemnation from the United Nations. I am passionate about freedom. When I see people oppressed, incarcerated, or killed over their political or religious beliefs, I take it personally because I feel their pain. As in the past, Jews are the first victims, but never the last.

⚜

My spiritual journey took a long curve as well. From my traditional Jewish upbringing to my intense faith during the war years to my loss of faith in God, the quest for knowledge, understanding, and meaning continues. For me, Christianity provided no more answers than Judaism to the problem of evil—I do not believe in original sin or that man is born evil. My humanist phase, and our association with our liberal Unitarian friends, was principally focused on social action and civil rights. As for my Judaism, it has taken me a long time to accept myself. One of the sadder aspects of discrimination that is barely talked about is that the target population accepts some of the lies and distortions aimed at the group, so that individuals and especially children incorporate it into their self-image. After the war, I thought I had to prove that I was not all the terrible things they said about me in their propaganda. That's why this inner journey of self-acceptance took such a long time. I am Jewish, period. I am no better or worse than anyone else. The values instilled in me by my parents are good values. Jews have made positive contributions to civilization and to the welfare of humanity in every field of human endeavor in spite of discrimination, persecution, and mass murder. Finally, the Jewish people have the same right to exist as everyone else, no more, but no less either. Needless to say, I remain very sensitive to anti-Semitism in all its forms, including the Boycott Divestment, Sanctions (BDS) movement that is aimed at the destruction of the one and only Jewish homeland.

Being Jewish was a hard way to grow up, knowing from an early age that I and the people I came from were discriminated against. Blessed with a long life, I have come to appreciate Jewish culture with its values and traditions: the sanctity of life, the importance of family, the love of learning, the respect for people of achievement in the arts and sciences, the quest for justice, and above all, the concern for the welfare of our fellow man. I also have emotional ties to Judaism and to Jews because of my early years in Vienna in our home, but above all because of shared experiences and shared values.

As for my beliefs, they are hard to put into a box. There is much wisdom in the Bible. It is part of our Judeo-Christian culture and heritage. It was Hillel who said, when asked to explain his faith while standing on one foot: "That which is despicable to you, do not do to your fellow [man], this is the whole Torah, and the rest is commentary" (Babylonian Talmud, Shabbat 31a). When it comes to religion, I also like to quote a parable from the Gospel: ". . . by their fruits you will know them" (Matthew 7:20). I do not close my mind to other sacred texts or to inspirational writings, be it the Bhagavad Gita or Kalil Gibran and more. They all reflect man's striving to understand the meaning of life and to fathom man's ultimate destiny. Ideally, the purpose of religion is to be a civilizing agent, to teach self-restraint, to hold us accountable for our actions, and to provide us with a code of ethics and a moral compass. In addition, religion meets a human need to acknowledge forces beyond our understanding, to help us rise above the humdrum of everyday life, to lift our eyes and contemplate the majesty of creation and the mystery of life.

Today, my axiom after much soul searching is that life has meaning, that all life is sacred, and that every soul is on a path. Besides providing a code of ethics to guide our behavior as is the case in the Judeo-Christian tradition, religions are an attempt to provide meaning—I just wish they could do so with less bloodshed. I also wish they were less self-righteous, as each one claims to be the sole bearer of the Truth.

As to what happens after we die? It's all a matter of faith. No one really knows for sure, and there is little sense in killing anyone over his beliefs.

Musings on Old Age and Transitions

We should go out in a blaze of glory after a life well lived.
Instead of aches and pains, we ride a glorious chariot into the sunset.
Instead of dimming eyesight, we see the beauty of the earth.
Instead of duller sound, we hear the music of the spheres.
Instead of the rush of duties, we enjoy a well-earned rest.
Instead of pain and sorrow, we only remember the lessons.

I know it's a long goodbye
But we shall meet again
And we shall meet friends from long ago.
Oh to be received with all the love we spread, past and present
To know the joy of reunions with loves thought lost
'Tis only a ride to a new adventure, a new life and new learning
Bathed in a sea of peace and beauty and ineffable love.

About the Author

Born in Vienna, Austria, in 1928, Edith Mayer Cord fled from country to country because of religious persecution. Separated from her family, Cord managed to survive the Holocaust in hiding. After the war, she focused on catching up on her education before coming to the United States. Cord worked as a college professor of French and German before becoming a securities broker, financial adviser, and certified financial planner. She is married, with three children and seven grandchildren. She currently lives in Columbia, Maryland.